MIND MODELS

New Forms of Musical Experience

Second Edition

Roger Reynolds

ROUTLEDGE
NEW YORK AND LONDON

Published in 2005 by
Routledge
Taylor & Francis Group
270 Madison Avenue
New York, NY 10016

Published in Great Britain by
Routledge
Taylor & Francis Group
2 Park Square
Milton Park, Abingdon
Oxon OX14 4RN

© 2005 by Taylor & Francis Group, LLC
Routledge is an imprint of Taylor & Francis Group

Printed in the United States of America on acid-free paper
10 9 8 7 6 5 4 3 2 1

International Standard Book Number-10: 0-415-97428-3 (Hardcover) 0-415-97429-1 (Softcover)
International Standard Book Number-13: 978-0-415-97428-8 (Hardcover) 978-0-415-97429-5 (Softcover)

Library of Congress Cataloging-in-Publication Data

Catalog record is available from the Library of Congress

Taylor & Francis Group
is the Academic Division of T&F Informa plc.

Visit the Taylor & Francis Web site at
http://www.taylorandfrancis.com

and the Routledge Web site at
http://www.routledge-ny.com

Contents

Introduction

THOMAS DELIO

It is an intensity of excitement which compels a man to work out a designd
feeling that variously arrives at stations on three levels: the presence in
the imagination in which the speech "comes," a mortality out of immortal
letters; the evident manifestation or trace we in the xxth century worship as
Art and declare immortal; and the return, the dwelling of the imagination
in the speech. So that powers and forms gather in the mind where it feeds
on any written thing.

—Robert Duncan.[1]

In *Mind Models*, Roger Reynolds documents the rich and varied landscape of music in the third quarter of the 20th century. Certainly, no book
has attempted a more comprehensive overview of this era. In it, Reynolds
brings together a body of work and a collection of ideas so fresh and so
startling in their implications that most scholars of music today are just
beginning to fully appreciate their significance. In addition, *Mind Models*
affords an opportunity for us to get inside the mind of one of our most
important composers and musical thinkers as he takes stock of the intellectual landscape of our time. This book is the product of his open-ended
search for new musical experiences, as well as the means to clarify and
understand those experiences.

Highly regarded as a composer, author, teacher and lecturer, Roger
Reynolds is one of the central figures in American music. Through both his
music and his writings he has embraced the world's inherent and, indeed,
essential pluralism. Rather than pursue just one medium, one compositional
method, or one cultural tradition – one creative stance – Reynolds accepts the
multidimensionality of the world that surrounds him. Throughout his career,
he has exhibited unbounded enthusiasm for sonic exploration (as reflected
in the present volume), and has embraced a great many of the most important contemporary musical developments. For many years he has used the
resources of digital technology for the purposes of sound synthesis, sound
processing, and algorithmic composition, and has used these resources
in a variety of contexts (instrumental, multi-media, and music-theater).
Moreover, he has been influenced by the music of various world cultures
(especially those of Asia) and has integrated these into his own work at the

deepest theoretical and philosophical levels. He has clearly absorbed various aspects of serialism (the second Viennese School and beyond), as well as the implications of stochastic composition, and is one of the very few composers to bring these contrasting visions of order into play simultaneously within his work. His drive to integrate such potentially contradictory impulses has enabled him to forge new conceptions of musical language and form.

Roger Reynolds is among a very small number of composers who have contributed to our understanding of contemporary music through their critical writings. In this regard he stands in the company of such American masters as John Cage, Milton Babbitt, and Roger Sessions. In *Mind Models*, his first book, Reynolds addresses questions central to our understanding of the contemporary world and the role of art in that world. This book constitutes a veritable roadmap for navigating the complex network of aesthetic concerns and compositional techniques with which every contemporary composer, writer, and artist must come to grips. When it was first published in 1975, *Mind Models* captured perfectly the extraordinary pluralism of the music scene from which it emerged, the hallmark of which was its overwhelming diversity of both musical styles and compositional methods. Indeed, *Mind Models* represents the first serious attempt to examine this central fact of our expanded musical world: its diversity. A quarter century later, this book seems truly prophetic, for the issues raised in it are of even more vital concern today than they were when it first appeared.

Mind Models is significant in two respects. First, in this book, Reynolds offers numerous observations on an entire range of music written over the course of the past century (from Varése and Bartók, to Reich, Xenakis, and Martirano). As in all his writings, he addresses this music from the perspective of trends and developments both technical and cultural in nature. Second, *Mind Models* serves as a mirror into the compositional thinking of the author himself. Each of the insights that he offers regarding the era in which we live, or the music of our contemporaries, also affords insight into his own creative development and concerns. In *Mind Models* Reynolds considers the then-current scene both from the vantage point of an observer as well as that of a practitioner; one of the seminal modernist practitioners of the last half of the 20th century.

Indeed, if one follows the trajectory of all of Roger Reynolds's major critical writings (*Mind Models, A Searcher's Path, Form and Method*), one finds this duality enacted along a clear line of evolution. *Mind Models* is a more general rumination upon the current situation in art and society and addresses this situation vis-à-vis the work of a variety of leading contemporary "experimental" composers (Alvin Lucier, Robert Ashley, Joji Yuasa, et al.). His second book, the monograph *A Searcher's Path* (1988), refines and deepens some of the arguments from its predecessor and begins a tentative examination of some of the composer's own strategies for composition.[2] Finally, his most recent book, *Form and Method* (2002), constitutes a full-blown, and quite thorough, examination by the composer of his own compositional practice.[3] In a sense, he reveals how his own music has embraced the many cultural and aesthetic issues first raised decades earlier in *Mind Models*. Reynolds's writings complement one another in a particularly significant way. Taken together they allow us to delve deeply into the mind of one of our finest musical creators. We understand the contemporary world through his eyes and then delve into his own creative response to that world. As such, it seems to me that it is essential to consider all three of these books as a single entity through which one can trace the evolution of this composers' thinking from the general concept, through the works of his most important contemporaries, to the specific details of his own compositions. I know of no other similar, or equally substantial, collection of writings by such an important figure.

At the time that *Mind Models* first appeared in print, no one else had attempted to rigorously define the issues raised by those composers who broke most deliberately with traditional European practice. This fact alone sets *Mind Models* apart from contemporary publications. Never before had anyone really attempted to explain the music of these composers in depth. (Indeed, rarely before had their music been taken seriously at all!) Reynolds was the first to clearly identify and consolidate into a single framework the vast array of forces (cultural, political, perceptual, and technical) shaping this heterogeneous body of work.

Mind Models is divided into seven parts. The author begins with an extensive examination of a number of issues of importance to composers and scholars at mid-century. He then moves on to more specific considerations of the materials of music. Finally, he concludes with an illuminating discussion of the morphology of music as it was conceived by composers of that era.

Specifically, in the first three parts, Reynolds raises a number of cultural and aesthetic concerns. Foremost among these is the question of permanence. As the author notes: "One of the most powerful shifts which we are now experiencing is that from the homogeneous ideal of standardization to one of diversity from the standpoint of both the producer and the consumer." Today we recognize that there are no absolute truths and that the world, as well as our understanding of it, are in constant flux. The most important composers and artists of the last half of the 20th century accept this as a fundamental premise for making art. Indeed, this is often the only premise that they share.

The author then considers the effect all of this has on the public. The audience for music today is truly fragmented, both with respect to its musical tastes as well as its listening skills. The emphasis on impermanence and transience has resulted in a proliferation of alternative art forms such as sound installations, environmental art, and site-specific sculptures. These are all manifestations of a general shift away from the production of fixed and permanent art objects, toward the creation of works that are more processes oriented, divorced from any specific instantiation; a shift of emphasis away from the objects of our experience toward the processes that enable and shape our experience. Such a radical re-definition of what an artwork is puts a great burden on audiences, who must adjust, or completely re-define, their most basic ideas about art. Listeners today are challenged as never before. Some, of course, rise to the challenge and are richly rewarded. Others retreat into the false comfort of the lowest common denominator, as exemplified in such current fashions as neo-romanticism and the like.

Following the logical trajectory of the first three parts of *Mind Models*, in the fourth part Reynolds focuses on a detailed examination of acoustics and psychoacoustics. He considers such interrelated topics as the structure of the ear and the elements of sound, including frequency, amplitude, phase, timbre, noise, and localization. He identifies new technologies that allow contemporary composers full access to all of these sonic attributes. Reynolds concludes this part of the book with his first detailed examination of a specific work, the electronic composition *Icon* (1966–69) by Japanese composer Joji Yuasa. The author outlines this composition's timbral and spatial designs and shows how these interact to project a unique sonic evolution over time. He demonstrates how Yuasa employs many of the elements of sound discussed earlier in the book in the creation of this remarkable, pioneering example of electronic composition.

"Music is a chronologic art ... [It] presupposes before all else a certain organization in time ..."[4] With this observation Igor Stravinsky, echoing the sentiments of so many others, underscores the primacy of time in the process of creating and experiencing music. In *Mind Models*, Roger Reynolds implicitly subscribes to this view as well. He devotes the fifth part of the book to this one element of music, emphasizing the need for more research into the very difficult question of how we experience time. He also encourages composers to work with psychologists in developing a greater understanding of our perception of time.[5]

At the conclusion of this part, Reynolds turns to examines *Piano Phase* (1967), a work by Steve Reich. Throughout his career Reich has been concerned with the identification of structure as a process of gradual transformation. *Piano Phase* enacts a process whereby one simple sonic image (melodic/rhythmic gesture) gradually moves out of phase with itself. Each resulting transformation is understood against the implied and constant background of its origin. In this case, the sonic image becomes its own frame of reference. Any alteration in the listener's perception of the original image is entirely the result of changes in that peculiarly self-reflecting frame of reference. The result is a surface of vibrations that acts as a generator for a fluctuating series of perceptual responses. Discussion of Reich's composition is particularly appropriate at this juncture. Through it, Reynolds is able to link his ideas on the temporal processes at work in *Piano Phase* to the more general questions of perception he has raised earlier in the book.

In the penultimate part of *Mind Models*, the author discusses an issue of particular concern at mid-century, notation. He first considers the traditional use of notation as a means of transmitting a composer's intentions to a performer. He then looks at alternative uses in experimental music where notation is often employed for the specific purpose of drawing the performer and, by logical extension, the listener into the creative act itself, thereby breaking down barriers that have always separated composers from performers and listeners. As Reynolds states, "between the creator's idea and the listener's response stretches a path along which a continuous process of decision-making occurs." Along this path, the input of the performer and/or the listener can be inserted to greater or lesser degrees.

The seventh, and final, part of *Mind Models* constitutes a summing up of sorts of all preceding parts. The author examines some of the truly unique conceptions of musical form that have appeared since mid-century, many of which seem to be a direct outgrowth of the social, psychological and technical issues raised in earlier parts of the book:

> An evident discontinuity with traditional Western ideals is upon us the moment we begin seeking contemporary forms in the traditional "closed" sense. Artists in all fields now seem less concerned with the production of contained, finished objects that reflect well-established structural models. The formalized nicety of clearly defined beginnings and endings, of announcing unambiguously that one was about to do something, was now doing it and had now finished, has been widely questioned. Experiences tend to evolve gradually (or sometimes commence arbitrarily), to end by simply fading away. The experiential implication is that one has, as a listener, sampled a process that existed before and will continue to exist after the immediate occasion has passed. The notion of clearly packaged forms of experience seems suddenly arbitrary to many artists who opt instead for less constraining modes of presentation: the sample adroitly selected.

If we fully grasp the implications of the issues raised in this book, we must inevitably conclude that traditional notions of form–notions rooted in a 19th century world-view–no longer suffice. As our understanding of the nature of both human perception and experience changes, we, naturally, expect that art will reflect these changes. As Reynolds took great pains to demonstrate in earlier sections of the book, perception is variable, experience volatile and both are entirely dependent upon a context that is constantly shifting.

> *Because the various world we sense is not*
> *Ever apprehended as one, or formed as one,*
> *Ideas are always wrong, always unfixed,*
> *And often their power to make the world real is lost.*[6]

These lines by the poet William Bronk capture perfectly the essence of the contemporary artist's dilemma; to illuminate a world which can no longer be viewed as fixed and bounded, but which is, instead, itself a process of perpetual reevaluation and realignment.

Art communicates through its modes of organization. From these emanate its expressive power as well as its meaning. Art that is built upon principles of closure reflects a view of experience that is fixed and absolute. In contrast, art that is built upon principles of multiplicity and opposition reflect the inescapable uncertainty of life. Composers who espouse such an open view of art are less concerned with projecting one fixed aesthetic viewpoint than projecting an infinite variety of possible viewpoints. Rather than seek to create one ideal compositional design, composers of such open works seek compositional designs that admit all possibilities as equally viable and expressive. Such composers reject outright the position that any one particular compositional choice may be inherently better, and therefore more meaningful, than all others. Recognizing that there is no single "correct" way to organize one's experiences these composers seek to express the full range of possibilities that their experiences engender. In this sense, multiplicity becomes the very fabric of their art, its *raison d'être*. Through their works, these composers seek to project the full richness of the material world. Their goal is to make art that revels in the chaotic, entropic nature of that world.

Of course, for musicians, the label "open structure" has curious and rather limiting connotations. It is often associated exclusively with various chance procedures of composition (statistical processes, improvisation, and the like). However, as I wrote over twenty years ago:

> *In its most characteristic manifestation the open work seems to be one in which perception replaces object. In other words, the focus of the open composition seems not to be upon the object of perception, but rather upon the process of perception.*[7]

Certainly, this condition can be, and often is 9, achieved in works that are fully notated, and non-improisional in nature, as is, for example, the case with Roger Reynolds' own music.

In the final part of *Mind Models*, the author examines a series of contemporary works, each of which exhibits a morphology that is rooted in the nature and processes of perception. Take, for example, a work by the American composer Robert Ashley that is presented here, *in memoriam ... ESTEBAN GÔMEZ* (1964). For this piece, a score was created that accepts any sonic context and generates a range of possible musical designs within very broad constraints. This score suggests only very general indications regarding the transformation of sonic materials. As such, the composition becomes a framework through which we may access many equally expressive and meaningful moments. This work is not merely a documentation of one particular compositional process (its product); it is process itself–process in all its manifestations (conceptual, perceptual, experimental and physical). Ashley's piece is a true reflection of the multi-dimensionality of the world from which it came.

In addition to Ashley's *in memoriam* ..., Reynolds examines compositions by such diverse contemporary masters as Iannis Xenakis (*Metastasis*, 1953–54), Krzysztof Penderecki (*Threnody for the Victims of Hiroshima*, 1960), Ben Johnston (*Knocking Piece*, 1963), Alvin Lucier (*Music for Solo Performer*, 1965), Gordon Mumma (*Hornpipe*, 1967), Salvatore Martirano (*L.'s G. A.*, 1970), and the author himself (*I/O: A Ritual for 23 Performers*, 1971). He concludes with a discussion of a work by architect Will Insley (*Ceremonial Space*, 1970) through which he demonstrates that the ideas outlined in his book transcend the local concerns of musicians and are of potential interest to all contemporary artists.

For young composers in the 1970s, the appearance of *Mind Models* provided a much needed breath of fresh air. Not only did the book constitute one of the first serious attempts to come to grips with the very latest developments in contemporary music, but it also pointed the way toward the creation of a viable method for teasing out the rich and complex implications of this music. In *Mind Models* Reynolds demonstrates that such new conceptions of music as those proposed by Lucier, Xenakis, Mumma, Martirano, and many others demand equally new and thoughtful responses, rooted in the latest developments in acoustics, psychology, philosophy, technology, and cultural studies. Consequently, we now understand that only through a comprehensive understanding of each of these fields individually and collectively can we possibly address the myriad implications of the music of such extraordinary composers. This music continues to challenge us today. *Mind Models* constitutes Roger Reynolds' own, very personal, response to this challenge. It is an essential work for anyone who cares deeply about the music of our time.

Notes

1. Robert Duncan, *Letters: Poems 1953–1956* (Flood Editions, 2003), p. ix. The poet's irregular spelling ('designd') is intentional.
2. Roger Reynolds, *A Searcher's Path: A Composer's Ways* (Institute for Studies in American Music, 1987).
3. ——, *Form and Method: Composing Music (The Rothschild Essays)* (Routledge, 2002).
4. Igor Stravinsky, *The Poetics of Music*, translated by A. Knodel and I. Dahl (Harvard University Press, 1947), p. 28.

5. The relationship between preceptual psychology and composition was extensively explored in a ten-year long collaborative interaction between (primarily) Reynolds and psychologist Steve McAdams and is reported on in: McAdams, S. and Battier, M. (eds.) *Perception and Creation of a Contemporary Musical Work, Ircam-Centre Pompidou, Paris* [CD-ROM] (2005).
6. William Bronk, *Blue Spruces in Pairs, A Bird Bath Between* from *the World, the Worldless* (New Directions, 1964), p. 2.
7. Thomas DeLio, *Circumscribing the Open Universe* (University Press of America, 1983; Italian translation, Semar Editore, 2001), p. 2.

Preface

Mind Models reflects its curious lineage. I had been abroad most of the '60's, in Germany, France, Italy and Japan, and resettled in the United States only in 1969. Shortly after taking up a teaching position at the University of California, San Diego, I was invited to be George Miller Visiting Professor at the University of Illinois. One of the requirements of that position, in turn, was the presentation of four public lectures. I decided to sum up for myself and my listeners the materials and perspectives that I had accumulated in my years of peregrination and then during early encounters with graduate students at the University of California, San Diego. The final chapters of the present book (on Sound, Time, Notation, and Morphology) are idiosyncratic compendia, and were presented with musical examples to fellow new music enthusiasts, students and colleagues in Urbana during the Spring of 1971. My listeners and I shared the desire to clarify through wide-ranging discussion a situation which seemed at once perilous and exhilarating.

As it happened, the eminent music historian Gilbert Chase, was in the audience and he encouraged me to publish my remarks, a notion that would never have occurred to me on my own. Chase contacted his editor at Praeger Press, and negotiations followed. Praeger felt that additional sections were required, sections in which I could propose a view of the social and cultural context that had fostered the sorts of perspectives that I was advancing from within the creative edge of the musical field. Such an undertaking was something for which I felt far less prepared than I had been for sharing current musical concerns with my peers. Still, I agreed to undertake this task and to do so in a parallel spirit to that adopted in my Miller Lectures.

The resulting book surprises me now, three decades later by the ways in which it remains relevant. Aspects of my argument that seemed rather adventuresome then have been borne out to a degree that I certainly could not have foreseen with precision. (I think especially of the discussions of Diversity, New Models, and Subgroups in Society.) Further, the care with which I attempted to check my perspectives with experts wherever specu-lation became perilous appears to have paid a dividend of continuing currency. In this revision of the 1975 publication, I extensively rewrote with a view to clarifying the line of argument. I have updated details where earlier perspectives might have proved misleading or irrel-evant but otherwise tried to leave the original opinions essentially as they were. In several cases, I would certainly not now place the same degree of emphasis on points that I did in 1972 (the potential significance of drugs to creativity or the importance of notational innovation which can now be seen as a period provocation). In general, however, the explorative and wide-ranging speculation in which Mind Models engaged appears to me to have been a healthy exercise. Though we seem now, in a new millennium, to be in a slightly more stable place, it is a place also marked by a relative timidity. It is clear, too, that there is still a role to be performed by those who – while maintaining an open mind in relation to innovation – seek an understanding of the context within which invention occurs, and the presuppositions of those artists whose aim is to lead us to new and rewarding aesthetic experience.

—ROGER REYNOLDS

Acknowledgments

The efforts of three individuals have been fundamental in the reappearance now, seventeen years after its original publication, of a substantially revised edition of *Mind Models*. H. Wiley Hitchcock, teacher, then colleague and friend, agreed to undertake this new edition as Director of the Institute for Studies in American Music. His editorial suggestions have been gratefully received. John Lauer (assisted, early on, by Keith Kothman) entered the text into a word-processing environment and resolutely overcame its most arcane objections to seemingly straightforward details in layout. Karen Reynolds was unflagging in her editorial service. To all of them I am deeply grateful.

Figures 1 and 2, courtesy of Reginald Bickford; Figures 3a and 3b, reprinted by permission from Manfred Clynes and J.H. Milsum, eds., *Biomedical Engineering Systems* (New York: McGraw-Hill, 1970), pp. 275 and 331; Figure 4, reprinted by permission from S.S. Stevens, ed., *Handbook of Experimental Psychology* (New York: J. Wiley & Sons, 1951), p. 100; Figure 5, reprinted by permission from George Miller, *Language & Communication* (New York: McGraw-Hill, 1951), p. 48; Figure 6, reprinted by permission from Rupert Taylor, *Noise* (London: Pelican Original, 1970), p. 63, copyright © Rupert Taylor, 1970; Figures 8 and 9, from unpublished research by James Beauchamp, University of Illinois, 1974; Figures 10 and 11, from Fritz Winkel, *Music, Sound and Sensation: A Modern Exposition* (New York: Dover Publications, 1967); Figure 13, reprinted by permission from M.V. Mathews, *The Technology of Computer Music* (Cambridge, Mass.: MIT Press, 1969); Figures 14, 15 and 16, reprinted by permission of Ongaku No Tomo Sha Corp., Kagunazaka 6–30, Shinjuku-ku, Tokyo, Japan; Figures 17 and 18, reprinted by permission from J. E. Orme, *Time, Experience and Behaviour* (New York: American Elsevir Publishing Co., 1969); Figure 19, reprinted by permission from E. H. Lockwood, *A Book of Curves* (Cambridge, England: Cambridge University Press, 1963); Figure 20, reprinted by permission from Evans and Piggins, *British Journal of Physiological Optics*, Diagram (Fig. 3); Figure 21, quoted by permission of Steve Reich; Figure 22, reprinted by permission from Paul Klee, *Pedagogical Sketch Book* (New York: Praeger Publishers, 1953); Figures 23 and 31, reprinted by permission C. F. Peters Corporation; Figures 25 and 26, reprinted by permission from Iannis Xenakis, *Formalized Music* (Bloomington: Indiana University Press, 1971; revised edition, Pendragon Press, 1992); Figure 27, reprinted by permission from *Source Magazine*, Composer/Performer Edition, No. 1, p. 41; Figure 29, *Source Magazine*, Composer/Performer Edition, No. 2, p. 85; Figure 30, copyright © 1957, Universal Edition. Used by permission of the publisher, Theodore Presser, sole representative, U.S.A., Canada and Mexico; Figures 32 and 33, photos by George Roos, courtesy of the Fischbach Gallery, New York, New York; illustration, page 237, copyright © 1954, Universal Edition. Used by permission of the Publisher, Theodore Presser, sole representative, U.S.A., Canada, and Mexico.

PART I
Rates of Change

Permanence

"The beauty of the rose is in its passing," wrote a Japanese master of N drama, Zeami. He was fascinated by transience as a dimension of scarcity, hence value. We now see that the acceptance of this pairing is culturally variable. Age is in one context positive, in another negative. Our own growing concern with recycling materials is based on an emergent understanding that new forms and functions can be imposed upon the same basic materials, as need decrees. Permanence is, in other words, a relative condition whose value depends on one's perspective.

As the pace of urban, technological life increases, the impact of individual objects and events decreases. Objects and momentary conditions, however striking, are not as solid as they once were. Some artists and industrialists pay tribute to this transience. They contribute to its effect by formalizing it and attempting to imbue it with value of its own. Such calculated rationalization of what one sees can provide a convenient excuse for drifting with and capitalizing on the social course. This is an understanding of convenience.

It is not necessary to abandon the idea of continuing relevance but, rather, to shift attention from the individual items of experience to the processes they populate and define. The event itself, whether earthquake, invasion, or court decision, is now quickly dissolved in the current of explanation and documentation that follows (demonstrating both the confluence of trends that produced the event and the radial implications it holds for the future). An occasional occurrence—a moon landing or fate's meddling with a figure of international importance—rises above the processes that contrived it, but these are increasingly rare. In the main, we are attuned to tides, to streams of events, and not to the individual item, whatever its magnitude.

Some more innovative artists have been taken to task for losing interest in the creation of "permanent" products and, by implication, of lasting values. But the physical object can be de-emphasized without sacrificing the peculiar insight possible through fresh conceptual perspectives on the forms of reality provided by a given context. For example, the sculptor Jir Takamatsu employs minimal materials—a sheet of canvas, a length of rope, to probe the flux of change within identity. Large quadrilateral sections of canvas are sewn together so that the outer perimeter of the whole remains square while excess material collects in the center. (The inside seams are longer than the outside edges.) Each time the entire mass is tossed, it falls into new patterns of prominence and shadow, an endlessly variable topography generated from unchanging substance and an eloquent commentary on the nature of permanence. Takamatsu's work generates implications with longrange value: a flexible surface, the skin of a potential dome, is made to accommodate a flat support—a phenomenon natural to one set of dimensions is thrust into another environment and transformed.

Critics of innovative artists should recognize that these artists are often groping toward the comprehension of process. They should realize that this is a reorientation rather than an abrogation of concern. Basic reorientation cannot be accomplished easily; especially since the focus on processes, on extended activities or evolving commentaries which abjure the particular object, is unprecedented and difficult for the inexperienced collector, critic, or museum-goer to comprehend. Processes are beyond possession; they separate the artist from his profitable involvement with prospective owners, the buyer from the satisfaction of possession.

Good art demands as one of its components an architectonic and allusive scope. This normally arises only out of the maker's confidence in the presence of his materials. Any major reorientation necessitates, then, a period of absorption and acclimatization by the artist. The public and the connoisseur must also adjust their attitudes.

Music in the West has occupied an unenviable economic position ever since the individual composer stepped from the servant's quarters into the metaphoric marketplace by attempting to replace services with salable goods (original scores). Though collectors may find the purchase of an historically valued musical manuscript a worthy investment, its value derives from the sonic worlds it has stimulated and from the current renown of its creator, not from its graphic substance. The manuscript defines a similar yet differentiated class of musical experiences that are implied but require the intelligent collaboration of performer and listener for realization. Unlike a painting or a piece of sculpture, a manuscript is not suited for direct public appreciation.

Collaboration presupposes a common set of terms, a context that is not in need of constant definition or fresh delimitation. Traditional painting and music continue to be appealing because of their sensuous uniqueness and structural generality. Their surfaces remain invitations and are organized in such a way that their inner patterns of relationships can be rediscovered as the context and emphasis in presentation change. Theatrical art has always depended on the willing suspension of disbelief. The spectator collaborates tacitly by agreeing to set aside the ordinary prerogatives of judgment, to accept events and consequences that might be patently absurd within the normal concourse of life. Hence, the play lends itself to abstract, general applicability as does, for a variety of reasons, the best of visual, plastic, and aural art.

This was possible because there was always an original context of some sort and it was a sufficiently long-lived and widespread shaping force to have been accessible to an individual through act of will, or inadvertence. What has happened to the assumption of firmly understood and accessible cultural contexts? Historically, creative artists have only on the rarest occasions broken with their own intellectual and social milieus; today the contemporary composer struggles to settle on a manageable selection of materials and to gain the attention of a small slice of an unprecedentedly massive public. Only then may he be tellingly productive.

In the past decade, there has been a geometric increase in the number of distinct subgroups within the world community and within each nation. Context is no longer inherited in the natural and, for all practical purposes, permanent way that formerly held true. To a certain degree, we can now choose our context. How this will affect the idea of style—or idiom-based art—is as yet difficult to fix with certainty. One imagines several possible trends. Human beings share certain anatomical and biological characteristics that are independent of cultural or racial factors. There may be, then, some avenues of direct sensory experience that could transcend the apparent differences. Another possibility is the use of general frames of reference, utilitarian structures such as cities, through which "guides" with special insight could help us experience in aesthetically pleasing ways. Finally, there is the notion of aesthetic experience individually tailored for small groups or for private consumption with materials derived from the participants. Attempts are already being made in each of these categories and we shall discuss them in later chapters.

Within and across the broad categories noted above, an abundance of possibilities is open to the creative artist. If the artist is faced with the dilemma of selecting limits, then each member of the public will have similar if smaller problems. He too will have a wide variety of choices, but even less time and energy to devote to selection. Consequently, he may recoil from the problems and make the simplistic choice: rejection. From a rational point of view it is difficult to see why this should be the case. Large-scale innovation in social and material matters is probably resisted less now than in the past. Moderate, unobtrusive change is embraced with progressive enthusiasm. But unfortunately, in the realm of art, prejudice towards change is indulged imperiously.

As our awareness of the rate at which change is experienced increases, we will pay more attention to trends than to the individual fact, which happens to result from their momentary intersection. We may find it more natural to cope with long-range processes, to surrender to the unfamiliar contexts, which they imply. The question, then, is how will the individual respond to life and the aesthetic experience in the next few decades? If we are less frequently obliged to exercise lifegiving or life-preserving judgments, should we not be more willing to risk the adoption of unfamiliar aesthetic frames of reference? If the security of basic life functions were to be guaranteed, the individual might well be both increasingly free to select from a variety of intellectual allegiances and more willing to adopt, if only temporarily, seemingly remote contexts for sensory and intellectual experience. The artist and his audience should enhance their mobility, range of concerns, and the willingness with which they adopt varied contexts in the interest of redefined benefits. One must expect less resonance from the singular event and privileged relational structures, accepting more readily the rewards of flow and process.

The basic issue is the speed with which experience can be consumed. As the rate of change increases, so must our concept of how we sample and process experience. Adaptability is reaffirmed as the evolutionary imperative.

Acceleration and Pace

A taste for speed is commonplace but an appreciation of acceleration is less often encountered. Let us assume that something is continuously increasing its displacement with respect to a reference point, be it intellectual, cultural, or spatial. Does the amount of displacement remain constant within equivalent intervals of time? If it increases with each interval, acceleration is involved. Acceleration is unrelenting intensification, an accumulative tendency. Acceleration is not necessarily uniform, however, since it can occur at different rates and may be continuous or discontinuous. Failure to recognize the by no means trivial possibility of discontinuous acceleration has subjected us to considerable hysteria and to sundry unfounded prophecies of disaster. Nevertheless, acceleration does involve larger perils than the unchanging nature of speed.

The glutting of the skilled-job market in the 1960's will serve as an example. A disruptive factor in American life then, this manpower surplus could not have been predicted on the basis of college enrollments alone, although they were certainly startling. (Attendance was up from 2.3 million in 1950 to more than 7 million by 1970.) While the bureaucratic mechanism of higher education was expanding, industry streamlined its operations through automation and computer speed. Specialized disciplines whose value had seemed unquestionable were obviated and new ones generated, as industry, oblivious to the content of formal education, forged ahead. Young people found themselves with fully developed sets of values incompatible with those of the business or government concerns which they were expected to join. How did these presumably stable and interdependent processes come to be so badly out of phase?

Part of the answer lies in the distinctive pace with which each increasingly self-contained and self-defined sector of society develops. Can we reasonably expect that the various areas of revolutionary change likely to occur within the coming decades will proceed apace? Is it likely that the rates at which various sectors of society make use of the products of revolutionary trends will correspond naturally? The inertial essence of self-generating and self-maintaining systems of public education and industrial automation, the predictive power of computer-generated models, constantly reforming lines of professional disciplines, and changing value systems of succeeding generations will lead to an increasingly more specialized and fragmented vocabulary of ideas and mores. It is becoming untenable to identify a condition or seek its roots within the confines of any one discipline. But although our awareness of alternate views and structuring of reality is beginning to breed caution, it is almost impossible to find an inter-disciplinary language that is general enough to provide genuine perspective. An initial step can be made by passing beneath the surface of descriptive systems to ways in which the subject material comes to us. The notions of acceleration and unsynchronous rates of change in themselves are useful in understanding how theories or visions are offered to societies, and the effectiveness with which they are likely to be absorbed. We are accustomed to think of speed in the adoption process as being at least moderately suspect and, more often than not, indicative of incautious naïveté. In this context, speed equals haste.

Is this necessarily so? Might we now learn to streamline the process by which we familiarize ourselves with new devices or ideas, new friendships or roles? Must we continue to use often archaic criteria to judge behavior in the face of new conditions? Adapting ourselves to the rate at which ideas, objects, and services become available now does not necessarily imply indifference or the abandonment of monitoring values. Cultivation of the ability to form and discard images of reality, comparable to the convenient adoption of contexts for aesthetic reward mentioned in the preceding chapter on permanence, might well result in an expanded sense of scope for mental life, a view wide enough to transform a quantitative dimension into a qualitative enhancement of the species.

On the negative side, consider the introversion implicit in the use of drugs, whether they be the mind-numbing agents of the young or the tranquilizing powders of their parents. The consumption of such isolating depressants effectively removes the users from a productive place in society. Yet, of course, a rapid pace of change cannot be governmentally mandated, customized for each segment of society. The most damaging effects of rapid pace can be moderated on the basis of attitude changes by a focusing on trends instead of events. Relief will not come from old perspectives in which the importance of individual moments remains inappropriately inflated. A redefined sense of what represents optimum participation in life is necessary.

The need for relief from the accelerative paces of the real world suggests a view of art as a refuge. This is a primary factor now operating to inflate the value of the older, socially accepted works of art. Certified by histori-cal selectivity, these are assumed to be understood, thereby releasing the spectator/listener from any obligation to exert effort. But the nature of the perspective that art gives to life as it is lived changes as human contexts change. Beginning as an agent of communal purposes, the artisan later became responsible to an aristocratic elite and in the process became what we call an artist. Egalitarian trends returned him to the service of a mass public but on a far less utilitarian, more esoteric basis. Now, as the capacity for the storage and retrieval of information expands almost limitlessly and subcultures proliferate, the artist is pressured to adjust his output to the variegated needs of a mass of subgroups, to learn to tailor and differentiate his products according to rapidly evolving needs and standards. The work of more than one important composer and filmmaker now clearly indicates the fascination that exploration of unfamiliar pace holds.[1] Where art, magic, and their attendant excitement may have once provided a highly stimulative contrast from dreary routine, we now face a turnabout, where certain types of art may become a refuge.

Diversity

If impermanence is an inevitable result of acceleration, diversity is likely as well. When the basic processes defining a society are in accord, they are integrated with relative ease. The functional interests of the individual and his society are served with maximum economy. When integration between, let us say, business, education, and ecological considerations, national and international priorities, or scientific and humane concerns breaks down or tends to become arbitrary, we lose the certainty of ponderous bureaucracies and the relative flexibility of our local communities. Although the content of formal education and the requirements of business may no longer be con-gruent, they still fall into some pattern of relationships, however incoherent. Institutions so basic to society as education and business *cannot* function in true independence.

A confusing diversity is produced as a growing number of intersec-tions between asynchronous processes occurs. The proliferation of techni-

---

1. Of course, slowness of pace and scale are linked. One need only consider filmmakers Tarkovsky and Sieberberg or composers Feldman and Glass.

cal specialties available at American universities during the second half of the twentieth century exemplifies this process. Programs in civil, electrical, and mechanical engineering have been joined by those in astrophysics, packaging, computer sciences, and so on. The same proliferation of categories can be seen in the humanities. At first, the traditional departments offer specialized degree programs. Faced with increasing demands on limited manpower and equipment, they eventually resort to "interdisciplinary" programs involving the cooperation of several established departments. A further step is already in use: the educational free market where there are no required subjects, only certain fields from which to select, and where students determine their own programs with the inconstant aid of faculty counseling. This is maximum diversity, to be sure, but can the tailoring of available guidance to a student's professed needs substitute adequately for those all-important, unexpected encounters that radically deflect and enliven the individual's education? Should an academic program be merely reactive?

Consumer industries and mass communications have been accurately designated the chief purveyors of homogenized tastes and of depressed standards. This was true while these gargantuan machines were in relative infancy. Now, however, diversity has become a feature of almost any field in which there is a profit to be made. Enlarged automated industry can introduce variations and mutations almost without practical limit. To understand this, one need not visit a major automobile dealer's showroom; it is enough to step into a car-rental office, once one has decided which of the dozen such agencies near any major airport to patronize. The range of models, named after planets, North American or African animals, folk heroes, and the like is literally breathtaking. The actual name of the manufacturer is never spoken, presumably for fear that the range of offerings might shrink to manageable and therefore image-damaging dimensions.

The eventual meaning to the arts of product differentiation will partially depend on the value attached to aesthetic experience by individuals undergoing changing patterns of life. To what extent might near-perfect whim-accommodation lessen one's aesthetic longings? If leisure expands, as now seems inevitable, there is no assurance that the largest or even an appreciable percentage of the public will choose to spend it enhancing or indulging their aesthetic dimensions. There will no doubt be formidable challenges from competitive and non-competitive sporting activities, gambling of varieties and on a scale as yet unknown, and from extensions of the service industries both of the impersonal sorts such as cable television and in the form of more directly interpersonal contact. Certainly the outcome will be based, in major part, on the actual stature and diversity of the new art.

In the '60's, the young rejected some of the sacrosanct assumptions of their parents, including the work ethic and other responsibilities routinely imposed from without. It is clear that pontification and admonishments about the value of aesthetic experience will not insure the public survival of the fine arts in a world when so many other more immediate gratifications abound.

In those years, it seemed as though the era of the internationally dominant virtuoso, the marketed star, would fade. Certainly cultural homogeneity, the acceptance of unexamined values that maintains broad cultural consensus, could no longer be taken for granted. One possibility seemed a return to the more functional, individualized production of the artisan: custom-made products for diverse tastes, more adaptive combinations of the agreeable and the challenging, responsive to each individual. There has been indeed a fuller response in all phases of life to the fact of diversified products and services and, hence, diversified need. In the arts, a wider experience with mixed media is available, but there has not been a return to anything approximating the informed amateur of the past. Because of the virtuosity and pervasiveness of communications technology, the listener is content to remain passive. The connoisseur of structural niceties, however, will no doubt continue to be served by subtly structured and carefully tailored music or sculptural objects.

Capability

A notable characteristic of *capability* as it now exists is the promise (or threat) that notions once comfortably hypothetical are now practical. Realization is often no more than a matter of financial backing or salesmanship. The ability to amplify the normal levels of human sensibility and strength by means of what Buckminster Fuller has termed "the mechanical extensions of man" increases both the likelihood and inconvenience of error. We ravage our own land and air, decimate the fields and forests of allies, and threaten to obliterate ourselves under the sheer volume of disposable products that industry, once unleashed, does not fail to provide. Foresight is no longer a virtue but an imperative. The long-range effects of trends we consider initiating must be weighed far more thoroughly than in the past. We can no longer take for granted relative human impotence in the face of the "permanent" mass of the planet and its evolutionally achieved systems. Too often for us now, the imagined becomes the real.

The bewildered individual is incessantly prodded by his own fallibility, his irreparable ignorance. He defers to the superior wisdom of experts who are, for the most part, oblivious to his individual values. In the light of present-day capacity, morality now involves far more than the evaluation of the immediate consequences of an act on the basis of locally inculcated values. Technology has provided the means for asking enormous numbers of questions and obtaining related "answers" under all kinds of shifting conditions. There remains the necessity to ask sufficiently astute questions. Unless one foresees the wide range of implications inherent in any process set in motion, a series of effects only remotely related to formally anticipated ends may well become overwhelming. Conceived as aids to commerce and communication, freeways divide territories and facilities, add to noise and air pollution, and confuse our already badly damaged sense of human scale.

The contemporary composer shares in the general dilemma and remains poorly informed about how his visions might be matched with present capability. He is inclined to conceive uses technologists would consider maverick. His attitude appears naïve to the technologically oriented observer, and the artist may even wryly join in self-denigration. The artist Robert Rauschenberg has observed that:

> ... most often *the artist himself is so seduced by the simple marvels of science that are really just utilitarian for the scientists* and for the industrial world, that the art concept doesn't match, it doesn't even compare to the level of scientific concepts because the artist just incorporates the phenomenon. He is seeing a *fact* as a romantic phenomenon, as filled with beauty, and if he touches it and says that's it, then that's his work.[2]

If he does no more than "touch," the result has no public value, is not a work in any useful sense. Note well the added italics in the passage above. How easily one may now become divorced from the consciousness of a role and its associated viewpoints. The artist, most of all, should assist us in nurturing the ability to assume and value a variety of stances. He certainly should not take his own position for granted. The "reality" of a phenomenon depends upon its context, and one cannot be interchanged with the other. The artist's interest in the long-term implications of processes set in motion by science is often neither economic nor moral. He has a different view of *utility* and this is the key word whenever the two worlds are brought into contact.

The Los Angeles County Art Museum spent five years (1967–71) implementing an ambitious program in "Art and Technology." In addition to a brilliantly compact and telling exhibition, a 400-page catalog resulted. Its impact goes far beyond the limited ability of words and diagrams to evoke the actual experience produced by contact with the works in the exhibit. Of overriding value is the way in which encounters between corporate technologists and invited artists are calmly and chronologically detailed. Monumental patience on the part of the museum staff, the considerable prestige of the institution, and its ability to promise large-scale public exhibitions supported the project (itself a process meriting exhibition), but

---

2. *A Report on the Art and Technology Program of the Los Angeles County Museum of Art*, Los Angeles, 1971, p.284.

few marriages were made. In the case of those collaborations that did result, the final product usually involved complete reshaping of the creator's initial (apparently impractical) aim.

Failure to achieve viable relationships stemmed from the sorts of business-minded rationales and intraorganizational blockages that a cynical observer might have expected. The artist's disruptive personal appearance, his technical naïveté or irreverent attitude toward the ends to which a particular machine was normally devoted, were often fatal to a proposed match. Acceptance usually hinged upon finding the right man within a corporation. Those companies whose higher executives were known art enthusiasts proved particularly unresponsive. In short, the degree to which preconceived concepts of the proper use of ideas and equipment, the proper function of art, and the proper behavior of men ruled responses on the industrial side clearly emerges as one reads the catalog. It is discreet in its editorializing but the indictment is unmistakable.

Siren calls, however, do not emanate only from science and its imagined wonders. Experts in one creative discipline are constantly wooed by elements from another. Musicians find that their ideas lead them toward mixed-media efforts in which sound alone is insufficient. Painters and sculptors realize that their evolving works—kinetic or process-oriented sculptures—necessitate coping with associated sounds, or, more unsettling, seem to require an organized aural dimension. The fine arts have entered the temporally structured domain on a fundamental level. Although the perception of paintings has always been a time-consuming process for a cultivated viewer, and sculpture gardens have always implied temporal as well as physical paths for the observer, this dimension has not been controlled. In too much experimental art of the 1960's, processes ramble on and undistinguished elements are expected to provide substance. The painter or sculptor is not trained, is not by habit skilled (as is a composer, a filmmaker, or a playwright) in gauging the order and spacing of events in time, let alone the interplay of contrapuntal, chronologically defined streams of events. The worker in the fine arts, not only the composer, must pay more attention to acquiring the expertise he requires from the other arts, from science, skills that his own evolving interests increasingly demand.

Varying rates of development and increased intradisciplinary specializing have resulted in loss of the synchrony once taken for granted.

The World's Fairs, beginning with Brussels in 1958 and, more notably, with Montreal's Expo '67 and the Osaka Fair in 1970, have stimulated nations and corporations to the use of technology to entrance enormous, mobile audiences. Most of these exhibitions have been devoted to salesmanship of one sort or another and were necessarily temporary. Multiple screen projections, complex presentations in which the viewers were polled to determine statistically the direction taken by a story, and total environments of sound, sculpture, and light have been used for undeniably strong if generally unrefined effect. These presentations have risen above apathy, exhaustion, and cultural barriers to make direct sensory touch with masses of individuals. A more germane example for our purposes is provided by contemporary approaches to the design of permanent entertainment parks.

Beginning with experiment in animation during the 1930's, Walt Disney was bent on the production of entertaining illusion. His efforts were not confined to two-dimensional studies; in the 1950's, he ventured into three-dimensional animation as well. Recurring, programmed sequences provide for high-volume traffic and independence from human performers. The collaboration of engineers, architects, artists, sculptors, and costume design experts resulted in an elaborate pirate adventure at Disneyland. This project, costing millions of dollars, was completed in the late 1960's.

"Pirates of the Caribbean" includes a sequential dimension so that spectators are moved on water-filled canals in individual, twelve-person barges propelled by water jets. The route winds through a bayou passage where Spanish moss drapes live oak trees, past full-scale ships and complexes of burning buildings populated by over a hundred life-sized figures. The latter are all sculpted and programmed to move in accord with the requirements of the scenario, a wink, a gesture, or an extended speech with appropriate grimaces. The complete twelve-minute cycle is produced with the aid of the environmental-scale manipulation of temperature, palpable dampness, and programmed multichanneled sound. It is all skillfully contrived, and each unnatural detail one notices is countered by the realization of how remarkable the illusion nevertheless is. An important initial effort in the production of large-scale programmed entertainments, "Pirates of the Caribbean" is a patently artificial experience that achieves an undeniably engaging effect. One is in an action of sorts, and though it is commercially inspired manipulation, to be sure, it is benevolently calculated, a forerunner, we may assume, of more compelling vicarious involvements.

As these massive, programmed entertainments improve, their makers will have to devote an increasing proportion of design thought to two crucial factors: viewer isolation and the control of sequence. Because of their many visitors and relatively restricted duration, environmental exhibitions at World's Fairs and museums have been unable to follow such an ideal course. Several of the more innovative plans for the Los Angeles Museum's "Art and Technology" exhibition were critically compromised by an inability to control the way in which the individual visitor made contact with the experience. We have paid so little attention to this fundamental factor in human aesthetic response that performance and exhibition facilities everywhere are ill-suited to attempts at any but the most rudimentary level of control. The Los Angeles Museum wisely restricted the number of presentations in its show and gave each a separate room with light traps and moderate insulation, but even these substantial steps proved powerless against the disruption of excited crowds of school children or the more subtle interference of a distracting remark overheard. The intent visitor marshals his attentive prowess but struggles in vain to clear away distractions. He must imagine, in private postvisit reveries, what might have been gained. In most of the environmentally controlled works, attentive absorption is a necessary condition. One needs to pass beyond surfaces that may seem trivial in order to find the genuine experiential depth offered. Sponsors of innovative aesthetic efforts in particular must come to understand how and why composers and artists are widening the scope of their efforts to control the nature of overall experience. Too many extraordinary attempts wilt and are discarded on the basis of inappropriately based judgments. Seemingly trivial incursions on what we casually call "mood" can be and frequently are ruinous to the dimension of an idea. As our technical capability increases, so must our ability to approach new forms of experience openly.

Acceptance of Context

When the imagined consequences of accepting an unfamiliar context involve bodily or psychic injury, where firmly grounded (though perhaps unjusti- fied) fears are conjured up in the individual, hesitancy is understandable. A child on his first day in school, the property owner confronted by repre- sentatives of a minority, the fieldtrained soldier who finds himself in jungle terrain—all have reason for apprehension. It is more difficult to understand a person's unwillingness to assume a flexible attitude in aesthetic situations, to understand, for example, the visceral fear that the devotee of Brahms felt when confronted with Wagner's music. The risk of real injury is slight even at the most outrageous avant-garde production.

Until recently, we have rarely been conscious of contexts on any scale, and almost never on the broadest. Contexts are intricately interdependent weavings of physical and cultural factors. Only the largest minds have upon occasions risen above their social conditioning. But the acceptance of contexts—especially those so broad as to escape our notice—determines beyond appeal those questions that can be asked and the answers it is possible to give or to utilize. Contexts elude discovery because they comprise the foundations of entire life patterns. They are sets of axioms inter- nalized past questioning. The Women's Liberation Movement of the 1970's impresses on us the degree to which custom and language itself condition the woman to subservience, infecting her capacity even to consider a broad range of roles and actions sanctioned for males. As desirable as complemen- tarity is, however much it underwrites quality in life, it must be admitted that sexual conditioning has become an anachronistic and arbitrary process that must undergo drastic revision. If we can be unaware of our adopted context on so fundamental a scale as biology, how many other subloyalties escape us and limit the flexibility of our minds? As the number of consciously apprehended contexts available to us grows and diversity accelerates, the ability to assume one or another at will may well become an evolutionary imperative. At one moment, we might need to be committed to a nuclear family structure, totally self-invested at another, and consciously members of a species at still other moments. These multiple stances need not conflict but could enable us to better serve the functions of each.

The Argentine writer Jorge Luis Borges has a genius for fastening upon stray stimuli and fashioning, by extension, visions of possible worlds. One of his striking, predictive short stories, "The Babylon Lottery," explores the implications of societal gambling. As a study in the acceptance of context it is hard to surpass. The lottery beginning as "a game of plebeian character" grows more compelling until all citizens are obliged to participate. Administered by the "Company," the drawings impose penalties and grant rewards. The use of pecuniary means to accomplish the lottery's ends are replaced by the consignment of each individual to a predetermined social role for the period between drawings. As for the citizen of Babylon:

> A happy drawing might motivate his elevation to the council of wizards or his condemnation to the custody of an enemy (notorious or intimate), or to find, in the peaceful shadows of a room, the woman who had begun to disquiet him or whom he had never expected to see again. An adverse drawing might mean mutilation, a varied infamy, death.

"Under the beneficent influence of the Company," Borges's narrator continues, "our customs have become thoroughly impregnated with chance." Fiction and reality, no longer simply confounded, become interchangeable.

> The Company, with divine modesty, eludes all publicity. Its agents, as is only natural, are secret. The orders which it is continually sending out do not differ from those lavishly issued by impostors. Besides, who can ever boast of being a mere imposter? The inebriate who improvises an absurd mandate, the dreamer who suddenly awakes to choke the woman who lies at his side to death, do they not both, perhaps, carry out a secret decision by the Company?

Borges's argument is fluid. There lurks in it the chilling specter of possibility.

The effects of conflicting allegiances are evident in everyone's daily life. In the 1960's, for example, young persons were intolerant of impersonal, formal contexts, of both the surface rituals and also their hidden, unconscious underpinnings. The outer trappings—habits of dress, decorum, and hair length, professed goals—were easy targets, easily discarded and, not surprisingly, replaced by glaringly different, but no less limited, alternatives.

More difficult to assess are the veiled qualities of a given context—old age, hard-hat fundamentalism, the limbo of partial legal maturity—those aspects of one's behavior that subtly confirm the "reality" or "truth" of professed (though usually unreasoned) positions.

It is no wonder that young persons bridle at formalism in concert halls and museums, but their rejection of what appears to them to be an arbitrarily imposed condition of quiet or awe at cultural presentations most seriously affects innovative efforts in art. By comparison, standard patterns and the repetition of familiar items in well-known idioms will not suffer. After all, the audience is undergoing a form of reminiscence in the latter situation. The materials are familiar; the level of redundancy is high. It is the *expansion* of experience that suffers from inattention and attacks on the formalism of cultural contexts.

Though a high value is placed upon the open directness of personal relationships, massive and seemingly impersonal rock festivals flourish. This is, in part, due to shifts in the structure of the traditional concert ritual. In the first place, amplification—the capacity to extend the intimate impulse to any desirable scale—is now capable of overcoming much of the isolation of distance. The loudness level is often so high that one has an illusion of proximity at odds with visual impressions. The apparent size of the performance area shrinks. Low frequency response in the sound system is utilized to such a degree that vibrations transmitted through the floor outweigh the audible frequencies traveling through the air. Vibration is heat-transmitting and tactile in a primitively collective way. It synchronizes the mass of listeners through an involuntary and irresistibly imposed calisthenic massage. Secondly, except for charismatic performers like Janis Joplin, Jimi Hendrix, or Jim Morrison, attention is often shifted from the stage, from the ritualistic center, to the minutiae of interpersonal events occurring within the audience. The music provides a background, the festival a comfortable context. Both serve to reinforce temporarily the limited sense of identity that a listener might feel in isolation. With its sensory immediacy and the social and moral commentary of its lyrics, rock music is able to virtually *impose* a context. It becomes not the objective center of a ritual tolerantly observed, as with the aesthetic fare of museum or opera house, but the sensual blanket, warming, coloring, and enclosing the listener.

New Models

The rock ritual encloses where that of the traditional concert radiates. One model is replaced by another more functionally suited to some of the needs of an era. The enlarged scope of sensory materials reflects not only a life that imposes on us greater familiarity with high levels of stimulation, but also the need for the creator to replace a larger percentage of the daily environment in order to involve people in a satisfying level of aesthetic experience. There have been numerous shifts in the primary models that we use to orient ourselves, and the number of new models continues to grow. One of the most powerful shifts which we are now experiencing is that from the homogeneous ideal of *standardization* to one of *diversity*, from the standpoint of both the producer and the consumer.

When large segments of populations still shared a closely matched frame of reference, when the contextual meaning of facts was relatively permanent, experience was transferable from one year to the next, from one generation or even century to the next. It is more difficult now to project the details of recollected experience onto one's present life. Thus, instead of direct transference from past to present, we depend upon an individual's *ability to abstract trends and processes* from the events of personal memories. More generally, knowledge might now be said to rest on the ability to generalize a constant stream of new information and new facts into whatever context the day brings. The value of any fact is reduced by the swift and effortless access to information provided by computers and electronic communications. But *facts*, of course, exist only in relation to a context and, consequently, can be genuinely meaningful only within that same context. Statistics have been used with such abandon that anything can be supported. One need only pick the boundary conditions cleverly: "four out of five dentists surveyed [if they agree to answer and are obliged to choose between evils] whose patients chew gum [and refuse to give it up]. ..."

The importance of temporal barriers has risen with the decline in significance of spatial barriers. As communication becomes inexpensive and rapid and the transportation of people and goods is done with increasing dispatch, the former primacy of distance, topographical features, the weight to be transported, and the duration of the trip tend to become insignificant. We become more conscious of the underlying influence of accelerated processes and enlarged experience on the few stable temporal guideposts that remain: a generally constant life span, the duration of day and night, the reproductive cycle, the seasonal shifts in the weather. If life spans remain constant, the structure of human life—infancy, maturation, mating, parenthood, old age, and death—remains more or less sequentially unchanged. But the meaning and weight of the intervals within this succession may change drastically.

It does not necessarily follow that the ability to move from place to place will be accompanied by the urge to do so. Communication techniques have improved not only in range and availability but also in quality. The fidelity of aural and visual information that one can now receive erodes the attractions of travel. The early Apollo moon flights provoked good-natured grumbling about the poor resolution and the lack of color or exciting topography provided by live TV coverage. Apollo 15, however, carried a new satchel-sized RCA camera that transmitted pictures of markedly improved resolution, depth, and color control. The attentive viewer began to share with the astronauts a lesser but quite tangible sense of extraterrestrial wonder as they moved over the surface of the moon. The *value* of direct observation derives from the opportunity to discriminate between what was expected and what is encountered. The thrill of walking the surface of another celestial body—an excitement that infects even the most laconic astronaut—*is not defined by its resemblance to other previous experience but by its divergence from those models.* As the quality of the picture improves, we begin, from the comfort of private homes, to make discriminations for ourselves. The homely familiarity of driving, digging, and walking on the moon provided the snare, not the revelation. In art, the listener's ability to make fine distinctions between the expected and the received is, of course, fundamental to the composer's ability to control the flow of events in a work for dramatic or innovative purposes.

In the past the most meaningful experience in each individual's life was direct. In our time, more and more stimulation is available, patterned into adventure, documentation, or fantasy. We are becoming more and more dependent on *vicarious* levels of experience. It might be argued that such experience is in some situations superior to the direct form; it can be more carefully monitored and is, in theory, infinitely more diverse. Vicarious experience can be edited and shaped for maximum impact. Who shapes it, however, and on the basis of what models? How has input been selected and to what purpose is the individual expected or allowed to respond?

The increasing extent to which we feed on vicarious experience parallels the business sector's tendency to shift toward the psychic gratification of services. At the same time, changing views of convenience and value lead us to reconsider the long-term worth of material goods. Tolerance of impermanence, for example, suggests the good sense in renting rather than owning. Acceleration tends to make us aware of skills and processes as opposed to individual items or specific achievements. This results in a proliferation of self-help manuals and crafts classes and a sharp increase in the sales of sporting goods, campers, and similar equipment. Can all this fail to influence our expectations in aesthetic situations? Diversity requires that we be aware both of the overall picture and the variety of detail if we are to orient and select efficiently. It also generates a participatory urge, a vague unrest with the traditionally passive reception of performance and plastic art. It impresses upon us the necessity for choice.

The Western desire for temporal quantization predated the clock. Mechanical calculating machines existed before electronics, and studies in encoding and information antedated the earliest digital computers and their necessary programs. Still, as operational, physical components of life, the clock and the computer have had enormous and pervasive influence on the societies they have served. They represent two of the major models in recent human history.

Observe how creative minds are stimulated by the *thing*, by the *physical form of the solution*, as opposed to its theoretical basis. Given the context, it is as though the clock and computer became physical shorthands for the processes they serve, provoking fresh speculative flights by their practical forms. Processes so objectified through science or in art may become catalytic models even though we only deal vicariously with their essence. Communication within society and within the human mind is not restricted to the languages of words.

PART II
The States of Art

Commerce and Excellence

Consider the words "art," "artful," "artist," and "artisan." The dictionary defines the first as "the production or expression of what is beautiful, appealing, or of more than ordinary significance," and attributes to it "skilled workmanship, execution, or agency." But "artful" involves the crafty and cunning before the ingenious. Skill is included almost as an afterthought. While both the "artist" and "artisan" have "superior skill or ability [and are] capable of a superior kind of workmanship," the artist is identified with the fine arts and the artisan with commercial or manual enterprise. Skill itself is "the ability that comes from knowledge, practice, aptitude, *etc.*"

A measure of unusual refinement in technique is implicit in each category, but the range of ends varies widely, from the abstraction of beauty through deceit into commerce. The creation of illusion (or deception) at some level is crucial. The recipient *accepts*—the implication is that it will be a temporary acceptance extended to events of "more than ordinary significance." He accepts, within a context, a set of values imposed by some agency for a purpose that he may or may not comprehend. Statements of purpose and the evaluation of that agency will not be sufficient to define whether "art" in any sense is involved.

Only a broadly conceived and constantly modified definition of "beauty" or "appeal" could be said to apply to much of the most meaningful sonic art of this century. The mature work of Varèse, penetrating, insistent, often raucous; the percussive, brittle music of Bartók's middle age; or the sometime glorious cacophony of Ives's multiple processes, stretching the confines of expectation within accepted styles and pitting one stream of "sense" against another: these are not considered "art" by virtue of any clear relation to beauty or by appeal in any usual sense. They are experiential monuments, unclear perhaps, complete nevertheless. These composers took the accelerating accumulation of materials that they found and banged them into often corrosive and apparently unruly shapes that had the evident merit of providing at least containment. Their works still offer public evidence of personal acts of courage and selective accumulation—models, questions, statements for us all. What were the intentions of these artists? Not, one would think, a desire to "appeal" in any direct way. By contrast, the artisan who traffics in local commerce is obliged to court the individual. His efforts are necessarily circumscribed. Extend this to the business world. Here products must relate to a need and demonstrate a superior ability to cope with it. Markets are defined, sales can be measured. The whole is quantified, and appeal measured on the basis of sales. Notice that the need may not actually have been served. It is enough that the customer thinks it has been. He has temporarily accepted the artful plea for his patronage regardless of whether his cooperation was gained by dint of cunning, ingenuity, or genuine merit.

In considering the quality of materials and techniques now commanded by the agents of commerce, one should bear the above in mind. For a long while, we have held a limited view of the functions assumed to be proper to art. Notions of mass production and obsolescence have been associated with business but far less with art. The public still expects the products of art to give prolonged service to a variety of needs that are far from easy to define. Art is thought to gratify dimensions of an individual that can be set apart from the mundane, utilitarian needs he is accustomed to satisfying.

Change is everywhere to be seen. Gratification can now be achieved in so many ways and competition for markets has intensified to such an extent that the engines of titillation manipulate us all daily. The individual's sense of aesthetic need undergoes constant buffeting. The entertainment-oriented products of technology at fairs or amusement centers are cunning, and it is the recognition of patent artifice that underlies the intelligent adult's response. One resists the invitation to recognize in these present attractions an art of the future. They certainly possess appeal beyond the limits of ordinary experience, but the elusive and non-utilitarian factor that the dictionary so cautiously terms beauty is absent. Do we require this dimension? Are we conditioned to recognize and value those subtle inferences caught in moments of particular awareness and reworked during islands of calm or reverie? Do these concomitants of beauty—form, inference, association, transcendence—still comprise an important component of our values?

Although brilliantly executed, attractive and evocative, the soft drink and beer advertisements on TV are not art. They are products of artisanship, designed to move us to physical rather than mental acquisition. They deal with the establishment and reinforcement of tastes as opposed to values. But, in the extraordinary level of their artfulness, they inevitably critique the quality of much that aspires to a more elevated status as art. The young composer or sculptor is drawn into mixed-media presentation by the richness of interdependent stimulation in his daily environment. When he completes a filmed component of a new work, working with a limited budget and unsophisticated techniques, the film's lack of brilliance, definition, and optical virtuosity is often so marked in contrast to the average products of TV and Hollywood that the audience is either unable to accept it as art or, conversely, embraces it *because* of its awkwardness.

A viewer accustomed to the virtuosity of commercially sponsored films can hardly be expected to find compelling aesthetic products that his experience brands as unskilled. It will not do to take refuge from this dilemma under the cover of antiformalism. Nonchalance cannot, in the end, function as art. John Cage, so often pictured as the arch antistructuralist, has never been careless. On the contrary, he has always planned and executed his works with meticulous deliberation. The sloppy pursuit of markets is intolerable in business, and, however much we may disdain commercial values, we will ultimately find careless efforts make for impotent art as well.

In past centuries or even in the early decades of our own, the artist and composer have generally been in easy command of their materials. This was possible because the evolution of instruments, of pigments, of sculptural materials, and of perceptual horizons has always proceeded at a moderate pace so that acquisition was accomplished naturally. At the same time, to the degree that they existed at all, techniques of reproduction and communication were so markedly inferior to an actual, aesthetic event that the stimulative, standard-setting value of the real thing was impregnable. This is no longer the case. The perceptual scale and quality of everyday, vicarious experience is enormously larger than was once true. Consider the speed and efficiency with which we now share in wonders and disasters through global communications, the perspective from the window of an airliner, or the way in which a good restaurant or discotheque marinates our senses. As means of re-establishing objects and events for our continued or repeated consumption, communications techniques have in some respects gone well beyond fidelity.

The skills necessary to achieve excellence in reproduction alone have been refined so that particular qualities of a subject can be intensified far beyond normal levels. Sounds are louder, the illusion of immersion in a recorded ensemble greater, colors more varied, definition sharper, selectivity almost perfectly enhanced. The technical standards to which we are accustomed establish levels of expectation for quality and intensity that neither the maker nor recipient of aesthetic experience has ever before faced. Most artists have had the sense to restrict themselves to those portions of the new materials that they can actually manage; by accident of training or association a few have been able to achieve a genuine specialized skill on a par with that employed in commerce. For the rest, there has been the distress of amateurism or the contrivance of supportive values—appeals to numbers or to history—that allow them to continue whatever it was that they were trained to do by the generally outdated and often irrelevant channels of education in the arts.

Powerful art requires the reinforcement and resonance of a social and stylistic frame of reference. The necessary support may come from the immediate temporal or physical locale in which the artist lives, or from some neighboring milieu. There is now not only a plethora of contexts for both artist and audience but also an unprecedented inequality of access to materials and ideas within the various fields of art. The reinforcement that normally acts within a discipline is limited because so few artists are familiar with the same contemporary materials or techniques. At the same time, the pressures to expand the dimensions of aesthetic involvement grow. The dilemma is profound. The artist requires not just familiarity with the skills of technology but an easy, informal involvement with them. He needs the shared experience and common knowledge of method that continually reestablish the accepted standards within which his individual taste operates. Most of all, he needs relief from an inability to match the level of sophistication with which business manipulates sound, vision, and tactility for its short-range, exploitive ends.

Subgroups in Society

In complex physical systems the *least* stable active element will often tend to dominate overall behavior. Stable subsystems tend to balance themselves, to cancel out perturbations within their own behavior, so one need not fear their effects. If one lives in a period of accelerated change, however, an error in judgment or an unfortunate inclination of growth will tend to wreak havoc much more readily than in other times. In complex eras, it is useful to inquire into the range and number of subgroups that exist; their self-contained value systems and the degree to which these diverge from the mainstream; and, finally, to appreciate their vitality. The concerns of many have been physical: surfing, skydiving, motorcycling, sailing, bowling, skiing, tennis, golfing, jogging, karate, and so on. But other groups are committed to Zen meditation, self-hypnosis, various treatment and rehabilitation programs, religious organizations of international or local scope, and often to community service. On the surface, these are all nonpolitical, not committed to social change or conservation. Unlike the Sierra Club, Nader's Raiders, CORE, SDS, The John Birch Society, or other transient activist organizations, their public posture does not mark their members as proselytizers.

These subgroups have, nonetheless, a decided effect upon public standards, on the very idea of art for "the public." They affect the individual's expectations of and tolerance for content in his experience and his taste for intensity. The young man who spends his summers surfing acquires a receptiveness to integrated patterns of sound, movement, temperature, and tactile stimulation that may well prejudice his response to any of these factors in isolation. Those who meditate or, in contrast, habitual users of marijuana may acquire a markedly increased tolerance for slow pace. They may have been led by alterations in their inner experience to limit the rate and intensity of sensory input so as to deal with it more satisfactorily. For a combination of reasons, they may have come to reject the whole aura of challenge and effort associated with current levels of urban stimulation. In a world of incomprehensible diversity, subcultural affiliations aid the individual in reducing to more reasonable proportions his obligations, choices, and patterns of activity. The specialized focus of these various groups is accommodated by industry and social structure but much less so by traditional forms of art.

Borrowed Models
In their need to move toward more satisfying values, in their suspicion of the work ethic, the disaffiliated groups in the West have been aided by dimly understood models of other human routes. Many of these have been drawn from Oriental societies. The most active distinction, the seductive kernel of such models, might be characterized as the Western tendency to *impose* and the Eastern to *receive*. Also important is the broad religious belief in powers surpassing those of the intellect, along with the suspicion that words cannot substitute for experience. As a rule, foreign idea structures are not fully embraced alternatives. They serve as an informal justification for the rejection of undesirable aspects of local life-styles. Yogic or Zen meditation and Sutra chanting put one in touch with exotic models that serve as comforting reinforcement of one's unstructured distaste. Meditation concentrates one's powers of receptivity, especially to internal sensations. It is hardly surprising to find that a fuller processing of feelings and images from this internal world can occupy the mind to the neglect of outward activity. This process can extend inertially, resulting in a wholesale devaluation of all input from the external world, a distinct though not necessarily hostile withdrawal.

Although it is impossible to generalize about the mores of Asia's varied cultures, it may be useful to elaborate one example to underscore the dangers of casual borrowing from even a familiar-looking cultural context. While living in Tokyo, I was involved in organizing a large-scale, international festival, "Cross Talk Intermedia," which took place in the winter of 1969. Throughout the course of necessary preparation, a host of experiences made clear the existence of primary differences in orientation and procedure between Americans and Japanese of roughly similar age, profession, and aims. Cross-cultural planning sessions were accomplished with relative ease. Intentions were outlined and goals agreed upon. In the process of moving toward fulfillment of these aims, however, incompatibilities began to emerge. The American solution was to adjust procedure, invent ways of circumventing—perhaps at the expense of elegance or propriety—unexpected obstacles. The Japanese manner involved only momentary reconsideration when progress was impeded, followed by continuation along the most natural, new, but deflected path. They were inclined to redefine goals in such a way as to match apparent and immediately available capacities. *Pressing towards a goal in spite of inconvenience* seemed to them not only unwise but boorish.

With incompletely understood or partially adopted contexts to guide behavior, one strives for the attractive surface without undergoing the formative processes, without absorbing that which underlies it. Similarly, subcultures do not supply their transient and part-time membership with fully fleshed out sets of values; they are usually concerned only with certain sectors of life. There is, in short, a loss of the deep roots that traditionally underlie both patterns of daily life and important public art. How many values do we still share? At what level do they operate? Each society creates an apparatus that equips the individual to cope with the problems he meets within its confines. This apparatus becomes—or, perhaps, evolves out of—an expression of values so refined that their manipulation through the culture's art can stir the individual deeply. Such shared depth of experience and response is also the basis for the parasitic art of negation, parody, imitation, and pastiche. A narrower focus on the content of the present moment is becoming more common than it used to be, not only by virtue of the strains of survival but because of the force with which we are all fed concentrated, prepackaged experience. It remains, as always, fundamental that art deal directly with materials meaningful to the individual. But the individual is now defined by an unprecedented confusion of powerful mechanisms. A common experience with materials and mores is much harder to anticipate than was the case in the past.

The Fragmented Public
As subgroups challenge the breadth of shared values, experience, materials, and skills, art may change its ways. The creative person cannot oblige his audience to conform to any prescribed mold. He works from within. He speaks to his audience's unspoken currents of need and idea. His works, then, will become either more specialized (more custom-devised) or less style centered (aiming at far more fundamental evocation). Let us compare the dilemma of art with that of social dissent, for example. The conversion of information and experience into a form compatible with a nation as diverse as ours requires the smoothing out of conceptual edges, the suppression of unfamiliar values, the use of analogies that foster the possibility of pseudo-consensus. The *appearance* of understanding is what matters, not the conservation of subtle reality. Such practice is not deliberately pernicious. Still, in order to retain more than a vestige of its original vitality, protest of any sort must remain out of sight of the media. Having suffered once the focus of media's explanatory machinery, the dissenter's message is lifted

out of the context from which it draws its force and pertinence; his rage is rendered futile. The process of seeking wider understanding is itself destructive. The style of dissent must be shaped, then, by its intended scope.

Art also suffers from its makers' unrealistic efforts to satisfy an inflated concept of audience. The artist should *make* his difficult choice between increasingly ruinous patterns of compromise and more realistically defined roles, for the effects of ambiguity and indecision are publicly as well as individually unfortunate. Note how easily the public accepts the inevitability of eclipse for popular musical groups and their styles. New groups approach and become a part of the popular scene by virtue of a freshness which, although it does not mean the same thing to everyone, is unique enough to suggest something new to each diversely experienced listener. As a novelty becomes familiar, it is vulnerable to challenge from a newer wave and is swept away, apparently with little regret on the part of its recently fervid supporters. One has a joyless understanding of the economic facts. For all practical purposes, the marketing of recordings, national television coverage, equipment transportation, large hall rentals, and so on are at the disposal of only the few. Those in the game appear resigned to its terms, welcoming renown and accepting eclipse with equanimity. The requirements of generality and commerce are at work here, as in the case of dissent. But art aims above artisanship. It has thought itself concerned with a longer-range utility. It has felt no obligation to meet the same tests or suffer the same easy manipulation as popular diversions. The serious artist has, after all, rarely achieved and hence rarely covets the level of notoriety and financial gain that exists for those in mass entertainment. He has pursued other rewards.

As I have indicated, maintaining the broad-spectrum audience may necessitate the generalization of materials or message. This may be one of the reasons why artists tend more and more toward mixed-media presentation. A curtailment in the complexity of information in any one sensory channel may be compensated by the addition of other reinforcing kinds of stimulation. A less style-oriented, more directly phenomenalistic approach to art experience may also lead to a shortening of the individual work's lifetime. An artist's style is, after all, more than a chosen coherence. Its evolution involves continual reevaluation and self-commentary. It fosters continuity of output and a form of longevity. If cultural alignments and values evolve more rapidly, it may become more difficult to retain particular stylistic allegiances for extended periods.

As a matter of taste or principle, some creative persons have chosen to bypass both the general public and the idea of permanence. They work within and for small segments of the public and allow any long-range impact of their work to accumulate as a result of the spectator's experience with a series of more or less informal presentations. The audience observes and assimilates a manner of operation, watches as a succession of efforts emerges from the continuously changed materials and interests of the composer, performer, dancer, artist, and takes home only a repertoire of personal impressions. *There is no stable, permanent representation of these efforts, no possibility of revisiting them.*

In sacrificing permanence of even a limited sort, one invites a major shift in almost every aspect of the assumptions of aesthetic traffic. A far heavier responsibility is placed on the individual listener; a gesture of confidence in and respect for his capacities is made. If there is to be no feedback— traditionally the most essential element of the intercourse between the continuing life of the artist's product and its receiver—then everything depends on the single presentation. Atmosphere, preparation, contextual identity, and clarity of presentation become even more than normally influential. The passing event, the disintegrating objects, the never-to-be-repeated sequence of sounds or movements take on the qualities in memory that we individually assign to them. This is familiar. The point of contrast is that the recipient imposes a structure and extracts the sense of the effort on the basis of a single sampling. The work becomes both more his own and less large. It is unable to resist or correct imposed responses by its continuing presence or return.

Drugs

The most provocative subculture in its size and implications may be comprised of drug users. Hardly a monolithic group, its members would object to being bracketed. Indeed, from the standpoint of apparent motivation, they should not be. Still, all seek relief of a sort and it would be difficult to state on an absolute scale which needs are most worthy of satisfaction. From the standpoint of art, most important are the masses of young marijuana smokers and drug ingesters; next, and by far the largest, is the group of middle-aged and older persons who are regularized by means of tranquillizers, stimulants, sedatives, restoratives, and other biochemical adjustments; finally, there are the hard-drug users whose lives are tragically beyond concern with such nonimperatives as art. The impact of the largest group is hard to assess, although it is clear that the dimensions of drug use by persons with middle-class values has had little influence on their opinions regarding the use of drugs for pleasure, expanded awareness, or escape on what they feel to be a more sinister scale. They continue to provide for their children an example that overweighs any number of contrary admonitions.

There are two separable aspects to the relations of drug usage and art: their potential *impact on the maker* and their *influence upon reception* of aesthetic experience. There is probably less controversy implicit in the latter. Drugs certainly change our perceptive or cognitive processes but both the degree and nature of the alterations show wide individual variation. Thus, though it is probable that one's receptivity to aesthetic experience (including notions of what qualifies as aesthetically pleasing stimulation) will change markedly under the influence of mind-altering drugs, it is difficult to predict the form of the changes. A particular drug will not lead, as a matter of course, to specific kinds of sensory intensification or distortion in a variety of subjects. A good deal of research has been devoted to uncovering such "drug specific" reactions but without success. Reactions to drug ingestion seem decisively influenced by the context in which they are taken. The user's psychological stability, his expectations for the experience, the nature of his surroundings, and the presence of reassuring companions are all important. Any one factor may disrupt or override the others. The complexity of interacting conditions and the consequent impracticality of controlling them make experimentation difficult, and contradictory results are common: under LSD, for example, color perception has been reported enhanced as well as impaired. The situation is further muddied by the frequent incompatibility of objective, nonparticipant reports with the claims of the drug user. That is to say, the drug ingestor's action may belie the sensations he reports experiencing.

Although the subject of drugs is not inappropriate here, given their historical role in many of the world's cultures, we encounter apparently insurmountable barriers in speculating about their *controlled* use in situations approximating the traditional public concert. Even the comparatively simple distribution of colored glasses at theaters attempting to display three-dimensional films is cumbersome and technically unsatisfying. A more likely path in redesigning the subjective range of an individual's experience during aesthetic events is to exert more thoroughgoing control over and perhaps radically enhance the contexts within which such performances occur. There exist auditoriums where listeners are literally surrounded by loudspeakers and visual projection devices. Assuming orderly audiences, physical context can dominate reception.

Even though uniform influence over an audience's receptiveness using drugs appears unmanageable as well as undesirable, they are significant in other ways. The emergence of psychedelic varieties of clothing and decor, waterbeds, and acid rock indicates that it is possible to reflect, in unaffected states, the special qualities of visual, auditory, and tactile experience originally encountered under the influence of hallucinogenics. Certain kinds of stimulation are particularly sought after as appropriate to drug-induced states. This process redefines the limits of sensory responsiveness and may therefore have fundamental relevance to art.

Beyond the admitted influence of drugs on an individual's input is the more basic question of whether or not a history of psychedelic experience or actually working during drug-induced states themselves can enhance creativity. W. Harman and his colleagues have reported that, under carefully controlled conditions, the "illumination" phase of problem solving was facilitated by the influence of psychedelic agents. Subjects attributed similar characteristics to their experience: lowered inhibition and anxiety, increased capacity for achieving larger contexts, high fluency and flexibility of ideation, high capacity for visual imagery and fantasy, increased ability to concentrate, high empathy with external processes, objects, and people, and accessibility of unconscious resources.[1]

The problematic element in evaluating such reports is always the degree to which the drug user is able to achieve meaningful communication or utilization of his experiences. There is a literature replete with reports of individuals who insist upon the value of efforts undertaken during drug-induced states. But they are often unable to recapture the basis of their excitement upon emerging from their temporary, biochemical reality. As long as art remains a shared phenomenon, we are obliged to judge on the basis of tangible output. The function of art is not only to display the creator's own visions but to concretize his ideas in such a way as to evoke similarly powerful response from others. The artist is society's *dowser*, and the communicable nature of his products is all-important.

Throughout history, many prominent artists, writers, and musicians have consumed hallucinogenic agents, some on a regular basis (including Coleridge, Dickens, Tennyson, and Aldous Huxley). Altered states of consciousness through other means—meditation, religious ecstasy, hypnosis, fasting—are common in societies all over the earth. The importance of such states as *models* of expanded awareness and embellished perception cannot be discounted. Early workers with the RCA Music Synthesizer (at one time thought capable of producing directly, with electronic circuitry, any possible sound) were dismayed to find how difficult it was to imagine unprecedented sounds in the absence of models. Production is incomparably more demanding than reproduction.

The problem in the case of drug-induced experience, then, is to fashion in the straight (or unaffected) state an array of stimuli that can reinduce the previously experienced pattern and level of response. There are limits to what models can provide, but their value in spurring us to look in otherwise unknown directions is unquestionable. An individual's retention of numerous models and their uniqueness is of enormous importance. I would argue that *mind models are the basis for the high-priority human capacity to view experience from a variety of perspectives and hence to achieve the unexpected association that has the power to resolve conflict and generate inferences.*

1. W. Harman, *et al.* "Psychedelic Agents in Creative Problem Solving: A Pilot Study," *Psychological Reports*, 1966.

The General Event

There is unavoidable divergence among our individual memories and therefore an inexhaustible variety of models on the basis of which judgments are
made. Points at which individual memories may approach one another are
the basis of both the creative act and the rewarding response; we need to
examine the nature and extent of useful overlap among individual patterns
and learn to what degree individuals immersed in the contemporary welter
of experience can share in a common responsiveness. To begin with the most
severe case, intercultural aesthetic impact is, of course, difficult to achieve to
any degree. As in the case of dissent, the attempt to bridge the gaps between
culturally distinct systems will inevitably involve the sacrifice of fundamental
aspects of each. Genuine translation would necessitate a complete reframing
of the logical-factual structure, the cultural context, and allusions present in
the original language. It would imply the recasting of the original content in
order to evoke a comparable pattern of affective and intellectual resonances
in the second linguistic-cultural context.

The unlikelihood of such a regeneration is apparent. We have always been
content with less. One catches an exotic flavor, a suggestive perspective
later utilized within one's own cultural system. Music and, to a somewhat
lesser degree, the visual arts have found it less difficult to pass beyond the
creator's experiential repertoire than have linguistically defined media. But
for the cultural outsider there are still almost impossible barriers to the full
comprehension and responsiveness fostered by an imposed congruence of
values and conditioned relationships. A person raised in Western society
does not, after all, have to attend formal classes in music appreciation to hear
and respond to unconsciously learned probabilities and their violation in
the music that fills his daily life. Conversely, one cannot anticipate a subtle
play on awareness in situations where the generative context of an event is
unfamiliar.

Although most art directs itself to a more or less particular facet of its
generative culture—and perhaps to a particularly trained sector of the
society as well—there are fundamental patterns, inherent accumulations
of norms, and violations that transcend such limitations. As outsiders, our
responses will not, of course, exactly parallel those of one who is a native
of a different culture. Nevertheless, we do respond to those facets of the
unfamiliar art that appear to correspond to elements in our own culture.
At the most general end of the spectrum, then, there are culturally based
phenomena that speak to all within their social context without regard for
special indoctrination. Certain forms of spectacle cut across intercultural
lines. These *general events* "mean" on a variety of planes, while retaining
their richest level of provocation within the culture of origin. General events
are as diverse as the bullfight, Mardi gras, the tradition of rock-throwing in
Korea, or the "potlatch" of British Columbian Indian tribes. They involve

the mutual and effectively classless indulgence of spectators, perhaps an element of subcultural contest.

Gambling may become a factor of major proportions in the life of the well-regulated man of the future—the man who needs a stake in events vicariously experienced but wishes to avoid personal inconvenience. The gamble may or may not be formalized. There are instances of societies condoning regular and large-scale excursions into high-risk terrain. Well into this century, Korean men and boys indulged in stone-throwing as a sanctioned national pastime. Maiming and death were anticipated and sustained although neither special formalization of rules nor structure of rewards was involved. The origins of such elemental indulgence in apparently unmotivated violence must have profoundly deep cultural roots. The very idea of stone-throwing invokes in us the horror of arbitrary terrorization or righteous retribution, but one could scarcely imagine such an event arising spontaneously between a cross-section of American males. We have no way of sensing what factors compelled the Korean man to behave thus.

The Kwakiutl Indians of Western Canada involve themselves in formalized, competitive giving as a means of establishing the dimensions of their honor, wealth, and psychic stature. Such a festive occasion is known as a "potlatch" and is characterized by the lavishness with which services and goods are distributed abroad. A participant who receives a gift is bound to match or to exceed the prodigality of his host. In certain cases, demonstrations of indifference to possessions take a less convivial form and one group destroys its own goods, blankets, livestock, money, and dwellings as a challenge to its rival's sense of competition and pride. The challenged group forfeits its honor or even civil and religious rights unless it destroys an even greater portion of its own material goods. The complex nature of social and cultural bonds necessary to sustain such a form of competition is obvious. Again, one is easily seduced, on an abstract level, by the outrageous bravado of the convention. In what other context could one wallow honorably in the pleasure of seeing selected rivals culturally bound to wreak havoc upon themselves? There is an element of gamble, no doubt, but it is limited by the giver's shrewdness in judging his opponent and by the power of pride to establish a psychological matrix beyond our comprehension.

Stone-throwing episodes or a "potlatch" are extreme examples of general events within cultural contexts that we can only vaguely appreciate. Each carries, however, a certain special flavor to us. We cannot know in what sense and to what degree our reaction to the physical facts corresponds to others' responses. Perhaps the appearance of communicable elements inherent in these ceremonies is no deception. Possibly they are artifacts. The important question is whether, given certain sorts of generality, persons with very diverse preparation could profit equally from the same event. The establishment of an experiential common denominator low enough to remain unaffected by culturally conditioned distinctions between human beings while remaining specific enough to resonate powerfully within the individual is the goal—a formidable one, indeed.

In the late 1950's, artists from various backgrounds in America, West Germany, and Japan began to work in an artificially contrived medium, seeking what I have called the "general event." Although studiously casual in manner of execution, conceptually formalized "happenings" rapidly became notorious among the young and disaffiliated. A form of theater achieved without (in fact contemptuous of) professional paraphernalia or trained participants, happenings attempted to invade the natural settings of the real world with ritualistic activity. These involvements were intended to over-reach boundaries of allegiance and insensitivity imposed by differing and stifling personal backgrounds. All spectators were required to participate, since passivity would have automatically enforced the fractionating influence of evaluation in midstream. One sought not to establish perspective but to immerse oneself. The best of the genre contained a compelling core of myth or ritual, sensory bombardment, or discomfort that operated at the level of a more general common denominator than would be normal. In the end there was not sufficient force in the medium to support its continuation. Still, happenings are worth examining in some detail as a significant effort to establish a less formal, more broadly affective means of creating aesthetic experience.[2]

Happenings seem to rely on one or more of three basic schemes, although they are certainly not so described by their makers: special focus, associative development, and *juxtaposition*. The first involves the illumination of one element through enlarged scale, proliferation, repetition, and so on. Associative development implies a sem-improvisatory, open-ended progress, from a simple beginning through more or less closely related, developmental stages. In juxtaposition, normally remote objects or processes, one of which may often be an archetype or myth, are brought together for simultaneous though not necessarily integrated presentation.

In America, happenings tended to do away with any passive spectatorship, husbanding the guest through some usually simple pattern of unskilled activity in pursuit of involvement. In contrast, anonymous participation in group art efforts is not a compelling ideal in Japan where joint involvements and endeavors, from the inescapable school uniforms to group vacations taken by all members of a given corporation, are an inevitable aspect of daily life. For the Japanese creative participant, a satisfactory sense of outlet or release comes more naturally in the form of individual action, even exhibitionism. Strictly impressed standards of personal decorum may be more

---

2. The following material is taken from Roger Reynolds, "Happenings in Japan and Elsewhere," *Arts in Society*, Spring-Summer, 1968.

easily violated under the banner of "art." The audience in Japan has not, as a result, been eliminated through cooperative absorption. It is, rather, essential as the passive element in the ceremony of display. Although very little is generally asked of the spectator, neither is he abused. Where "individualism" and the patterned sterility of suburbia in America leads to the need for the release of "participation" and chaotic settings, Japan's crowded, tightly group-structured society naturally leads elsewhere.

Here, for example, is a description of a Japanese event that relates to the schemes of special focus and associative development: Toshi Ichiyanagi's *Experimental Music* was included on a program of "Happenings" at Tokyo's Sgetsu Art Center in the fall of 1966. Four persons were seated in straight chairs and contact microphones (picking up vibration directly through physical objects) were fixed to the surrounding floor. The performers leaned sideways in their chairs, as slowly as possible. At the end of the time period which they privately had judged to be four minutes, they were to have reached a point of imbalance such that they crashed to the floor. At this instant began a second four-minute period during which each performer was directed to struggle violently but silently with his chair.

When the second period was up, each individual froze in whatever position he found himself. Then, when all four were ready, they resumed their original positions, leaning gradually to one side. The curtain slowly descended, falling completely before balance was lost again. The sounds of this mute, stoic, four way struggle were electronically amplified and broadcast throughout the hall.

Though not true of the event described above, it is a provocative notion that a verbal, written, or photographic report often makes a stronger and more evocative impression than does the actual experience of the happening. Descriptions operate selectively, instinctively avoiding all that distracts from the reporter's perspective. At a distance, amidst the comforts of one's chosen surroundings, even interfering or disagreeable elements can be relished.

People tend to be bored with, embarrassed or annoyed by activity they recognize as clearly unskilled, unless they have some personal stake in it (as, for example, with a "Father and Son" talent show). The same is true of environments confused by a clutter not our own and of time dimensions that prove inappropriate for planned events. Consciousness of time (and hence boredom) arises from the effort to achieve continuity. If there is not sufficient motivation for the observer or if there is too great a profusion or paucity of events, he loses interest and passes into a state of daydream or discomfort. Unless he is deliberately attentive, he will not derive detailed or meaningful impressions from a confused jumble of new experience.

For the most part, activity results in satisfaction to the degree that it involves the successful use of skills. These need not necessarily be professional, practiced skills. By "skill" I mean a personally established capability—the meeting through effort of some self-recognized standard. The most rudimentary instances of human gregariousness include no more than rhythmic handclapping, swaying, and chanting. These are tasks geared to a common denominator. Personal satisfaction comes from doing something in a way that rates well on one's own scale of values. Why should people be moved, altered, or enlightened by observing an inept performance or by participating in activity—not so taxing as to require real effort, unlikely to elicit satisfaction—which does not effectively challenge their personal capabilities?

In the 1960's, other means for establishing something like the general event emerged, in spite of interpersonal disparities in skills and background. Two such methods were the encounter group and the commune. Both addressed themselves to the necessity of establishing and enforcing a common context of values and constraints like that required by the "potlatch" or Korean stonefights. (In the case of happenings, such a matrix was usually either absent or inoperatively frail.) Fundamentally, the encounter-group phenomenon stemmed from the work of J.L. Moreno and later that of Carl Rogers. The encounter group assumed the necessity of seeing things, at least for a time, through another's eyes and opening oneself to a wider and more relaxed contact with sensual experience through non-verbal and intensive group interaction. Though a leader might guide or introduce material, he was often no more than a facilitator. Groups tended to generate their own subject matter out of personal concerns, out of the needs that motivated them to make the association in the first place. The intensity of exchange possible in small groups where a neutral setting and broad temporal horizons are assured was both revelatory and traumatic. The group aimed to force each individual to a more candid level of statement and reaction than normal social contexts would ever allow. The encounter group was, of course, heavily dependent upon total submission to the prescribed context. A resistant member was quickly expelled or forced to comply with the group's understanding of its function and terms. An individual's attitude toward submission will be colored by his motivation. On what basis does he make the decision to submit?

One of the primary functions of the group is to establish the areas of similarity—the shared experiential norms—between its members. One must become part of the flow, immersed in the emotional, subjective climate of words and actions. Establishing common context between two persons is normally a very drawn-out process and, more often than not, the resulting relationship may, in fact, be artificial for both. Its functional success does not ensure its genuineness. In the encounter group, the process of seeking a common level was greatly accelerated. Defenses had to be lowered much more quickly.

One of the primary currents in the artistic activities of the '60's was the mixed-media experience. In it the total reliance on niceties of structured relationships within one mode of perception (sound, sight, *etc.*) is replaced by a lowered concern for detail, a less formalized dependence upon a broad front of sensory input. The participant in encounter groups also made an exchange. He sacrificed, at some real peril, certain individual protective mechanisms in return for a more intense, hopefully rewarding experience of interaction with and response to other human beings. The greater his act of trust and submission, the greater the possible rewards. Though this form of general event comes about with no history of commitment to understanding or living in a particular, preparatory context, the normal social process is replaced by the always dangerous gift of oneself. Is intimacy false because it is short-lived? Is aesthetic experience insubstantial because it takes place on a broader, less intellectually formalized sensory front? Probably. The long-term impact on one's behavior will be limited, in any case, by the usefulness with which one extrapolates from an occasion.

The commune went a step beyond the flirtatious intermittency of the group encounter. No matter how intense an experience one might have within an encounter, it was still, like formalized public art, a fragmented, "unnatural" episode within the larger pattern of one's daily roles. An effective withdrawal from a social milieu that one feels to be adverse, or, on the other hand, the search for conditions that allow a freer exploration of the emotional, human aspects of life requires a community of support. In practical terms, it frequently happened that communal experiences, although far more protracted than the normal domain of formalized art or sensitivity training, were still only episodes seen against the backdrop of the whole life. For reasons of internal imbalance or external pressures, the particularly felicitous interplay during communal episodes inevitably seems to have been disrupted; the commune disbanded or was forced to become benevolently repressive in order to survive.

Certainly the arts provide a less perplexing, more easily implemented alternative to *ad hoc* groupings or chemical intervention. Public art in the historical sense is becoming increasingly impossible to support, however. Aesthetic experience may now be channeled either into a service tailored for specialized, small-group tastes or towards more elemental, more apparently rudimentary and unadorned manipulations worked upon polyglot audiences. These developments could be effected through the use of increasingly flexible and powerful communications and through the use of sophisticated technology in live performances.

However enlarged our awareness of process and intersensory experience becomes, we shall not, I think, wish to abandon the inexhaustibly useful, the general or the quite particular *event*. The luminous disruption and sudden skewing of event patterns to which we are accustomed is essential. Individual or social reorientation and adaptation require a clear, though perhaps distant and incompletely understood, mark of reference. The development of thought and the enrichment of experience on a nonmaterialistic plane proceeds by regenerative feedback in ideas, by the processing of continuing resonance from events that stand out from the otherwise unexceptional, unmemorable conformity with established patterns of behavior and experience. In the presently overstimulative cacophony of sensory input with which the individual struggles, it is important to consider how to conserve the special moment. There are clearly limits to the method of trying to command attention by exceeding and elaborating upon normal levels of sensation.

PART III
The Public and Private Realms

Alternate Forms of Art

Even a cursory awareness of the nature of aesthetic experience in cultures remote in time and cultural space should suffice to convince us that art has meant and most probably will mean a wide variety of things. From iconic object to public ceremony, the ancestry of art forms, large and small, is veiled. Though the functions vary at each extreme—from the individual's solitary interaction with the qualities of a purposefully made but static object to the socially reinforced, tribal response to fluid, interactive human performances—the circumstances always include the possibility of profound immediate and long-term impact on the recipient. Meaningful aesthetic acts, of whatever sort, however, have occurred within homogeneous cultural milieus. As suggested in the preceding chapters, it has become increasingly difficult to maintain this shared base of conditioning, the common acceptance of values that fostered an unparalleled expansion of public art during the past several centuries in the West. The dominance of the museum, the theater of words, and concerted music made by hundreds for the consumption of thousands needs to be finally broken. All these forms depend upon the grand manipulation of and a subtle play within clearly mapped areas of cultural overlap. As these areas apparently enlarge, their actual depth is reduced. They become illusions lacking actual function. Art is losing its most imperative fundamental: a shared cultural base.

During the past thousand years, the scope of style and method in Western music has widened, both through the evolvement made possible by extensive and unhurried exploration of forms and through those occasional revolutionary changes accomplished by new juxtapositions of familiar means. Still, both processes required the listener's possession of a common structure of rules, acquired either through formal education or informal habituation. As the scope of distribution for art of all sorts expanded, these organizational systems were strained. They were forced to accommodate, at one moment, the esoteric level of the connoisseur and, at another, the more general level that mass subscription necessitates. We all need to face the impossibility of further strained attempts to serve these essentially

different masters if we are to allow the creative forces in society to better
serve their fellows.

Art as Event

The General Event: Breadth of vision necessitates an unimpeded view. Note
how large a proportion of transcendent experience involves the sense of vista
that accompanies the removal of boundaries. The mountain top, the desert,
and the night sky are not only physical contexts conducive to elevated states
of emotion and awareness; they also serve as metaphors of release for the
internal experience of one who is confined. Depending on circumstances,
space in this boundless sense can suggest isolation, majesty, or oneness.
What does seem constant across individual and cultural boundaries is the
evocative power of scale, the situation in which lines of sight and the rever-
berations of sound pass to their human limits without barriers.

There are other factors, not all physical of course, that possess a level
of cross-cultural, archetypal significance. These are basic to the notion of
the general event discussed in the preceding chapter. Though the exact
meaning—the continuing implications of suicide or of space, of violence
or isolation—is peculiar to a cultural milieu, there will be, nonetheless, a
significant overlap in weight and value, even between persons of radically different experience. Although our gradual and halting awareness of
the functional depth of cultural disparity cautions us against any dreams
of facile communion, the rapid growth in the physical understanding of
the human nervous system is certainly provocative. The sense of balance,
the limits of aural perception, and the mechanism of visual illusions are
given, no matter how a society has weighted its members' response to them.
It would appear that fundamental knowledge of this sort, combined with
an increased understanding of the operation of memory and of language's
mechanism, might allow the artist to contrive experience of previously
unimaginable generality and viscerality. Such an art could go beneath
cultural factors.

At MIT's Center for Advanced Visual Studies, Gregory Kepes led a group
dedicated to the absorption of technology as an artistic medium, the enlargement of artistic scale to urban size, the development of media geared to all
the sense modalities, the incorporation of natural processes like the flow of
clouds and water, and the participation of spectators in such a way that art
becomes a confluence. This group jointly undertook the planning of a large-
scale project, an animated, luminous, environmental sculpture involving the
entire Boston Harbor.

On another level, composer Robert Moran and artist Paul Crowley
engaged—to some degree at least—the entire San Francisco peninsula
with a performance of their "39 Minutes for 39 Autos" in August 1969.
They utilized not only the performing automobiles but also local radio and

television stations, lights and receivers in private homes, and a light show realized through synchronized use of the illuminated facades of downtown buildings. As aesthetically limited, as necessarily ill-defined as these efforts were, they imply a good deal. So, too, do the roar, the heat, and the vibration of electronically powered rock music events. The category of general event that I am sketching has not yet emerged but the portents have.

The generality of aesthetic events involves not only the means by which they are achieved and the scale on which they operate but also the attitude with which they are received. Public performance art has developed—as have spectator sports, political rallies, and mass religious gatherings—a central dependence on the sharing of experience. The human resonance that can be generated within crowds, the often frightening and sometimes tragic delving beneath the civilized, imposed surface of constraints that is accomplished in these situations is poorly understood but it cannot be discounted. To what degree is this collective level of response necessary to the operation of public art? To what degree, in fact, may it have supplanted truly aesthetic content in much that we have continued to designate as art? Efforts to answer these questions should begin with an understanding of the nature and breadth of the actual shared base in any context. The more primitive the level of spectator communion, the more difficult it is to control (and the performing arts have always been manipulative, to some degree). The artist entering the vast arena I refer to here will need to exercise great caution. He will be operating below what is normally thought to be a necessary level of formalized organization. He will need to be comfortable with both a more primary level of intuition and a more elaborate physiological map of human potential.

The Specific Event: At its most extreme intensification, the *specific event* corresponds to an invocation of what neurophysiologist Robert Livingston of the University of California, San Diego, has called the "now-print" mechanism. Given a sufficiently powerful confluence of emotional and intellectual factors—for example, the moment at which an American was informed of the Japanese attack on Pearl Harbor or the assassination of President Kennedy—the brain is apparently capable of issuing unwilled commands that result in the storage of a detailed representation of that moment. It is an autonomic process that is irrepressible. The content of the representation is, of course, entirely individual, dependent upon a person's history of involvement with an image of the President and, more particularly, upon the actual context within which he hears the news. The representation is specific to a degree probably unattainable through conscious effort and it is indelibly retained for decades. Such "now-print" occasions happen in each individual life, of course, and the phenomenon is not particular to national or international scale. Just the reverse: in less extreme forms, the specific event retains the quality of a mix peculiar to the individual's repertoire of experience, while losing the public dimension entirely. In other words, although the general nature of the response might be classed with that of other individuals, the actual substance departs fundamentally. A specific event is nonsocial, private. It does not involve the shared quality or the substance on a universal level that the general event does. Although all human reactions are, to a degree, idiosyncratic, they tend to possess whatever level of congruence is necessary to assure the normal functioning of society. Though my "red" may not match yours when selecting wall paint, we do concur sufficiently at stoplights. No such general utility of concepts or responses need be involved in aesthetic matters, however, at least not insofar as reception is concerned.

Assume an image of art as an individual service. The maker is then no longer bound by the limitations of speaking to a general audience, although this should by no means inhibit his use of the deep reservoirs of myth and archaic substance so basic to much that has been called art. It implies no renunciation of craft. Rather, within and out of the knowledge he might be given (by means of electronic sensing and data storage devices) of a spectator's or a listener's personal history and habituation, the artist could guide the basic selection of materials as well as shape his execution and style quite precisely for maximum individualized effect. Such improbabilities, ultimate connoisseurship, no longer seem *necessarily* impossible. There is always, as in the past, the possibility of an alliance between an artist and a small audience that has itself chosen a certain pattern of allegiance. A particular assemblage of values, skills, and tastes, achieved for nonaesthetic reasons, could certainly still form the basis for a specialized aesthetic responsiveness. But such alliances now could exist with greatly enhanced technical and psychological flexibility, and could come about by voluntary selection rather than by dictum. More radical, more to the point of present tendencies, is an extended notion—that a repertoire of materials and needs could be drawn from within the individual's own mind and body.

Techniques now exist whereby several levels of information within the body—of varying specificity and differing character—can be electronically monitored from without simultaneously. Dreams and less natural states of altered consciousness have long done this internally. Though the claim is not made here that dreams are art, neither would I resist the idea that they or other forms or items of experience drawn from within might not become the materials of an art. We are not obliged to arbitrarily limit aesthetic experience to those moments in which it is directly stimulated by external input passing through our sense organs. Might it not be possible to introduce electrical impulses directly into the afferent nerve fibers themselves, to access the contents of memory capriciously, to explore the effects of temporarily disrupting the integrative mechanisms of various sensory channels in the body? It is not necessary to have a complete understanding of exactly what is taking place in such situations before beginning to explore them. Although we are in no position to exert anything like fine control over the operation of the brain, this kind of startling exploration is already taking place in laboratories and hospitals. The internally generated mirage or illusion is a recognized fact. Such multiple, simultaneous use of the cerebrospinal and autonomic nervous systems goes on daily within each one of us even as we daydream or drift into sleep. What technology has done is to improve our ability to identify a certain process, and this, in turn, is a key to utilization (see Biofeedback Training below).

How might all this concern art? In the same way that any increase in materials and awareness, any accumulation of values and alteration of attitudes, always has. Aesthetic functions do not depend upon the source or content of materials. Rather, the qualities of art stem from the particular ways in which events are selected and arranged, the patterns by means of which our absorption and interpretation are guided. There is no substance too rare or too common to be transformed by art, no idea or set of circumstances too ordinary to be set in a newly revealing light. Both our increasing capacity for handling and tailoring information to suit our convenience and the constantly more revealing picture science is constructing of the operation of intelligence and emotion support the potential of an individually formed, essentially *private* experience within what has formerly been the domain of the public performing arts.

Initial efforts to produce the illusion of three-dimensional sound recordings were undertaken by means of earphones. "Binaural sound" possesses stunning spatial qualities, far more compelling than those attainable with loudspeakers under any but the most extraordinary acoustical conditions. One might speculate that it was not only the superior convenience of speaker systems that caused the virtual eclipse of earphones but also a certain uneasiness on the part of the listener, stemming from the unearthly vividness of the binaural sensation. Binaural sound was, of course, a purely personal sensation.

Closed-circuit TV learning and cable transmission for commercial purposes raise other issues that are not very remote. In a provocative report written for the Carnegie Commission on Educational Television, J.C.R. Licklider fixed upon the essential incompatibility between possible viewer-program interaction and the mass media. This parallels the drawbacks of the present tradition of public art that I have mentioned earlier. Licklider counseled the quite practical alternative of providing an ensemble of transmitted alternatives so that each listener, even in the case of relatively large audiences, could select the sequence of segments that would best suit his own capacities. The subject matter would retain its larger identity in all selectable forms, but the level of professional knowledge, the pace of presentation, and the viewpoint could be adjusted suitably by the listener's choice of segments. Simplistic attempts to realize such selectivity—this is still by no means an interactive dimension—were instigated as early as 1967, at the

Czech Pavilion in Montreal. The audience voted at several key junctures as the plot unfolded, and electronically tabulated results determined which of several possible segments would be shown until the next bifurcation point.

As will be seen, it is now feasible to monitor viewer response in much more direct ways, determining, almost before the subject does, that his attention is wandering and automatically adjusting the nature of the experience in counteraction. The practical applications of these techniques in programmed learning are obvious. Their utilization in art may be, for the moment, less realistic, but with our already staggering capacities for storing information and for modulating its presentation (pace, intensity, and so on) digital control devices could be programmed to respond to and follow the contours of individual interest, discomfort, pleasure, or alarm.

Some distance beyond is the specter of aesthetic experiences that are derived from the surface or primordial substance of the individual mind. In the following sections on altered states of consciousness, it emerges that although fine control is still very far off, the capacity for meddling at a crude level with perceptual and mnemonic functions has been with humanity for a long while, and knowledge about such means is growing rapidly. Perhaps the occurrence of extra-normal states will not remain indefinitely either utilitarian or indulgent.

Art as Process

The preceding discussion considered the explicitness of events, the senses in which they are meaningful, and the novel ways in which they might be presented to us in the service of aesthetic intent. In considering overall states of consciousness, consistent mental biases with temporal extent of their own, we move from events to the processes they populate. General and specific events I regard as having a quality of unified brevity that suggests containment, though resonance of response within the crowd or the individual may continue long after the enactment. These events can be characterized variously: at extremes, the mythically radiant social sharing or the personally tailored and privately decisive. But under a translation from the normal to an altered state of consciousness, the entire apprehension of significance may change. We are no longer concerned with more or less singular events or with successions of them (archetypal threads: oedipal, heroic, sacrificial) where classes of reactions can be enumerated with relative ease. Now not only the apprehension of the moment but succession, retention, value, tolerance, causality, need, and motivation will require reexamination. Nothing can be taken for granted.

"Does it emerge? Or do we enter in?" asks John Cage about the music of Charles Ives. He leans towards the former and observes that we would nowadays prefer otherwise: to do it ourselves. "The difference is this: everybody hears the same thing if it emerges. Everybody hears what he alone hears if he enters in." This is a quantitative distinction that may or may not reach the qualitative level. In recent years, there has been a marked increase in the number of aesthetic situations that are multi-layered by design, instances where the creator's technical competence and outlook have not turned him toward singular statement or argumentation. Here, the recipient's attitude (the conscious and unconscious state of mind with which he approaches an experience) can be decisive long before one begins to consider the possibility of manipulation. In the case of Ives, the polytonal, polyrhythmic musical substance allows a rudimentary form of selectivity by presenting a larger number of simultaneous strands of sense than a listener can handle. Since it would be patently impossible to apprehend the whole in its manifold detail, we are effectively released from the traditional listener's obligation and allowed to search, indulge momentary fancies, and move on as other events cajole or command our attention. The work itself remains unresponsive, of course. As with the CATV smorgasbord of the future, alternative paths, here, are limited in number and there is no provision for midstream modification on the basis of sensed response. But CATV selectability would involve less fanciful movement of attention from one strand of sense to another. The complexity of simultaneous demands is itself of interesting potential, but may be only an interim step in the evolution of aesthetic situations which include feedback, hence listener modification.

In some works produced during the past several decades, composers have concerned themselves with autonomously evolving process rather than with the description of a succession of precise sounds, all of which are elements of a quasi-narrative. The composer has been content to set up a certain matrix of conditions, of well-behaved processes that can be set in motion to bring about a foreseeable class of results. He does not claim to know exactly what will occur at any given point in the overall experience nor even, perhaps, to predict the succession of factors that is admissible. All that is said is that he will accept as fully representative of his intentions any situations that arise as a result of the process(es) undertaken as specified. Of course, in such cases, the composer is under the demanding obligation to *foresee* the ways in which his materials may interact and to adjust the required conditions so as to optimize and characterize the possible results. The chosen processes will have to embody a freshness, a fascination, a just tolerable level of frustration. They will need, in short, to engage and reward.

These *process pieces* are to some degree analogs for the still fanciful notion of art experience based on shifting modes of perception. Nevertheless, it has already been demonstrated that, given the proper care and context, process pieces can be alluring. Let us go much further. In classic Western tradition, carefully selected and ordered materials are offered to individuals who are assumed to be in a more or less "normal" frame of mind while listening. Consider a reversal where the *materials* are assumed and the receptive frames of mind are chosen by an artist. Various extra-normal, but inherently consistent, modes of perception might be defined, imposed hypnotically, for example, and allowed to modulate in prescribed ways the largely unpredicted content of each listener's chance experiences. Ordinary events, sights, sounds occurring naturally would be perceived through inventively contrived perceptual filters. The results would be influenced by the listener's particular experiences, of course, and also by his unique physiological makeup. The chance that one individual's immediate experience or derived meaning will coincide significantly with another's would appear to be slight. The result could be a form of private art. At a rudimentary level, this already occurs daily in the drug subcultures.

It is not necessarily true that the duration or starting point in time of an experience aspiring to art must be preordained. In the case of architectonically, discursively organized music, one is required to follow a certain chronological sequence in order to comprehend what amounts to an argumentative or contingent process. Here, it will assuredly matter if the planned succession is disrupted. One must hear the premise, the stages of alteration, the occurrence of departures, of returns. But, if the creator's viewpoint shifts, his presentation might cease to be dependent upon a predetermined grammar of any sort. Complex processes, it would appear, may accommodate a virtually infinite number of approaches. The listener, in a sense, guides himself rather than being more or less successfully compelled by the emergent articulation of the music. Such processes could be made cyclical, or circular, for example, so that no matter where one entered the stream he would in time come upon the same sets of conditions. Certain types of music (particularly in Asia) tend to be purposefully redundant so that one may come and go as circumstances dictate without losing the essence. In such cases it may in fact be difficult, impractically taxing, to remain in attendance throughout the performance and to adopt an attitude of serious responsibility to each moment. Could music or other combined media presentations not operate continuously as a sort of psychic refuge to be used when and for as long as needed? Each individual communes according to need.

Within the present revolutionary exploration of biological processes, an effort is being made to avoid the moral indifference that insulated many of those involved in the early experiments with atomic energy. The failure to consider human and social impact inherent in the developing reality of atomic energy has led to suspicions regarding its use in service roles. The direct utility of art is admittedly slight, but its example has been of profound consequence. It appears to me that, through a combination of circumstances perhaps beyond the control of any one sector of society, art is now failing its obligation to humanize the materials, conditions, and needs of contemporary man. I have not been considering the detail of how art is created, nor the stylistic vehicles by which aesthetic ideas travel, but the raw, the present or prospective circumstances within which it could act. By and large, public art remains much too essentially antiquarian, gradually but irrevocably dooming itself to impotence.

The Experience

In undertaking some brief comments on the function and meaning of aesthetic experiences—of objects or periods encountered and explored—I will attempt no structure of aesthetic philosophy. A few informal observations regarding the effect of art on individuals are necessary, however. Much of the material presented in this book is based on these deliberately utilitarian points of view, adopted in the hope of effectively redefining our categories of art and our range of receptivity. The most basic and still expanding capacity of human intelligence is the ability to retain images of experience and to influence subsequent behavior by drawing upon them even in the absence of conscious volition. Not all of our behavior, of course, is governed by practical imperatives. In the modern world, a vast proportion—one might argue the most significant sector—is no longer directed toward the acquisition of protective conditioning or the necessities of existence. We are increasingly free to seek and to accept forms of experience on the basis of other criteria.

Sheer sensation, unsupported by larger design or transformation, can, of course, be satisfying; in some cases it is sublimely so. It is not yet art nor of more than peripheral importance to aesthetic questions. Still, the tangible vividness of strong sensation is a component of what are termed rewarding encounters with art. It is not only the appreciation of the exquisite shadings or vibrancy of sound or light or form or motion that I refer to here. It is, rather, the sometimes almost febrile sensation that a particular sequence of events evokes in its timing and unprecedented balance in each dimension. Only partial comprehension is required—the fragile, tantalizing sense that a particular moment or span of experience is, the intuition of something beyond the expected serving of function or the recognition of agreeable materials. The substance of this kind of moment may be rational on the surface (a sudden structural comprehension, an astonishing relationship caught) or it may occur independent of any easily formalized means of understanding (the suggestions of an attitude, a poignant interaction of elements beyond language). In any case, the experience of which I speak must contain an unavoidable, concomitant realization that one cannot fully fathom or completely register its content. Such moments are unique, *certainly* lost, even as they occur.

Again one can go beyond events to processes, to the empathetic sharing of a sequence or gesture within which the individual components are scarcely noted. Gossamer or grating, breath or bow-bound, the outrageously correct, the slyly deviant, the seductively lilting: the skilled use of the listener's attention promises but may not deliver the hoped-for satisfaction.

It is possible, of course, to engage the listener without achieving these *special moments*. In this case, as I have suggested, the substance of response will tend towards empathy or vicarious movement within some field of possibilities rather than toward the necessarily brief, revelatory instant. A particular state of elevated identification or absorption cannot be sustained for long under normal circumstances. One needs the relief of contrast or slackened pace. We are still concerned here with experience, with one's sensations *during* exposure to art in some form. But the recognition of unusual moments or absorbing episodes alone will not suffice.

In Retrospect

What is still wanting is long-term retention. Somehow, the individual must be able not only to code and store away the chronological order and apparent meaning of items in aesthetic experience, but also to have continued access to them. Art is for our benefit, whether it reveals or entertains. But where it is sought and only serves as a form of release or indulgence we need have no continuing interest. But ongoing service is provided an individual's mental life by models of alternative ways, unfamiliar occurrences, sometimes unimagined standards. The size of one's mental space, the vividness of its references (on the basis of which judgments are made and actions initiated) is determined by the clarity and variety of experience one has undergone; more particularly, by the success with which one has been able to retain it.

This is the great advantage of familiar styles and formal patterns. The listener is aided by general schemes, by codes more or less consciously understood. It is a far more formidable task to grasp even fleetingly the form of events whose logical or habitual underpinnings are unfamiliar. In experimental art, provision for this fact should be made. Care in introduction, a sufficient level of redundancy, and particular attention to the memorability of crucial instants, spans, or points become unusually decisive. These not only guide the responses that accompany a performance but determine the use which each listener can make of the experience in retrospect. When what I have called an argumentative scheme is used, similar problems will apply during the actual period of contact between performed music and a listener. The audience's ability to weigh, even to notice, relationships is limited by their musical memorability. During contact (whether a performance or a period of observation), moments of arrested fascination or puzzlement are succeeded by troughs in attentive level. These may become occasions for reflection, the generation of anticipation, and so on. More important is the extended resonance which an aesthetic experience is able to engender. In the end, the continuing fidelity of an aesthetic event is less imperative than its memorability—that is, it is less important to recall an event correctly than it is to retain a vivid image of one's own that was sparked by a given experience. The impact of art must extend beyond temporary distraction, however pleasant. It should strike sparks within the individual, and one cannot expect to control precisely what is ignited as a result.

Alternate Approaches to Art

It is probably not rash to assume that a given form of art arises or flourishes in response to the creative individual's intuitive apprehension of needs within himself. By virtue of a well-nurtured sensitivity, the better artist will often anticipate the emergence of similar general needs on the part of his fellows. The existence of an aesthetic methodology, even its brilliant consummation, insures little in the absence of social responsiveness at some level. An elite reaction can function as a holding action, but a more general response will still be crucial for fruition. Some of the human conditions discussed below raise perplexing issues in regard to this previously natural interplay of proposal and disposition.

Does the need for beauty—in whatever sense one may intend this beleaguered word—arise from its absence? Do we actually relish only that which we cannot fully possess? Given the assurance of an unlimited supply of transcendent ecstasy, privately experienced and self-induced, the wary person would undoubtedly hesitate to commit himself. We are heavily conditioned to believe that restraint in the face of desire of any sort is admirable. The inhibitory force of this conditioning has been weakened, however, and it is no longer as clear as it once might have been that restraint is always necessary. Drug addiction is compassionately (often, to be precise, condescendingly) attributed to deficiencies in the addict or his cultural background. A compelling arsenal of arguments is mustered to demonstrate this. It would be unacceptable to admit for a moment the possibility that the state of drug-induced euphoria might be preferable to reality for some portion of humanity.

Various forms of addiction are by no means rare in this increasingly ambitious, goal-oriented, industrialized world. Little is yet known about their physiological mechanisms, although they often seem to involve the avoidance of descent into a painful state of physical imbalance as much as a drive towards the "high" condition. In animals, there is ample evidence that electrode-induced stimulation is desirable and addictive to the degree that only complete exhaustion and/or imminent death by starvation will serve to stem its self-inducement. On the human level, there is as yet little information about the long-term effects of similar forms of crude electronic manipulation, let alone the vastly more complex pleasure-inducing constructs that are within technical grasp. These facts should be directly faced and openly explored at a time when choices are still possible, when controlled experiment can precede uninformed, underground distribution. A lack of wisdom in the case of hallucinogenics is already history, and unfortunate repercussions are still with us. We have been led to believe that addiction is a condition beyond reasoned choice, but what of the emergence of stimulative contexts (these do not, of course, need to be confined to simple sensation but might engage the mind strategically as well) which are rationally preferred alternatives to normal patterns of existence? Since monolithic industrial societies of various ideologies are now in a position to support a subsistence-level existence for vast numbers of people, the option of genuine, radical choice regarding the use of one's life becomes feasible. What alternatives will be offered, and which will be preferred?

Various societies have sanctioned abnormal states of consciousness, absorbed them into their fabric of life to a degree that seems unlikely to the unprepared observer. The stabilizing influence of dream interpretation by the Senoi people of the Malay Peninsula is such a documented example. We have no reason to assume that their dreaming is unlike our own. There as everywhere, it would appear to represent an exceptionally unimpeded form of psychic association and play. What is unusual is the careful training each child receives in order to formalize a social acceptance of the personal dream world as valuable public information. Although the general picture is clear, it would take considerable investigation to determine the veracity of detail in the report. What of dream fabrication to achieve one's ends? If someone reports a dream in which an undesirable relationship with another person has occurred, the content of the dream is revealed to its object and steps are taken by either or both parties to release harmlessly the implied aggression, danger, and so on. Feelings of anxiety producing such dream sensations as falling are recast by the Senoi elders, who condition the child to enjoy and accept the sensation on the grounds that everything in dreams has a function—in the case of falling, liberation. The dream world is interpreted as the product of rationality and is used as a positive resource.

Altered States of Consciousness
In hazarding even the most general of discussions about unfamiliar or altered states of consciousness, one must sidestep the significant question of their durability. We have no occasion to consider the robustness of our usual experience with daily events. The normal state of affairs seems perfectly stable. But altered states of consciousness involve not only initiation—a relatively untroublesome matter—but also maintenance. All the literature in this field implies *temporary* or *short-term* alterations. The actual adoption of an extranormal frame of consciousness on a long-term basis creates questions of another magnitude altogether.

To reverse perspectives for a moment, certain conditions *are* also required for the maintenance of normal consciousness. It is precisely the organism's failure to remain within the relatively placid shoals of these optimal limits that results in the so-called altered state. A certain range of sensory input and variety is basic to normal, waking consciousness. Extended, this implies the importance of sufficiently varied environments and motor activity. By means of these, presumably, acceptable levels of cognitive and emotional activity are initiated. When ideal levels are exceeded by too great a margin (by sufficiently rapid and intense, hence chaotic and inescapable, sensory bombardment) or we fail to maintain them (as in purposeful sensory deprivation), mental aberrations will result. Similarly with the exercise of high levels of attentiveness for prolonged periods (as in special vigils) or extended periods of decreased alertness (hypnogogic reveries while resting or sunbathing, for example). Finally, there are psychochemical factors. Some of these may occur naturally, as with sleep deprivation, dehydration, or starvation. Others can be induced by ingested materials (drugs or other substances in excessive abundance or deprivation). All involve violation of acceptable levels of concentration for particular chemical substances in the body and the consequent chemical disruption of psychic processes. It should be noted that many of the above sets of conditions are openly and easily accessible to anyone wishing to experiment, and that it would be quite hopeless to attempt to prohibit such efforts. Neither can one responsibly encourage experimentation in ignorance. It might be the case, however, that the exploration of more accessible extra-normal states—meditative modes, for example—could have musically useful results.

Although their proportions vary markedly, certain characteristics are shared by several of the altered states of consciousness: *disrupted thought processes*, including decreased involvement with causality, logic, memories, or the conservation of opposites and *a disturbed sense of time*, directly related to the capriciousness of memory, the loss of concern for temporal passage, or an inability to pay attention to the deductions that normally help us fix chronology and speed of passage. An awareness that *personal control* is being *relinquished or lost* can be terrifying or profoundly satisfying; *changes in emotional expression* run both toward greater intensity of experience and expression and to quiescent disengagement in the presence of emotional materials. The *body image* is often *altered* so that one may feel that a particular limb or the entire body is separated from the mind/ self, or that the body has undergone physical transformation. *Perceptual distortions* are common as a part of many of the preceding items and particularly in the direction of hypersensitivity and synaesthesia. Partly as a result of the many foregoing psychic changes, there are changes in the quality of interpretation the mind achieves with data it receives. One can be understandably overwhelmed by the vividness or novelty of an objectively mundane perception and attach elevated meaning to it as transcendent discovery or universal truth. In some cases, this may be accompanied by a sense of the ineffable nature of the experience so that the subject presents himself as unable to express to anyone without similar experience the uniqueness of his own. There is a certain convenience in this since it is often impossible for the subject to demonstrate elevated states, even without words, or to recreate them internally once he has emerged from the altered state. Naturally, in a condition of perceptual confusion, unaccustomed power of experience, and loss of self, a person may be particularly prone to suggestion or guidance from without.[1] In such a state of wonder and release from boundaries, it is natural to find an absence of critical attitude or capacity.

Brain Waves: It has long been known that extremely low-level electrical signals are generated by the human brain. Only recently have experimentalists begun to collect certain firm bits of information in this awesomely difficult but uniquely exciting study. The major impediment to research is no longer the lack of precision monitoring capacity but, rather, the inaccessibility of functioning human brains for test purposes, except in rare and accidental circumstances. Ultimately, there is the sheer complexity of neurological mechanisms, unparalleled by any other known structure. This fact promises to frustrate anything like a comprehensive picture for a long time to come. Still, it is not necessary to understand the mechanism of phenomena that can be identified and measured in order to gain the ability to predict and influence within limits. Experiments on animals have achieved some modest objectives, but the enormous qualitative distinctions between the brain of man and that of the lower animals mark this road as one of limited utility.

The electrical activity of the brain is of extremely low voltage, at the most on the order of 10 to 100 microvolts (1/100,000 volt) for a particular frequency component. The periodic nature of these signals has resulted in the establishment of four general frequency bands within which more or less prominent activity can be measured in most subjects.

0–3 cycles per second =delta waves	unconscious
4–7 cycles per second=theta waves	
8–12 cycles per second=alpha waves	conscious
13–30 cycles per second=beta waves	

The mechanism by which these electrical potentials are generated is not understood. Nor is it even certain that there are actually generators for the four commonly cited frequency components. That is to say, they may simply be artifacts of some other more complex (or simple) and, as yet, unknown function. The alpha component is generally strongest and, as the most easily detected element of the waking electroencephalogram (EEG), it has been the subject of the majority of laboratory work (and, sadly, uninformed

---

1. Much of the preceding discussion is drawn from Arnold M. Ludwig's "Altered States," in Charles Tart (ed.), *Altered States of Consciousness*, New York, 1969.

commercial exploitation). In perhaps 95 percent of subjects who display an alpha component, the frequency is approximately 10 cycles per second. The disarming follow-up to this convenient instance of orderliness is that between 5 and 10 percent of the population appears to have no detectable alpha, while a similar percentage has it almost constantly.

Normally the EEG varies continuously in time; each four-second plotting, for example, appears noticeably different.

The EEG consists of multiple, constantly varying traces drawn by an oscillograph on a roll of paper that is being constantly advanced mechanically at an even rate of speed. The traces record fluctuations in electrical potential in the brain measured from various points on the surface of the skull. The number of channels of information being simultaneously recorded influences heavily, of course, the completeness and accuracy of the representation. Such equipment is expensive, and many experimenters count themselves fortunate to have a four-channel capacity. The overall picture is this: a constant graphic record of carefully limited frequency-range and extremely small amplitude (signals of such low electrical strength are prone to interference of many kinds) from four electrodes placed at more or less equidistant points on a subject's skull becomes the standard source of information about a teeming, convoluted, incessantly active, and changing web of signals traveling through billions of neurons. It is hardly an ideal circumstance for the neurophysiologist. The statement that a certain proportion of the population has no measurable alpha components refers to the fact that none can be detected by visual inspection of such a graphic print-out. Recently, it is important to observe, more elaborate monitoring devices have come into play, where potentials from a larger number of electrodes are constantly monitored and analyzed by a computer. Naturally, this is vastly more promising than previous instrumentation.

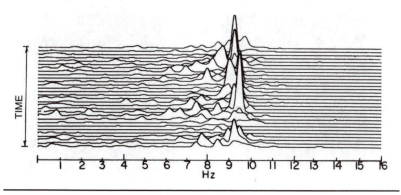

Figure 1. Spectral display of the alpha rhythm of a normal subject by "hidden-line" method.

The foregoing should sufficiently warn the overzealous—as any of the reputable researchers in the field will. One simply cannot state that a particular EEG frequency corresponds to a specific emotion or mental state.

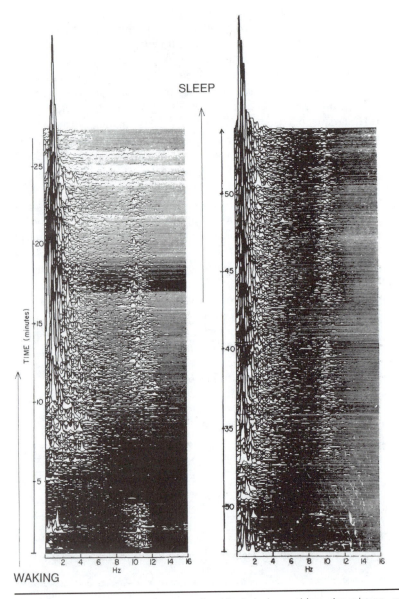

Figure 2. Spectral display of a normal subject during waking, drowsiness, and sleep (slow wave phase).

It is generally true that a subject can learn to recognize very reliably the presence of alpha in his mental activity, and that he will, in general, relate its presence to a pleasant, relaxed state of awareness which he enjoys. (He will, in most cases, have considerable difficulty in verbally describing the states.) The EEG component, then, helps to *identify* the presence of a general condition. There is no evidence that it *produces* the state. Alpha waves are the subject of excessive enthusiasm because of their practically desirable concomitants, but they remain perplexing to researchers. Unfortunately, the 10-cycles-per-second frequency is similar to numerous muscle potentials also generated in the skull (related, for example, to facial expression and visual accommodation) and this has necessitated very careful electrode placement and narrow band filtering to insure that one is actually measuring alpha. (Amateur experimentation with alpha detection devices is more than likely to run afoul of such pitfalls.) It would appear that the visual orientation procedure—the reflexive search for the source of any sensory item of interest—may act to suppress alpha activity.[2] Normally, alpha waves will be absent or greatly attenuated when the eyes are open and appear spontaneously when they are closed. Grey Walter speculated years ago, in The Living Brain, that they might represent some sweeping search function that is obviated by visual fixation when the eyes are open. Whatever the truth, it has been amply demonstrated that subjects can be trained to recognize the presence of alpha and, as a result, to increase their control over its presence or absence even with their eyes open. It is worthwhile to reemphasize that they are, in this case, adjusting their bodily state in such a way as to re-create conditions favorable to alpha, not the other way around. Alpha is an indicator, not a switch.

After alpha, the most intriguing EEG component has been the theta activity that appears between 4 and 7 cycles-per-second. (Alternatively, one might say that activity within this band is designated as theta.) With untrained subjects, theta is normally associated with the semiconscious, hypnogogic state that precedes sleep. In contrast to the flowing ideation associated with alpha, theta images appear to pop into consciousness quite abruptly and may seem quite arbitrarily composed. They are difficult to remember. Time associated with such electrical traces from the brain shows less consistent activity than do alpha periods. Experimenters have proposed a relationship between the unlikely and sporadic imagery of theta-associated states and the mechanism of creativity. As mentioned previously, theta accompanies the drowsy state preceding sleep and is therefore experimentally elusive. Subjects have been taught to retain the desired condition without lapsing into sleep (the

---

2. Very particular gratitude is due Dr. Joe Kamiya of the University of California's Langley-Porter Neuropsychiatric Institute for his remarkable patience and generosity in discussing much of the following material with me.

delta range) or rising to a fully conscious state. One training mechanism involves the simple but effective stratagem of asking the subject to balance an upright forearm on its elbow so that the toppling limb counteracts each momentary loss of consciousness.

Biofeedback Training: Reference has been made to the capacity for eliciting from subjects a greater than normal control over certain complex physical states. These states have, in turn, been associated with general psychological characters and further with frequency bands in an EEG record. Such teaching takes place by means of a basically simple mechanism, variously termed autogenic feedback training, biofeedback, or physiological feedback. Though the mechanism used varies, the outline of the modern forms is similar: sensing devices monitor the psychophysiological function one wishes to influence (heart rate, for example), and an indication of the presence or absence of the target function (low activity, high activity, *etc.*) is given constantly to the subject. With sufficient practice, the subject is able to recognize, at some level, the "feel" of the desired bodily circumstance and, subsequently, to achieve it through his own volition. In the end, then, the monitoring device and associated signal is no longer necessary, and the subject is able to influence directly a function previously beyond his conscious reach.

Although J. H. Schultz published the successful results of autogenic training procedures in 1926, it was only recently, with the addition of the feedback element, that they came into wide use. Schultz relied on the very gradual development of inner sensitivities and will through the reduction of exteroceptive stimulation, the mental repetition of physiologically adapted formulas, and an attitude that he described as "passive concentration." Though results were obtained, the regimen proved too intangible and arduous for most. With the addition of electronic monitoring capacity, the process has become convenient. Electrodes detect relevant potentials and concentrations, and these signals are amplified to drive a light or sound signal easily noticed and understood by the subject. The *feedback* loop is simply an aid that increases the speed with which accurate recognition of autonomic functions can be achieved.

For a long while, work in this field was inhibited by traditional learning theory: the belief that the autonomic nervous system—including such factors as body temperature, blood pressure, brain potentials, and muscle tension—were only capable of an inferior sort of learning, classical conditioning. Here, as Pavlov's salivating dogs remind us, reinforcement must be an unconditioned stimulus which produces the same type of response that one is attempting to teach. Superior types of learning, like operant conditioning where reinforcement is accomplished by rewarding any occurrence of the desired response, were thought to be the exclusive domain of the cerebrospinal nervous system. This view has been decisively disproven.

Patients have been treated for chronic tension headaches by learning to relax directly the muscles producing them; one case of insomnia was mitigated by teaching the sufferer to warm her feet by conscious command; others have been able to achieve, within limits, positive influence over their blood pressure and heart rates.

In response to direct questioning about the limits of biofeedback techniques, Dr. Kamiya confirmed that wherever enervation exists in the body, biofeedback means could, in theory, be used to alter or bring under control related processes. In short, the system will work. Restriction is imposed only by the physical limits of body systems and by developments in measurement instrumentation. Although psychological states result from exceedingly complex interactions of physiological processes, relatively simple conditions can account for certain altered states of consciousness—periods of extraordinary relaxation, for example. In view of this, one might train persons to gain control sufficient to allow them to achieve an unprecedented state of total relaxation. One would, in effect, be capable of introducing the conditions for mental aberration by decision alone. Experiments with the total exclusion of muscular activity in an arm—at a level well below what one consciously feels to be "relaxed"—have already been performed. They were accompanied by subjective reports of various perceptual illusions, including, prominently, sensations of floating and disembodiment. One could easily construct a more potent chain of possibilities. One can, in fact, anticipate a point at which volitional influence upon general psychic states could obviate the current dependence on mechanical or chemical means.

Meditation: The meditative condition is essentially concerned with receptivity, with quietly paying attention, but it can effect profound changes in human behavior. The ability to enter such states is hard-won, even though one can eventually learn to accomplish this transition with relative dispatch. At the outset, training involves traditional methodologies, both for Yogic and Zen skills. These programs antedate and were reflected in Schultz's autogenic method. Until recently, science has paid only the most cursory experimental attention to meditative phenomena, so that very little factual information is available. EEG records of normal individuals and Yogic and Zen meditators have produced an interesting comparative picture, however. If a representative of each of these three groups is asked to sit quietly (meditating in the last two cases), and loud bursts of sound aperiodically interrupt the calm, the following contrast results. The normal individual will gradually respond less and less to the annoyance, eventually ignoring it; note that this implies the gradual, *directed inhibition* through efferent nerve paths of responsive signals from the auditory receptors, even though they are still under bombardment. After a time, the interruptions fail completely to ruffle the average course of EEG traces. The Yogic mediator's EEG pattern, however, indicates no response from the outset; once in his trance, he is oblivious to distraction. For the Zen master, on the other hand, the EEG registration is always uniform, not fading at all after numerous repetitions.

Clearly the scope of meditative practices is considerable. Simple experiments have been done with ordinary persons exercising quiet attentiveness in controlled circumstances, and the results, in very short periods of time, are extraordinary.[3] Meditative approaches, then, offer an exceptionally congenial method of altering normal states of consciousness, although the term meditation is generic and far too general to designate with any practical force how several different individuals might react to a given situation.

Hypnosis: Science has also been remiss in informing itself about the mechanisms of hypnotism. To date, there is apparently no single indicator or collection of signals that will allow one to state (on the basis of an EEG, for example) that someone is in a hypnotic trance. Hypnotic depth appears to be related to three factors: the degree to which role-taking involvement on the part of the subject has penetrated below the level of consciousness (he must be living fully, not dutifully playing the part of a subject); trance depth, or the extent to which his awareness of the structure of ordinary reality has faded; and archaic involvement. The last factor concerns the critical relationship between subject and hypnotist. The absence of an archaic dimension to this relationship will inhibit the production of "fireworks, or evoked primitive meanings."[4] Since art is concerned with such fireworks, this point merits special attention. Within several of the altered states, relinquishing the self is a prominent feature. In meditation, one renounces normal intellectual activities but is in a position to return to the real world as one chooses. The hypnotic subject, however, must totally surrender his willpower to the hypnotist, and there may result a partial identification of the hypnotist with archaic authority, parents or teachers. This, in turn, leads to an investiture with omnipotence, to the desire to please, a heightened suggestibility, and so on. The archaic factor, in short, penetrates most deeply into the self and has therefore the largest potential to transform experience.

It would be useful to know in greater detail the importance of the intermediary, the agency to whom conscious control is relinquished (need it be human?). Presumably such a step is undertaken only in the expectation

---

3. Dr. T. B. Mulholland of the Preception Laboratory, Veterans Hospital, Bedford, Massachusetts, has studied in detail the alpha relation to visual attention. "Changes in the EEG previously attributed to 'visual attention' can be explained in terms of changes occurring in the cortical regions that are important for visual control processes," he writes in an unpublished paper. This is important because of the widespread tendency to attach alpha suppression directly to attentiveness.

4. See particularly reports by Arthur Deikman in *Journal of Nervous and Mental Disorders*, Vol. 136, 1963, and Vol. 142, 1996. He describes a wide range of sensory distortion from multiple sessions with five to thirty minutes of meditative attention. An ordinary blue vase in an otherwise empty, dimly-lit room is observed—not analytically studied.

of valued returns, as is the case with full participation in encounter groups. Does such a figure not have the power to increase the subject's openness or dedication to the task and the opportunity of perception? If so, posthypnotic suggestion might influence one's responses to a given aesthetic presentation. A level of actual control might be possible, producing programmed enhancement or modification of perception on an individual basis, as desired. Hypnosis, like meditation, is a term that covers a panoply of conditions, methods, aims, and experiences. Correlations for which there are no adequate explanations exist, as between high alpha production and good hypnotic subjects. Not all persons are vulnerable to hypnotic suggestion and only a few are unusually so, but one's receptivity to trance can apparently be enhanced through biofeedback training in alpha production.

Self-hypnosis appears to be related to meditative experience but there is no effective way to gain a very sharp or comprehensive picture of what is happening to a given individual within such foreign realities. These unfamiliar realities are individual phenomena and share only the necessary insulation from normal, conscious states of reality that nurtures their existence. What is their attraction? Are they more complex than reality, engagingly oblique, or is there a simplicity that allows comparatively greater intensity or clarity to be generated? Some subjects credit altered states with a rejuvenating influence. Reports during the course of an extranormal experience are impossible to evaluate since we have no way of establishing equivalences. Reports after the fact are marred both by amnesia and the inevitable violence worked by any translation. In the end, the question remains private; at some level a decision is made that allows at least a temporary commitment to another way.

Altered Perception

The most fundamental alteration that our interpretive perceptions may undergo is to find temporary release from the tyranny enforced by conditioned patterns of expectation and structure. The way in which one interprets messages received at the cortex through afferent nerve fibers is established by an individually unique process of conditioning that begins at birth. The earlier and more powerful the conditioning, the more resistant it is to alteration and, in fact, the more difficult it is to believe one is dealing with learned factors.[5] Long before adulthood, reactions become structured in the interest of efficiency (defense, communication, decisiveness, and so on). These categories speed response and insure a coherence for the personality, but lessen one's acuity in detecting perturbations in anticipated patterns. Meditative activity has been seen as a means of temporarily disrupting such automatic functions, allowing adult intellectual processes access to

---

5. See two articles by Renold Shor in Tart, *Altered States of Consciousness*.

seemingly fresh input. Such a condition may constitute not so much an altered state of consciousness as an unfettered state of access to otherwise incompletely processed sensory input.

Other basic alterations have been successfully attempted, one of which is the distention of subjective time. Through hypnosis, it has been possible to alter gradually a subject's impression of subjective time by suggesting, for example, that a reference metronome was gradually slowing down. As a result, the subject may be convinced that each governmental minute is ten or even sixty times that long. Some evidence suggests that efficiency in problem-solving tasks can be improved dramatically under influences of this kind. In any case, art traffics in impressions as often as facts, and the potential of altered frames of reference for the temporal dimensions of experience is considerable, even if it is an illusion entirely unsupported by behavioral testimony. One might be led to accept chronometric indicators that were in turn responsive to the aesthetic design of a performance, so that sensations of temporal speed, disruption, or expanse could be manipulated with unprecedented freedom and breadth. The present experimental evidence concentrates on the utility of time distortion and has left untreated such questions as what would result if the hypnotist attempted to make a subject under hypnotic trance aware of practical discrepancies between concept and action in temporal terms. In the case of hypnosis, this may well turn out to be impossible because of the substantial trance depth necessary in order to achieve time distortion. The general phenomenon—retaining the real-world context while operating on accelerated time—has already been reported under the influence of LSD.

Psychochemical changes drive the body systems in a way that more passively induced states of altered consciousness do not. Under the influence of LSD, not only can an ordinary flower take on implausible aesthetic radiance but imperfect objects may become literally intolerable. Intensity of sensation has complementary effects, revealing positive and negative qualities with impartial inevitability. From this fact arises the imperative need for guidance and care for the setting (mental and environmental) within which one has hallucinogenic experience. If drug-induced perceptual alterations are generally the most spectacular they are also the most difficult to control. Color, spatial, and temporal distortion is common under powerful drugs. The same is true of the milder influence of marijuana. Since the latter also decreases the strength of all levels of memory and the functions of expectancy and anticipation, the user tends to focus on the present moment and his own sense of it. The social dimension of experience is muted. Since a concern with chronometric measurement of time is a socially reinforced function, it too is weakened. All objective accuracy, measurement itself, becomes largely irrelevant to the private experience of the drug user.

In a less dramatic sector of the spectrum, depersonalization, hallucination, visual distortion, and so on have been readily produced, at moderate levels of intensity without sensory overload or chemical catalysts, by rudimentary exercises in meditation or unusual attentiveness. These experiments suggest a potential for altered perception of the world by ordinary persons (with limited personal investment) that is truly surprising. This is immediately pertinent to the development of new and more productive attitudes on the part of individuals toward aesthetic experience. The private arena, if explored, might provide a larger and more rewarding prospect than the public one. This is the first of two primary new means for altering spectator experience: *manipulating the level and pace of receptivity, storage, and interpretation accorded incoming materials from the outer world.*

Altered Materials

The second path involves *finding new sources for the materials of aesthetic experience*, drawing most heavily on the individual's internal world: previously stored or spontaneously generated items that, again, may undergo any number of normal or altered forms of processing as they become, in some sense, "understood." Manfred Clynes has undertaken a promising examination of cortical potentials, using a rosette configuration of electrodes to establish four axes, each rotated by 45 degrees from the last.

The four channels of information derived from these electrode pairs are analyzed by a computer employing a subtractive method that leaves the traces relatively independent of one another so that a dimensional picture is derived. Clynes believes that every perception has a "unique counterpart as a space-time code in the brain."[6] Although there may be general validity to this—and, indeed, at some level there must be—it is difficult to see how it could have more than a rudimentary, physical importance. We must all share a basis for interpretation—items, resonances, tested against a map of memory that is, in each case, decisively unique. There would appear to be little likelihood of an identical code developing in several minds for even so simple an item as "dog." These reservations, of course, would not necessarily apply in the case of basic emotions or what Clynes refers to as "sentic" states, and a good deal of intriguing material and conjecture has come out of his efforts. We are indebted to Clynes for the vigor with which he pursues his idiosyncratic interests. Item from Clynes's work for reflection: The strength of a reaction as recorded by an electrode configuration is not dependent solely upon the intensity of the input. The configuration of the stimulus may be a more powerful releaser, and, further, a visual configuration can be equally forceful regardless of the area it subtends on the retina (regardless, that is, of how large and/or close it is).

Clynes has apparently had some success in predicting by computer analysis of electrical activity in the brain the nature of the stimulus a subject is receiving at a particular moment: the color red, for example, as opposed to blue. He has, further, utilized (by means of a two-dimensional recording in time of finger-pressure patterns) gestural expressions of emotional states to test his belief that these states are unaltered by cultural influences. The use of the physical gesture instead of an EEG map, for example, is explained by the fact that one needs an integrated form for representing an emotion. These "sentic" states—love, anger, sex, *etc.*—are not equivalent to single items of sensory input. Single events may trigger complex emotions but in doing so,

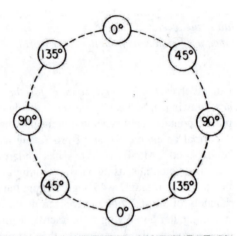

CIRCULAR ELECTRODE CONFIGURATION

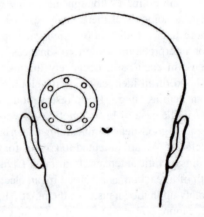

Figure 3a. Circular array of eight scalp electrodes (rosette) to measure spatially evoked potential. Measurements are taken simultaneously between opposite pairs of electrodes, resulting in four traces.

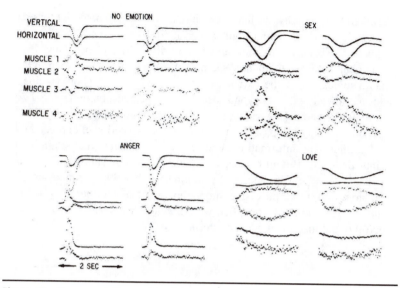

Figure 3b. Representative pairs of trace patterns for several basic emotional states.

they are, of course, acting in combination with vast amounts of previously stored information.

Other less controversial scientists have made more pragmatic use of internally derived materials. Their attempts range from the amusing to the chilling. In 1969, Elmer and Alyce Green of the Menninger Foundation adopted the straightforward device of electronically multiplying by a factor of 200 the potentials from each of the four primary frequency bands in the EEG. The resultant frequencies were thereby raised into the audible range, producing what they wryly termed "music of the hemispheres." Other neurologists are experimenting with the electrical stimulation of an apparent "pleasure center" in the septal region of the brain. This is not the evocation of pleasure. It is rather direct operation in and on the brain, the self-initiated but externally induced triggering of powerful sensations within a human being. Experiments undertaken in the area of sleep have revealed something of the mechanism whereby stimuli are incorporated into dreams. Tactile items seem most easily integrated by some subjects rather readily. One may assume that when such an ability exists in several subjects, it could be trained and enhanced in others. Apparently the earlier notion that external events *cause* dreams is unwarranted, but all forms of stimuli in sufficient strength, and tactile events in particular, can strongly influence the direction and content of an individual's dreaming. Since it is a relatively simple matter to detect some dream periods that are indicated by rapid eye movement (REM) and allied EEG activity, we have here another interesting potential for using, husbanding for desired effects, the internally derived stuff of dreams.

There has been no attempt here to describe in detail the many diverse phenomena referred to in this section; the intent has been to provide a general indication of the extent to which activity in psychophysiological fields has already moved beyond speculation. The question remains: to what use will this rapidly expanding capacity to manipulate directly human experience be put? The past few decades have been a period of unprecedented bombardment by information, and we have suffered the strain of its various demands. But all has been indirect. We remain capable of rejecting as we wish—at least in theory. The coming wave will be far more intimate in its approach, more pervasive, more capable of direct operation on areas of human life and intercourse that were previously beyond all but the most fanciful or unthinkable modes of interference.

PART IV
Sound

Natural Sound and Its Limits

Sounds and Their Use in Music
In order to accommodate a workable level of discrimination, an information-receiving system must operate within limits. This is true of the human visual apparatus, of television, a thermostat, or a telephone. Stimulation at too low a level passes undetected while that in excess of the system's inherent capacity becomes chaotic, painful, or even permanently damaging. What are the most prominent physical limits of the auditory system? Sensitivity to frequency, or pitch, the subjective sensation of "high" or "low" sounds, varies with age and sex but tends in adulthood to range between 20 and 16,000 cycles-per-second (cps) for practical purposes. The upper and lower thresholds of sound pressure, or loudness, vary with frequency.[1] A pure, sinusoidal pitch corresponding to a note in the bottom octave of the piano keyboard must be much more intense than one in the piano's top octave (the ear's optimal sensitivity range) if it is not to escape detection. The upper extreme of sound pressure (intensity), a range of loudness where sensations become physically painful, remains at a constant value throughout the audio-frequency spectrum. There are also limits to the speed with which the organs of hearing can respond to and recover from stimulation: for example, how rapidly a series of similar, brief sound pulses can be presented and still heard as separate items, or the rate at which a sequence of distinct events—let us say a series of different pitches—can be presented without losing its sequential identity. These rates differ markedly depending on intensity, frequency, and so on. In addition to the enumeration of range extremities, one must consider such functions as resolving power within each area of the established spread. The smallest change in pitch that can be detected alters as a function both of frequency and sound pressure; so too does the ability to determine which of two sounds is louder or when a change in intensity has occurred.

---

1. Although the distinctions are treated in more detail later, it should be mentioned at the beginning that pitch and loudness are perceptual measurements, based on human judgments. They do not correspond exactly to physical parameters such as frequency and intensity.

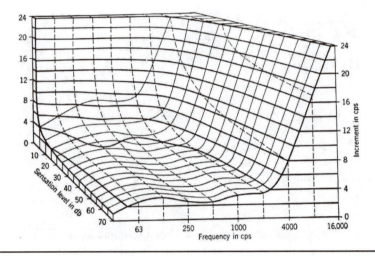

Figure 4. Three-dimensional surface showing the differential frequency threshold as a function of the frequency and the intensity of the standard tone. Frequency discrimination is poor at intensity levels near the absolute threshold (rear part of figure) and at high frequencies (right-hand part of figure). At sensation levels above 30 db and at frequencies below 1,000 cps, however, a change of about 3 cps can be detected.

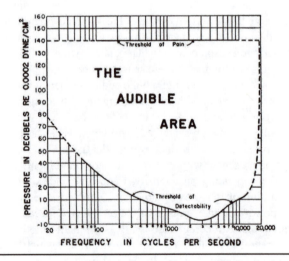

Figure 5. A graphic representation showing how sensitivity to the pressure of a periodic sound varies with its frequency. Sounds at the lower end of the audible frequency range must be far stronger in physical as opposed to psychoacoustic terms than those with frequencies around 3,000 cps if they are to be heard.

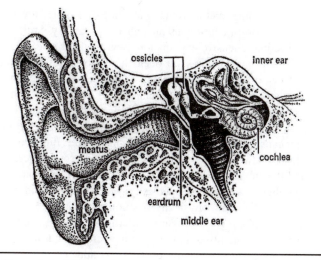

Figure 6. X-ray view of the human ear.

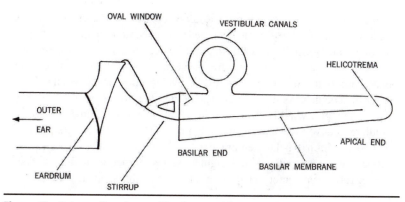

Figure 7. Schematic view with the cochlea uncoiled. Incident pressure waves beta against the eardrum causing displacement that is transmitted by hammer, anvil, and stirrup to the oval windows of the cochlea. Movement of the oval window (at the basilar end of the cochlea) induces movement of the perilymphic fluid which in turn stimulates hairs along the basilar membrane. Frequency sensitivity runs from high at the basilar end to low at the apical end (near the helicotrema).

The ear is preeminently a time-sensitive organ and its capacities are astonishing. It is far more rapid and accurate in temporal matters than the eye, which has a relatively long receptor latency period, and is able to deal with distinctions involving periods as small as 1/10,000 of a second.[2] Visually, on

2. The integration of such durations between the two ears is partially responsible for our ability to determine the apparent position of a sound source in space.

the other hand, a motion picture running at a rate of 24 still shots per second produces the illusion of continuous movement or stability. Still, the overall picture defies comprehensive explanation. Several theories of hearing have proved productive but none has yet been shown to be fully adequate. The difficulty is at least twofold. First, there is an unavoidable interconnectedness that frustrates attempts to measure crucial factors in isolation. Almost every sort of aural sensation varies with frequency, intensity, and duration, so that statements are inevitably cloaked with layers of modification. Second, there is no direct means of establishing, to a satisfying degree, uniform patterns of correspondence between physical facts (frequencies, sound pressure levels, timings) and the subjective sensations within an individual that accompany them in a nonlinear way (pitch, loudness, speed, duration, and so on). The traditional implication that, physically, any complex sound can be described as the sum of simple, regular pressure patterns has misled many investigators. There is no such additive simplicity at the perceptual level.

Although sound waves can, of course, be conducted in such media as wood, water, and metal as vibratory patterns, musical experience deals almost entirely with patterns of pressure transmitted through air.[3] Common to all contexts, finally, is the rise and fall of pressure transmitted to the oval window of the cochlea, a snail-shaped organ central to the workings of the inner ear. Normally, a series of sound waves beats against the eardrum and is transmitted mechanically by an elegant arrangement of three small bones comprising the middle ear to the oval window at the basilar (large) end of the cochlea. As the membrane covering the oval window is deformed inward, the perilymphic fluid within the cochlea flows in response and stimulates tens of thousands of small hair cells. These hairs are situated along the inner partition (basilar membrane) of the coiled cochlea in such a way as to produce, when stimulated, a weighted series of nerve impulses. These, in turn, reflect and interpret to a certain degree the acoustical nature of a pressure impulse or periodic waves of pressure.

The hair cells on the cochlea appear to be far more highly specialized than was originally thought; as the nature of this specialization becomes better understood, many of the still perplexing physical problems related to hearing may well dissolve. There is only one kind of signal that a nerve cell can transmit up the auditory nerve bundle: a brief electrical impulse, always of the same strength and duration, traveling at the same rate of speed. The awesome variety and detail of information that these cells supply to our higher centers result from the location of the cochlear partition of the transmitting cells, any further specialization of these cells,

---

3. A limited account of the ear and its response to sound will aid in understanding the subsequent material in this and other chapters. Fuller descriptions are available from numerous other ources. Bearing in mind the several cautionary perspectives offered in the present treatment, an exploration of the better literature is stimulating and rewarding on a practical level.

the number of impulses sent individually or in group volleys, and the point in the auditory cortex to which each message is sent. The brain's decoding of an auditory experience, then, depends entirely on the accuracy with which trains of identical, minute electrical impulses—traveling up the hundreds of thousands of neurons that comprise the auditory nerve—are counted and their patterns of interconnection (innervation) integrated.

The simplest form of pressure disturbance in the air, sometimes known as a pure tone, is a *sine wave*. Its familiar recumbent s shape results from graphically representing a perfectly even and continuous rate of pressure accumulation and release in time. One complete cycle of this process is followed by another, and if each takes an equivalent period of time, it is possible to determine a stable average: so many *cycles per second*. Roughly speaking, the frequency at which these equivalent, continuously repeated cycles of pressure and release occur is translated into a sensation of pitch by the brain. As mentioned above, the unaided human hearing apparatus responds to frequencies between approximately 20 and 16,000 cycles per second. Concurrently, one must consider the magnitude of the pressure peaks upon the eardrum. A greater pressure (higher peaks) produces a larger deviation, or *amplitude*, is more or less independently of the frequency with which it is applied. For a single pure tone, we need only know frequency and amplitude along with how they change in time to be able to predict rather accurately the subjective sensation that will result. This all assumes a continuous phenomenon. If the pressure impulse meeting the eardrum is very brief, the situation is seriously complicated. We will, for example, lose the sense of precise pitch.

Nothing that we notice is of infinite and unchanging extent. A constant pressure on the eardrum will come to be interpreted as silence. Alternatively, we are attuned exclusively to change: starting, altering, stopping. The perfectly smooth and continuous fluctuations discussed above are never encountered in the real world. A pattern of pressure waves must begin and, at the instant in time that it does so, it must set previously resting objects in motion. This process of initiating even the most orderly pattern invariably introduces unevenness and discontinuities, *transient* conditions, that damp out in a relatively short time, leaving the system—at least potentially—in a regular, steady state of fluctuation. Again, the pure and ideally simple pattern of the continuous sine wave does not occur in nature. Physical systems tend to produce complex patterns of vibration because of their imperfect elasticity and symmetry. In turn, these vibrations initiate complex patterns of pressure waves in the surrounding air.

Complex sounds can still be periodic, of course, but the fluctuations of amplitude with time during each cycle are less continuous and symmetrical. To the degree that they remain repetitive and periodic at some frequency, they will retain a pitch-like character. Most naturally vibrating

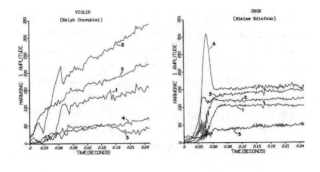

Figures 8 and 9. Graphic representation of the complex nature of initial transients for oboe and violin in a similar pitch register. During the initial phase of each tone the individual harmonics making up the composite sound begin, then wax and wane in individual ways. No composite attempt to synthesize sounds by general formulas—each harmonic bearing some constant relation to the last—will result in timbric cues as subtle as these naturally occurring ones.

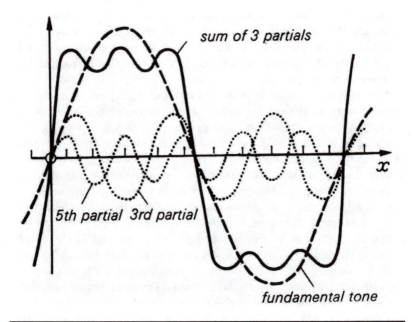

Figure 10. The addition of odd-numbered partials (3 x the fundamental frequency, 5 x the fundamental frequency ...), each a pure sine wave, will gradually approximate the angular square wave.

systems—bells are a prominent exception—obey simple rules regarding the generation of *harmonics* (sometimes called partials or overtones). A family of harmonics can be described as integral multiples of its lowest member or fundamental.[4] The characteristic pattern of any complex but periodic wave may be physically described as an algebraic sum of sine waves at these prescribed "harmonic" frequencies. In order to designate completely a continuing, complex wave in a physical sense, one must know the frequency of each harmonic (or nonharmonic) component, its amplitude, and its phase, as well as how these change with time. This information can be included in two forms of representation: wave form (or time analysis) and spectrum (or frequency analysis). Such a conglomerate of information might also be said to include what subjectively is called *timbre*. This term is a general designation for that aural attribute by means of which we recognize that two voices or different types of instruments whose sound outputs seem identical in pitch and loudness are yet clearly dissimilar.[5]

Phase relations are of considerable importance in physical descriptions of sound phenomena, although the ear appears relatively insensitive to them when their relationships remain constant. Since a periodic fluctuation must begin at some point in time and pass from a state of maximum pressure to one of maximum relaxation and so on, it will regularly pass through an instantaneous state of equilibrium halfway between the extremes. The points of balance are referred to as zero crossings or *nodes*, and the zero crossing just preceding the growth half of each cycle is taken as the starting point for the period. A particular element's temporal correspondence, its synchrony with the starting points of each other component of the overall sound complex, is measured in time and can be expressed in terms of a *phase angle*. Changes in the amplitude and/or phase of the pure tone components of a complex wave will change its shape dramatically. To re-emphasize a cautionary note: the shape of a wave in graphic display is not necessarily an accurate guide to its subjective quality. That is, wave representations that appear similar may differ strongly in sound quality while those that look unrelated may sound almost identical.

---

4. The midrange A to which many instrumental groups tune before beginning to perform completes 440 cycles each second. This could then be the fundamental or first harmonic in a complex tone that may include 880, 1320, 1760, 2200, 2640, 3080, and so on. Although a system may contain a very large number of physically detectable harmonics, it is generally impossible for the unaided ear to discriminate more than five to seven of them. Those of a higher order are perceived collectively and contribute to the discrimination of timbre.

5. The character of an instrument's sound is most economically determined for purposes of recognition by two other factors: *transient characteristics* and *formant bands*. It has been suggested that pitch judgments are physically made on the basis of two kinds of pattern recognition, one temporal (periodicity detected in the firing of nerve impulses), the other spatial (positional templates along the basilar membrane). The latter mechanism is critical in timbre perception.

Several points from the preceding outline are worth reviewing. Sounds naturally occurring tend to be complex but often can be described physically in rather straightforward ways. All sounds in the real world begin with transient periods, the most crucial of which is the first 50–100 milliseconds (1 millisecond equals 1/1000 of a second) after onset. This segment is the most decisive in the life of the sound. Not only the fundamental, but also each harmonic (or inharmonic, which is to say, nonintegral multiple of the fundamental) component of a complex sound begins in its own way and at its own time, creating a strongly colored and therefore characteristic *cue* by means of which instruments, vocal sounds, and speech consonants are recognized. So-called steady-state conditions are extremely rare in naturally occurring sounds even for brief periods of time. The overall regular variations in frequency that we call *vibrato*, the complementary periodic change in amplitude known as *tremolo*, and the constant introduction of minor discontinuities and unperiodic (or *noise*) elements through human and mechanical instabilities all contribute to an imposed randomness. This, in turn, is basic to the sensory richness that serves to engage the listener's attention.

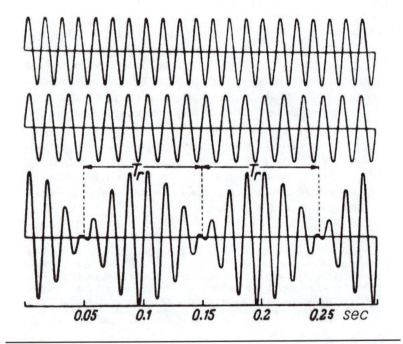

Figure 11. The combination of two sine waves of slightly different frequencies results in a strongly amplitude-modulated result. T$_r$ represents the period within which the sum of the two upper wave forms gives a zero amplitude.

Of similar influence to that of transient cues is another characteristic of resonant systems, *formant bands* or regions. A formant region is evident in the overall distribution and strength of frequency components, though there may be numerous resonant peaks, or points of special sensitivity, contained within one such region. By virtue of its dimensions, a voice or a musical instrument will have certain resonant properties. Particular bands within the overall audio-frequency spectrum will invariably be stressed or amplified by these natural regions of resonance. Formant bands are defined by a center frequency, and each operates symmetrically upon a range of frequencies above and below it, although with rapidly decreasing strength. The center frequency does not change unless the characteristics of the resonant cavity do. Thus, each time a complex tone with its attendant structure of overtones occurs within such a resonating structure, any fundamental or harmonic falling within the formant bands will be selectively reinforced or amplified. A physical system may have more than one formant region and there need be no harmonic relationship between these or with the fundamental of any affected tone. One could foresee that pitches in the upper register of an instrument will be less clearly influenced by its formant properties since the majority of harmonics for these tones are too high to be affected. Experience confirms that our ability to distinguish between the sound qualities (timbre) of different instruments tends to weaken as they enter the highest portion of their compass. When a variety of pitches is sounded, a characteristic pattern of stressed frequencies will emerge, some relating to fundamentals and others to higher harmonics. Along with the transient phenomena described above, this characteristic stenciling of all sounds processed is largely responsible for our ability to recognize instrumental families, performers, or even individual instruments.

The emerging picture of a given sound now includes an initial transient period, a relatively stable aftermath (during which a number of more or less periodic fluctuations in overtone structure, frequency, amplitude, and phase relations will take place), and, finally, a cessation. The sound may end in a variety of ways, at extremes with an abrupt cutoff or through a gradual dying away. The release transient is apparently less crucial in cuing than the initial one, although it is not clear that this is entirely for physical reasons.[6] The

---

6. Similar patterns are characteristic of physiological processes. Response to the introduction of a voltage or chemical factor is, in general, much more rapid than its dissolution. For example, the detection of a *decrease* in concentration of some substance within the cell or blood stream is generally accomplished by a different class of nerve channel than for an increase. Biological specialization is again in evidence here. Two sets of control channels will probably exist for each process, one to stimulate and the other to inhibit. Apparently the organism places more functional value on initiating a condition than on terminating it, although this might be a culturally dependent factor in some situations. A functional and spatial separation of command in the nervous system further promotes, as Manfred Clynes has observed, the existence of differing concepts for aspects of one variable like hot and cold, light and dark.

overall way in which the amplitude of a given sound grows, is maintained, and passes away with time may be described schematically (making a plot of amplitude against time) and is referred to as the *envelope*. Allowed to run their natural course, such percussive events as a gong or piano sonority will begin more or less suddenly and forcefully, gradually fading away. Conversely, a pipe organ will tend to build more slowly at the beginning, stopping rather abruptly whenever the key is released. Although it is possible, with most instruments or other sound-producing devices, to vary the quality of the initial transient (attack), sustained section, and the decay time (release), each domain nevertheless retains a quite characteristic envelope shape.

Variance during the central, sustained portion of a sound is most familiar musically as the phenomenon of vibrato, a slight periodic alteration of the basic frequency at a rate of about six or seven fluctuations per second. The process by which this quality of warmth—when discreetly used—is imparted can be called *modulation*. In aural contexts, modulation may be defined as the process whereby the frequency or amplitude of one sound or group of sounds is varied in accordance with the frequency or amplitude of a second sound or group of sounds. Whatever approach one takes to describing the mechanism of such interaction, the important point to recognize is the ability of events in one process to impose prominent aspects of their character upon the membership of another simultaneous process—a certain coloring, a synchronization of change, but always the overlay of new information. A modulated product will, therefore, usually be more complicated than either component; in electronic manipulation one runs the risk of obtaining a result so lacking in clear periodicities and harmonically related overtones as to be incoherent.

The admissible sounds in musical contexts are those that please or effectively engage the ear, that cohere in such a way that they can be identified and, hence, that simultaneous strands of them may be tracked without unmanageable confusion on the part of a reasonably experienced listener. Note the extensive use of modifiers in the preceding definition, a warning that the substance of the statement is more than usually dependent on context. Within the Western musical tradition, the definition of permissible sounds and combinations of them has evolved constantly. With the exception of minor stylistic fluctuations, the course of this development has been unidirectional, aiming toward a larger inclusiveness. Each increment of breadth has necessitated a practical reworking of guidelines both in terms of methodology and aesthetic sensibility. Even more fundamental disjunctions of taste have been continuously in effect between cultures. It is not only with regard to the ways in which sounds are employed but in their very physical nature that divergence obtains. The powerfully focused musical continuum of the West from the seventeenth century into the twentieth produced an intolerant adherence to a timbric homogeneity of restrained latitude sometimes dubbed *bel canto*. This ideal stressed a sedate, uniform smoothness of instrumental and vocal response and favored musical materials that best displayed these characteristics. Although notice was taken of registral properties, particularly in the case of the clarinet or the violin, for example, the professional performer aimed at an even roundness of sound. Each step up through the compass of an instrument was matched as closely as possible to the last. Discontinuities were noted and averted whenever possible in the selection of instruments and the composition of music.

Homogeneous material establishes its own justifying inertia. It masks the mediocre. More indispensable to art are the potential differences arising between diverse phenomena, roles, or ideas. Homogeneity of materials fosters unhealthy emphasis upon relationships internal to a given structure, at the expense of attention to the actual sonorities by which aesthetic substance is delivered to the spectator. Further, it shrinks the limits to which a performer or artist may go in search of an idea's proper fruition. Indiscriminate alteration is not sanctioned here. Whatever the range of sensation used, discontinuities—contrasts between materials—are fundamental to any experience of scope. Not only inflection but also the abrupt translation of a quality from one clear level to another establishes the aesthetic space. Asian cultures have habitually adopted a rather more accommodating posture toward materials, trading upon inherent qualities. The Japanese *shakuhachi*, a vertical flute made from a bamboo root, has five fingerholes and is capable of producing a twelve-note scale through the trained adjustment of mouth and finger positions. To our ear, its most striking sonic feature is timbric heterogeneity. In an ascending scale, successive steps are found to vary drastically in timbre and strength, one bold and clear, the next tentative and muted. Each note of the *shakuhachi* literature is allowed to live naturally, to reflect unashamedly the facts of its acoustic origin. While the Western wind player devotes years to the elimination of inconsistencies, his Japanese counterpart finds acoustical quirks a richly expressive resource. The latter cooperates with the instrument as it exists, highlighting its facets without attempting to impose unnatural standards.

The influence of musical Impressionism from the end of the last century opened the ears of the musician and listener alike to new densities and mixtures of familiar instrumental sounds. Most prominently associated with the French, particularly Debussy, whose personal achievement actualized in a vivid way what might have remained an impotent idea, the influence of Impressionism was substantial. Involving as it did not only new emphases on materials but a profoundly rebellious attitude, Impressionism set itself apart from the personal expression of the boisterous ego. More than in any previous period, musical sound became an expression of itself, an evolved experience reflective of the artist's relatively uninflected mental and emotional life. The impressionist's position might be seen as a step away from the compulsion of spectator or listener; it was a move toward the creation of objective though highly colored depictions to which each individual might come with some expectation of recreating or recapturing the artist's privileged sensitivity. Impressionism invited both the unashamed use of the sensory substance of materials and a willingness to reconsider one's stance regarding the structuring of music as well as the interpretation of responses to it. No wonder that musical minds as diverse and searching as Ives, Bartók, Respighi, Vaughan Williams, Boulez, Falla, and Stravinsky were deeply indebted to its force.

Impressionism raised afresh the level of sensitivity to and perhaps tolerance of a wider exploration of timbre. For example, harmonic parallelism involved the extraordinary shift from transformation to translation. Instead of restructuring the frequency relationships (the harmonic substance) from moment to moment, an attractive structure supporting a moment in a line of music might be maintained and moved higher or lower in parallel fashion. It could be moved without damaging its sonorous identity; chords were no longer statistical instants snatched from the logical progress of some accepted harmonic succession. An expanded percussion complement within the orchestra, the ubiquitous industry of machines, and years of bitter social disillusionment suggested the introduction of brutal and aggressive elements into musical language. Musicians questioned more easily and more regularly the necessary supremacy of a uniform and refined instrumental sound. Increasingly basic questions regarding the "proper" materials of art were raised within each of its disciplines. Of particular importance to enacting such insurrection was the availability of electrical and mechanical assistance. It was not imperative that an innovator like John Cage convert an entire ensemble to sympathy for his stance, although his ability to do so was a further demonstration of his pragmatic genius. In the late 1930's, he and other experimentalists were in a position to use Hollywood sound-effects records and, later, radios, phonograph cartridges, tape machines, and other electronic and mechanical devices. These allowed, in one sense of Buckminster Fuller's phrase, the mechanical extension of a man—the conversion of private fancy into public impact. Social problems arose with the next step: the implementation with groups of human performers of experiments first realized mechanically.

If Debussy, by example more than by design, emancipated musical sound from traditional structural obligations, John Cage was concerned with securing the acceptance of noise in the late 1930's and early 1940's. Both composers operated in public musical forums so that their products spoke unambiguously. Their music compelled response by its existence, by maintaining unmistakable profile in experience. Debussy succeeded more easily, for his concern was a realignment of obligations, while Cage struck at previously sacrosanct assumptions about the very nature of musical sound.

Cage was by no means the first to be accused of coddling noise, nor even the first to mount a systematic effort to introduce noninstrumental, seemingly raucous, or abrasive sound into formal musical contexts. His position was unprecedented, however, in its radical inclusiveness. It did not rest upon the fact of industry, the need for an enlarged palette of expressive materials, the desire to shatter cultural conformity, or any other such rational, limited, and therefore vulnerable basis. Remove all restrictions, he said; sound and silence are the stuff of music, and silence itself is a relative condition. If we are physically capable of hearing a sound, we cannot have silence, for it is excluded even in an anechoic chamber by the sounds of our body in operation. *All* sounds are admissible, not just the natural ones that might evoke, or the shriek of machines that might intimidate. Each and every disturbance that reaches the ear, whether intended or not, is the musician's concern, his natural substance. Cage undercut the possibility of argument by observing that purpose too had no place in art. One could no longer counter that a certain category of sounds failed to serve expressive functions, for, he said, let them express only themselves. Remove yourself as central, as manipulator, and assist sounds in their own work: to establish their physical status. They remain unavoidably open to interpretation, to the imposition of imagined intent, but this will be controlled by the individual who experiences, only inadvertently preordained by the composer.

Cage's deliberate assumption of total admissibility was concerned with materials. It was a pragmatic position that generated but did not flow from philosophical discourse. His acts forced upon him the position of justifier, and his acceptance of this role has been of crucial importance to the development of art in the second half of this century. His concert activity often involves collaboration with some type of theater, whether the organized activity of dance or a less artful inclusion of incongruous, joyfully arbitrary events or movement in normally restrained contexts. Because of his unique personality ("I have been gifted with a sunny disposition."), quickness of mind, and an ability to seize upon and transform common items, he was able to realize publicly events that could not have had so prominent an influence as speculation, however witty.

In admitting all acoustic material, one incurs other tacit obligations. Sounds not produced to specification, as they are for musical performance, tend to come equipped with contexts. Little occurs in natural isolation, so the admission of one sonic item practically implies acceptance of its habitual and often distracting companions. Noises, after all, are not necessarily loud or even annoying. On the other hand, musical sounds *can* be irritating when reproduced too loudly under inappropriate conditions. Although we have tended to use the word "noise" in a pejorative sense, the dictionary does not exclude a more general understanding, covering "soft, confused sounds" as well. Physically, one might assign such an appellation to nonperiodic, which is to say, excessively complex structures.[7] No matter which is chosen, however, utility and habituation are central to any definition. Quite understandably, we guard ourselves from those stimuli with which we are unfamiliar and for which, as a result, we have no use. A flaw in human reason permits us to categorize all unfamiliar items within one class— whether the sounds of language, the faces of another race, or the habits of another generation—and to see them as undifferentiated. It is a notorious but pervasive error. When we expose ourselves to unknown masses of events, they begin to resolve into subsets long before we are capable of identifying the basis upon which we differentiate. One might fervently hope that an argument as familiar as this is unnecessary—but each day impresses upon us the boundless capacity for intolerance.

Each generation of initially frightening innovations in art is soon proved docile. Of course, the materials and their distributions do not change with time, but our capacity for recognition, retention, pattern-making, and hence value-adducing does. If noise, then, is simply an appellation for the inadmissible and we are prevailed upon to be more tolerant, another brand of dissonance can emerge. The difficulty in accepting unfamiliar phenomena represents only a first stage in the confrontation with unknown contexts or sequences. While one might be persuaded to accept certain previously excluded sounds if they were treated in understandably "musical" ways— one thinks of a disagreeable parallel in the way Disney cheapened the observation of wildlife by anthropomorphizing its ways—the reverse is not true. Experience informs us that even the most common materials can become remarkably unsettling in unfamiliar contexts. We are addicted to familiar forms of continuity.

From the acceptance of all sounds as *potentially* but, of course, not neces-sarily useful elements in musical experience, another development followed quickly. Artists of all sorts began to experiment with entire environments. Several ordinarily independent but well-known processes were combined, or short fragments of several realities rapidly interspersed. The Dadaists, for example, introduced urinals or collages of scraps of newspapers and maga-zines into art galleries with studied sobriety. The perceptual dissonance in-troduced here was greater than would have been expected from the materials alone. In theory, the spectator's dilemma could be further intensified by com-binations in which both materials and contextual abutments were unfamiliar. "In theory," because dissonance is something that obtains *between* items or

---

7. Numerous efforts—not infrequently undertaken by scientists who are nostalgic, amateur musicians—have been made to uncover a physical basis for "dissonance" as it is presently defined. A reasonable case has been made for modulative interaction by sets of harmonics that lie within a *critical band width* (approximately one-third to one-fifth of an octave) of each other. In any case, attempts to define "dissonance" can often be reduced to attempt to explain physically some out-of-favor subjective characteristic

ideas. If one rejects the elements of a situation, one can hardly experience the intellectual or emotional interplay that can arise from the superimposition of well-known but novelly disposed materials.

Borrowing from the fine arts, as in the case of Impressionism one might label the foregoing method "montage." It is characterized by the superimposition of several previously organized items or fragments or, alternatively, by the rapid, sequential sampling of several preexistent series of events. Here the artist is in an optimal position not only to use the qualities inherent in individual physical sensations and to construct relationships and sequences that serve his purposes, but also to manipulate the resonance of each fragmentarily presented snippet of reality. He may play upon the potentially rich repertoire of associations that exist in the mind of the listener for the original context from which a segment has been lifted. Depending upon the context in which it occurs, montage can be rather easily absorbed. It allows a facile expansion of the range of aesthetic manipulation without making great adaptive demands upon the listener. Used more boldly, in combination with demanding materials, it may well be the most powerful affective means available to art. Its limitation is precisely this response-insuring topicality.

A Wider Field of Access

The limits of aural perception need no longer keep us from examining and perhaps incorporating vibratory phenomena that may be too slight, too rapid, too complex, or too lethargic for normal processing. The useful range of vision was expanded long ago and we have by now grown quite accustomed to the impact of information gained through telescopes or microscopes. Though there may have been little direct use of such modes of expanded apprehension in art, they are of incalculable value as models, as I have repeatedly stressed. Until recently, extension of aural limits has been concentrated exclusively on the transmission of useful but ordinary forms of information over great distance, as by means of telephone or radio. It is easy to understand from several perspectives the increasing use of *amplification* in music. Certain historically important instruments, like the clavichord (a keyboard instrument in which *tangents* press against—but do not strike or pluck— strings to produce minute but subtly gradated sounds), are for all practical purposes useless within huge modern concert halls; so, to a degree, is the more familiar harpsichord. Building larger and therefore acoustically more imposing models on the same principles does not guarantee a faithful translation. Acoustics is a complex subject and, as explained above, the acuity of our response is dependent upon loudness as well as the physical structure of the sounding source.

Electronics has provided an important if not a final solution to the problem of gaining access to small sounds. Using a variety of microphones that exclude unwanted signals (ambient noises and distortion), it is possible to amplify instruments selectively. Although excessive amplification can distort a sound to the point of qualitative transformation, discreetly used electronics can distribute and make available an otherwise inaudible or poorly balanced component of a musical performance. The process of amplification—with the essential proviso that the signal is properly distributed through loudspeakers—effectively moves a given sound source closer to us, allowing it to function for a far larger audience than would be possible under ordinary circumstances. The exquisite subtleties of a natural guitar or clavichord can be made *present* in the sense to which we have become accustomed through recordings and home high-fidelity installations. Natural imbalances between members of an instrumental group may be discreetly corrected. Beyond this—and of greater importance to musical innovation at the moment—there is the possibility of utilizing extremely small sounds, those that even careful attention in everyday circumstances might not reveal. To begin with a conservative application, instruments are capable of producing extremely slight sounds. This range of possibilities was never exploited for the reason that these sounds are unsuited to projection in public performance. As we shall see, entirely new areas of instrumental performance technique have become feasible with the advent of electronic amplification. Further, a composer may investigate and choose to employ sounds too soft (the whisper of wind currents) or too remote from normal aesthetic contexts (the raging of a blast furnace or the sound of children at play or even the incessant activity of a brain cell).

Given access through amplification to any acoustic output, how may we capture it so as to produce the desired sound-moment on command during a performance? Respighi employed a phonograph recording of a nightingale in *The Pines of Rome* in 1927. Since then, tape recording and, most recently, digitally coded memories have made it possible not only to store indefinitely any given sound or sonic environment with excellent fidelity but also to select a listening perspective. That is to say, one may achieve the illusion of varying acoustical spaces (from cathedrals to closets), movement within environments, and proximity or remoteness, all with relative ease. With the ability to control and opportunely release any extant audio signal comes an enlarged responsibility for selectivity. The only limitations at the moment are imposed by inexperience and the moderate level of knowledge involved. The sounds to be treated can remain entirely natural in and of themselves; it is only the circumstances of their presentation, of their participation in music that are novel. They may undergo amplification so as to fall within the situational limits of our hearing, be stored until the moment they are needed for use in performance, and be reproduced in an appropriate manner. Not all sounds, particularly those that occur in remote or feeble form, are easily identified or attached to a real context. As a result, the use of naturally occurring sounds does not necessarily imply a montage-like effect. They may still fall gracefully into abstract, nonrepresentational use.

Recording tape may be cut or electronically edited by instantaneous gating[8] procedures so that sequences unimaginable in real life can occur as prescribed in a montage presentation. The musical utility of superimposing layers of recorded materials or of recorded and live performance events is limited only by the constraints of human attention and response character-istics. Another useful technique now readily available is *filtering*. By means of electronic procedures, one can overcome, within limits, the objection raised earlier: that we tend to find naturally occurring sounds surrounded by other less desirable sounds. The filter is a frequency-sensitive device by means of which portions of the audio spectrum—for example, all sounds low in pitch—can be removed without a trace. If a desired segment of sound material occurs within a relatively narrow pitch range, it is possible to filter out all frequencies except those in that range, in much the same way that optical filters can limit or enhance the content of an image transferred to photographic film, or that one can crop the resulting print to a more desirable configuration. One further method of gaining access to natural oscillatory phenomena (for example, the previously mentioned periodic but sub-audio discharges occurring in the brain) is by modulation. Here, not the original signal but its influence is made audible through combination with another signal in the audio range. It is now also possible to achieve multiplication or division of a signal's frequency, while preserving the original wave form, or to change the speed of a succession of events without altering their sound qualities. This allows, over a much wider range and with precise control, the kind of transformation that results from playing a phonograph record at a faster or slower rate than was intended. In the past, such mechanical transpo-sition has usually been done at the expense of the particular qualities of wave form and spectral content present in the original. Now, vibratory phenomena ordinarily too slight, too fast, too slow, or too remote can be translated into the normal perceptual arena, becoming *sounds* that can be heard without losing their inherent peculiarities: new yet natural materials.

Enhanced Instrumental Resources

The drive toward new instrumental resources has persisted without interruption since the impulse to make instrumentally assisted music itself first arose. Those periods that were particularly turbulent due to changing methods or values, the effects of cultural crosscurrents, or the impact of

---

8. Gating refers to a process whereby the passage of some form of electrical signals—control functions or audio materials—can be allowed or blocked by reference to another signal. At root, it is simply a convenient way of turning a given switch on or off. The efficiency and speed with which new electronic devices allow gating to take place in synchronized patterns can achieve very complex results.

fresh mechanical expertise probably produced a wider variety. Curt Sachs has observed that the sixteenth century was uniquely rich in instrumental hues, far more so than any succeeding age. As one might imagine, contemporary efforts have been shaped by the enlarged attitudes toward admissible sounds discussed earlier. One of the most unpretentious and charming of modern developments, Cage's "prepared piano," introduced in 1938, involves the simple expedient of inserting various metallic and rubber objects between the strings of the piano's multiply strung pitches. An efficient, varied, and to some degree predictable ensemble of percussion events results, a kind of idiosyncratic reduction of the *gamelan* ensembles of Java. Others of courage and imagination have designed and realized whole families of instruments. The music of the American Harry Partch involves an expansive, dance-like gestural content as a result of deliberately choreographic instrumental designs that he developed over the course of his mature creative life. In Partch's case, as in a majority of experimental forays of this sort, the impetus would seem to have come from a variety of dissatisfactions, not the least of which was unhappiness over the tuning restrictions imposed by the normal complement of Western instruments. In France during the 1950's, Fran ois and Bernard Baschet developed *Les Structures Sonores Lasry-Baschet*, more on the basis of sculptural and engineering insights than out of musical necessity. Although these constructions, probably because of their extramusical motivation, present a somewhat more unprecedented array of sounds than do Partch's, they have been, to date, only sporadically and unimaginatively used. They assert, nevertheless, an as yet unexplored position: that contemporary materials and fabrication techniques could produce synthesis equipment on other than electronic bases.

Of more general interest are innovative performance techniques that can be readily applied to traditional instruments. These techniques have genuinely enlarged timbric scope and control of the subtlety of microtonal pitch. Although dynamic range may be freely manipulated by electronic means, instrumental and human mechanisms, upon which the limits of speed and the capacity for duration continue to rest, have not changed significantly for a long while. The fact that instrumental design—reeds, bore characteristics, and key mechanisms—have evolved as a response to the demands of one stream of stylistic persuasion does not exclude the possibility of their serving other masters. An instrument produces sound when either its resonant materials or contained columns of air are set into (usually) periodic motion. There is, of course, a wide variety of ways, not all of which occur in the Western tradition, by which basic vibratory patterns can be induced. With their intricate venting mechanisms, woodwinds offer a particularly broad spectrum of complex sounds. One needs only to move slightly beyond the normal and well codified limits of instrumental technique to find sounds of surprising diversity and stability. The variety of new resources includes some that are percussive, some sustained or minutely graded microtonal pitch deviants, some timbric hybrids. Most interesting, perhaps, are the large families of "multiphonics" available on any woodwind instrument.[9] These effectively dispel the common assumptions that woodwinds are exclusively single-lined (monophonic) in nature, that timbric homogeneity is inherent in an instrument's construction, and also the notion that traditional Western instruments are necessarily bound to one set of tuning imperatives. The number of multiphonics revealed within a brief period of exploration is already very large. Many are as reliable as normal sounds on the instrument, have pitch stability (though not necessarily corresponding to normal equal-tempered scalar resources), and a considerable dynamic range. Significantly, they are more diverse in character than the sounds of the usual, deliberately homogeneous instrumental output. Instruments like the clarinet or oboe have suddenly become vehicles for a surprisingly wide variety of timbric subtlety, polyphony complexity, and unexpected pitch relationships—all of which are by no means accidental or unrepeatable. No work has yet been done on a physical analysis of the growing multiphonic repertoire—and one looks forward to much investigation. Some of these sounds have a

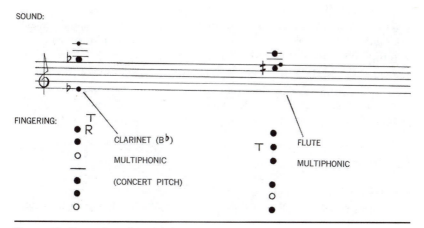

Figure 12. Examples of multiple sounds that may be reliably produced from standard instruments. Sounds are notated at actual pitch. Smaller noteheads indicate weaker components. Suggests a microtonal raising of the pitch. Fingerings show which key (including trill and register keys) are depressed, and which remain open.

---

9. The term "multiphonics" was coined by Reginald Smith Brindle, editor of the English translation of Bruno Bartolozzi's uneven but important pioneering volume, *New Sounds for Woodwinds*, London, 1967.

distinctive, ethereal consonance about them in spite of the fact that they are based upon objectively "dissonant" pitch relationships.

Production of multiphonic sonorities on the clarinet—or, alternatively, microtonal scales containing over a hundred distinct sounds between two equal-tempered semitones (*F* and *F-sharp* near the throat register, for example)—can be accomplished by alternate fingering arrangements, sometimes in combination with altered embouchure or adjusted pressure on the reed. They do not necessarily entail any acrobatic extensions of normal methods and are, therefore, not limited to use by particularly skilled players. In fact, beginners seem to adapt rather easily to producing them. Perhaps they are spurred on by the more immediately tangible rewards of the unexpected and strikingly evocative multiphonic result as compared with traditional sound ideals. The multiphonic sound is accessible and reproducible, and it can vastly extend the expressive compass of the woodwind family.

The use of such devices by exploratory composers is steadily increasing. Those results too soft for normal use can be amplified; those that are too unreliable can be recorded, edited as desired, and played back as needed in a musical context. Work in this terrain is bounded only by statistics: the outrageous number of combinations that await trial. At present, acousticians are unable to prognosticate reliably, as the distressing number of inadequate new concert halls attests. Experiment proceeds on a pragmatic level, by trial and error. Again, one might interpret multiphonic sonorities—and the analogous phenomena to be found by exploring other families of instruments—as a form of mechanical as opposed to electronic synthesis. A device of limited physical extent is manipulated in order to produce whole families of sounds with properties varying from the simple to the complex. These may, in turn, become the materials upon which other compositional operations are imposed.

Synthesis

Initial Efforts

A confluence of factors—including the twentieth-century instrumental and coloristic innovations discussed earlier, the rapid strides in electronic technology brought about by World War II, and a body of scientific literature devoted to perception and, in particular, psychoacoustics—has served to suggest the possibility of direct sound synthesis through electronic means. Prominent investigators following Helmholtz in the late nineteenth century had used the mathematical techniques of Fourier to demonstrate that, to an apparently adequate degree, any sound could be described as the algebraic product of a sufficient number of sine waves. We have seen earlier that this proved too simple an approach for musical applications. It was, nevertheless, an attractively straightforward invitation to researchers. On the basis of Helmholtz's clear and reassuringly orderly assumptions about the nature of sound, devices were built, some early ones electromechanical in nature.[10] All in all, it was a felicitous simplification, responsible for the relative vigor of early efforts in synthesis. Still, it is unfortunate that some of the early attitudes continue to limit the development of realistic scope for experiment. Considerably more information than was first at hand, and hence more elaborate equipment, is needed if genuinely satisfying musical materials are to be achieved through electronic synthesis.

Efforts to understand the mechanism of hearing stemmed from medical and communication needs. Unfortunately, models that were adequate for these utilitarian ends fell short when required to match the naturally occurring richness, the kaleidoscopic variation of aural microstructure that our ears take for granted in and out of musical contexts. Understandably, early efforts at producing marketable electronic synthesis were based upon engineering rather than musical criteria and were spurred on by hope of financial gain. There are two basic aspects to compositional sound synthesis: the production of sound material and its distribution into meaningful patterns. In both cases, simplifying (economical) assumptions were tempting and regularly indulged.

In its first stages, electronic music was derived entirely from oscillations produced electronically. The term was later applied also to music recorded on tape as a result of montaging sounds collected from the natural world (musique concrète), to music that involved a combination of live sources and their electronic modification during performance ("live electronic music"), and to modified and taped materials of any origin. At the outset, however, synthesized electronic music always involved processes whose final results were permanently fixed on magnetic recording tape. The basic electronic signals normally came from bands of sine-wave generators. These, each with manually adjustable frequency output, could be set to correspond with the fundamental and higher harmonics of the complex tone one was attempting to synthesize. That is, the approach was to construct along lines suggested by mathematics and physics. Complex tones were sought through the addition of sufficient numbers of pure signals whose amplitudes had been adjusted, so that as one ascended from fundamental to first, second, third, and higher harmonics the intensity was lowered by a constant amount.

Imitation of instrumental sounds also began, less on an empirical basis than upon information abstracted from psychoacoustical analysis. For example, the attempt to reproduce a clarinet-like sound used only odd harmonics, as physical analysis of the instrument—a cylindrical bore with

---

10. An absorbing documentation of the efforts of the American Thaddeus Cahill appeared in the first issue of *Synthesis* magazine (1972). In spite of its practical limitation to three simultaneous voices and a wearisomely invariant timbric range, the "Telharmonium" was enormously heavy and cumbersome.

one end closed—predicted; a flute-like sound with a prominent fundamental was attempted for parallel reasons. The results were amusing to engineers but entirely unsatisfactorily to musicians. The process of achieving even one acceptable tone segment by means of setting and balancing a dozen oscillators or more was cumbersome. No effort was made to incorporate formant structures, characteristic phase relationships, or transients of sufficient complexity. Yet, as we have seen earlier, these factors, along with a variety of continuously fluctuating pseudorandom deviations from steady-state conditions, are crucial to establishing a timbric identity for a series of sounds intended to carry a line, and to attaining a satisfying semblance of actual instrumental sonority. Gradually, tremolo and vibrato were added but, again, in perfectly or nearly regular patterns; the results were cloying. Simplistic approximations of the natural envelope structure of sounds were made, but, to keep matters simple, these were applied to the composite wave form, not, as in the natural case, to each component harmonic or nonharmonic element individually. Envelope generators later provided a range of rise ("on-set") times, steady-state durations, and decay lengths, each manually selectable. Results were thereby improved, but they were still unsatisfactory because of their simple, pure, and regular structures. The quality of natural sounds was increasingly seen to be based upon their incessantly shifting *approximation* of certain orderly norms, but the practical problems involved in the generation of such complexity electronically were virtually insuperable.

Another early effort at achieving more appealing materials was found in beginning at the opposite extreme. *White noise*—familiar to us as the broadband hiss audible when shifting a radio dial between stations—consists in a random, constantly changing sampling of frequencies from the entire audio band. It is, in a way, analogous to white light, which is made up of energy from all visual wave lengths (colors). If one starts with white noise and cuts out sections of varying *center frequency* and *band width* by means of filters, one can circumvent the painfully slow additive methods.[11] Bands filtered out of the full frequency spectrum are called *colored noise*. As one might expect, the narrower such subtractive bands, the more orderly the wave shape, and the more nearly periodic or pitch-like the wave shape becomes. Colored noise was expensive to work with because of the elaborateness of sufficiently flexible filtering devices, but it was more convenient than additive synthesis and had the merit of a ready coloristic freshness. Initially unfamiliar, the timbric range of colored-noise bands and bursts was limited by the uniformly chaotic, therefore indiscernible, makeup of their material. Further, it was thoroughly

---

11. *Center frequency* is a convenient way of indicating the position of a given band of noise in the audio spectrum. This term corresponds to the frequency halfway between the outer limits of the band. The *band width* designates the numerical difference between the frequency of the upper and lower limits of the band.

impractical to achieve, as one easily could by additive means, a selective harmonic or nonharmonic distribution of upper partials.

Developments have continued in the area of material construction, but so far as individual component analog equipment is concerned, they remain centered upon two basic sources: simple tones and noise bands.[12] A selection of orderly geometrical wave forms (square, triangular, sawtooth, and pulse, in addition to the basic sine wave) was common in early synthesis equipment. These were added to one another, producing still regular but more angular wave patterns; or, for example, a sine wave was gradually transformed into a square by the incremental addition of properly weighted odd harmonics. Filters have improved in flexibility and lowered in cost, and modulation is used more frequently for the easy conversion of two simple components into a far more complex wave form. (The number of effective additional components depends upon the type of modulation and the frequency range of the components.) Modulation, however, continued to be limited by its arithmetical nature. Amplitude modulation, the most practical form, produces extra pitches ("side bands") by the addition and subtraction of component frequencies from the two modulating signals. But pitch changes *geometrically* with frequency, so that an octave is twice the frequency of its fundamental while a double octave is four times the fundamental. In the octave surrounding middle-*C*, the lower *A* vibrates 220 times per second. Compare this to the *A* octave straddling the soprano high-*C*: *880* and *1760*. A modulated process retains its absolute relationship throughout the audio spectrum, not the frequency *ratios* inherent in pitch shift with natural sounds and their harmonic complements. The meaning, as sensation, of a modulated product of two tones differing in frequency by 200 cps, for example, will be totally different in the lower octave (where that spread nearly equals the octave pitch spread) and the upper one (where it is less than one-fourth). Although modulation procedures do produce complex resultant timbres economically, the nature of the timbric and dynamic character changes depending on the frequency range within which it takes place. Two mid-range tones close together, within a critical band width, produce the most dense and vibrant results. Although the barriers encountered in synthesizing rewarding sound materials may be easily ascribed to the ear's extraordinary sensitivity to constant variation in transient cues and subtle steady-state fluctuations, these barriers remain formidable. An *acceptable* result will never stimulate the transcendent, illuminating responses that we expected from art. Adequate is not enough in aesthetic matters.

Unfortunately, a similar sort of problem arises with respect to the second major aspect of synthesis: the distribution of materials in meaningful patterns.

---

12. The distinction between *analog* and *digital* processes will be discussed later. The latter is the basis of almost all computer installations and includes, therefore, its own characteristic potential.

The ear is accustomed to and able to discriminate among a welter of simultaneous sources of informative or randomly occurring sound events. Although we have limited capacity to process information completely, our remarkable selective abilities allow us to make sense of even the numbing cacophony of a party in a crowded apartment, shifting at will between conversations, street sounds, or familiar strains of music (and, in the latter, among lyrics or melodic subtlety or instrumental backing). Just as the trained ear expects and receives complexity of organizational detail, even within the materials of a common and simple musical experience such as the sounds of an unaccompanied flute or folk singer, so it demands an equal suppleness in textural and temporal design.

At first, sound synthesis was done by the laborious process of manually setting large numbers of dials, recording the composite results on tape, cutting these materials into segments of appropriate length (and therefore desired duration), and rerecording them in acceptable combinations. If one coherent and acceptable train of prepared segments was difficult, complex polyphony was so in the extreme. Although traditional Western ideals of music performance do not demand a perfect beat-by-beat synchrony, a minimum level of coordination is required. When one tried to add one line of music to another by recording successive tracks on the same tape, a satisfactory degree of synchrony was surprisingly difficult to achieve. Slight differences in the speeds of different tape machines and slight inaccuracies in measurement accumulate destructively. Again, the ear's ability to detect nonsimultaneity is uncanny, and sounds that do not come sufficiently close to simultaneity will be felt as distinctly separate. As observed earlier, it is also difficult to produce material that retains an interesting and continuously identifiable timbric quality throughout a reasonable pitch range. A music of several independent lines or of primary lines and supplementary accompanimental design is, therefore, also difficult to achieve satisfactorily by the techniques still most generally in use.

Even if one did produce an agreeable store of materials that suited more complex *polyphonic* (multiple-lined) treatment, a satisfying degree of synchrony involved additional difficulty. On the one hand, assuming perfect synchrony is attained, it is at first dazzling, and then quickly becomes transparently mechanical. The listener needs the easy flexibility of the individual human operator or the disciplined but still comfortably imprecise ensemble of musical groups. On the other hand, it is more difficult than might be thought to figure out *how* synchrony and regularity of pulse or rhythmic pattern should vary so as to feel (while not being) natural. The designers of component, analog synthesis equipment approached this problem by way of keyboards that allow a human operator to call forth preselected sound materials at will by assigning each to a selected key and then tapping out rhythmic patterns as desired. They admitted, in short, the hopelessness of uncovering and implementing satisfactory automated alternatives. Other parts could be added similarly to materials previously stored on tape in order to achieve a full musical texture.

A second development, more interesting in its implications, was the *sequencer*. Here, again, preselected sound events were triggered but not, this time, manually by human operators. A normal sequencer might include sixteen steps. Each step could activate three or more different electrical signals that correspond to this position alone. These, in turn, could call forth a particular pitch, dynamic level, and envelope shape, for example. Each of the signals or voltages corresponding to a given step was still set manually, but, once set, access to their control information could be gained automatically and continuously through the electronic sequencer. An electronic *clock* signaled the sequencer output to advance from one step to the next at whatever rate the user specified, and over a wide range. In this way, one after another sound—each predefined as to pitch, dynamic, and envelope—would be selected in any chosen sequence.

Unfortunately, the auditory cortex in combination with short-term memory is also remarkably retentive. Even as many as forty distinct sounds following each other one after another at a moderate rate of speed become familiar and predictable almost immediately. They result in what a musician refers to as ostinatos—regular, repetitive sequences of notes. Although ostinatic elements have played a significant role in activating earlier stylistic periods in Western music, they tend to suggest a rather formalistic and inflexible attitude and are best suited for accompanimental (*i.e.*, secondary) functions. Recently, more and more complex sequencing has come into use; some devices have very large numbers of steps. It also became possible to advance the count at proportionally unequal intervals. That is, in contrast to early devices where one was limited to an equal time interval for each unit of the sequence, it became possible to vary the temporal proportions by prearrangement. The clock rate itself, of course, has always been subject to continual alteration by manual control. If the overall clock rate is thought of as analogous to tempo and the individual step durations as analogous to rhythmic relationships, vastly increased flexibility can be anticipated.

In traditional music, partly as a function of the size of the performing group, tempo is relatively, though not completely, constant. Not only are rhythmic details irregular, however, but the extent, the bounded range within which variation occurs, is as well. We will not remain engaged by rhythmic relationships, however intriguingly asymmetrical, so long as they recur in too brief a period relative to their length. Ideally, a sequencer-generated succession is useful only for one or two repetitions before we begin to discount it as redundant. Even within the most motoric live musical context, irregularities are constantly happening. They not only serve to maintain our attention but, naturally, as a means for the performer to transmit extremely subtle shades of implication. Products of an automated sequencer are rapidly unmasked and as automatically relegated to a textural function by the discriminating ear. This being so, the basic motivation in developing the sequencer—to allow the more economical generation of musical expanse—is frustrated. We are unlikely to escape from the need for irregularity and a subtle form of variation. As a result, the search for a more acceptable product from the sequencer principle has led, primarily, to new means of triggering events irregularly. Random or pseudorandom control signals can produce an attractive fluctuation in the microstructure of sound and, for a time, may also be effective on a rhythmic level. There is still a great and significant gap between bounded randomness and the kind of *directed* although irregular alterations introduced by the nervous system of the performer for expressive purposes.

Methods of producing patterns of sound by semiautomatic means were sought in order to overcome the wearisome process of manual construction. The development that made such automation possible was the principle of *voltage control*. Voltage is a property of electrical force that can vary continuously under precise control. Recognizing this fact, designers contructed electronic devices whose sensitivity to variations in incoming voltage eliminated the necessity for manually adjusting external control knobs. With a voltage-controlled oscillator (VCO), the frequency of the output could be made directly proportional to voltage input over a wide range. Thus, a low voltage could result in a low frequency or pitch while a continuously rising voltage was paralleled by a similarly ascending pitch output. Similar means were applied to envelop control, modulation, amplification, and filtering. Control voltages can be derived by many means (including periodic sampling or envelope detection performed electronically on any input signal) and can be used to achieve continuous or *analog* variability.

All audio signals vary more or less periodically and continuously and are therefore analog signals. All control signals, however, are not analog as they are in the voltage-controlled units just referred to. The sequencer proceeds step by step, from one setting to another, without intermediate gradations. It may be operated by pulses, or relatively brief signals of constant amplitude. The signal, then, is either off or on. It changes in sudden discontinuous steps, and only at precise moments, equally spaced in time. Such a system is referred to as *digital* and the sequencer is controlled (or "pushed") by a digital clock. Each pulse causes an abrupt switching from one step of the sequencer to the next. The digital principle is at the root of most of the present computer technology because science is profoundly committed to quantized, countable phenomena. Science has aggressively pursued ways of approximating continuous processes digitally for easier mathematical manipulation. Analog computers exist but are not at present in favor. For musical purposes, analog output is required and, thus, earlier efforts at synthesis were directed into this area. As described, however, it proved difficult to achieve sufficiently sophisticated analog techniques for satisfactory sound synthesis. This is true not because analog methods are inherently weak but because industrial technology has concentrated on the more readily manufactured and reliable digital concept. There remains a more basic measure of the dilemma. Designers know too little about the mechanism of hearing and the nature of complex audio signals: they know too little about the aesthetic standards and needs of serious musicians.

Computers
Computer technology is variously thought of as a menace or as a panacea that will provide final answers to previously awkward impasses and untenably time-consuming processes. Not surprisingly, its capacities have been brought to bear on the problem of sound synthesis, particularly through the efforts of M.V. Mathews and his associates at the Bell Telephone Laboratories during the mid-1960's. Earlier work in speech synthesis had prepared them for the dimensions of the musical task, and by 1967–68, they had developed a *program* called MUSIC V that subsequently became the standard for work in computerized sound synthesis. A program is a compilation of rigorously logical, step-by-step instructions by means of which a computer organizes the nature, order, and interaction of its calculating operations. Programs must literally foresee everything at a minimal level of completeness, for *a computer takes nothing for granted* unless it has been instructed and given the means to do so. Programming requires not only a completely considered sequence of orders but knowledge of the properties of a special "language" by means of which the computer can be made to understand directions economically. The language usually used in synthesis work was called FORTRAN IV and comprised a complete collection of specific conditions delimiting the nature of words and statements that could be made, the manner in which ideas and processes could be encoded. At this time, a computer is unable to deal with even the most concentrated and logical progression of commands unless they are translated into a language that it is already programmed to understand. The complexities of our daily language—especially idiomatic and topical trends—make it too formidable a system for secure comprehension by computers.

Although the authors of MUSIC V went to considerable pains to make their program general, it was inevitable that their assumptions should have colored in fundamental respects the ways in which music could be made. It is difficult for the uninitiated to detect the nature of the basic assumptions involved, particularly in the case of computer programs. We are not working, now, within an absorbed codification of practice and inference that is the product of hundreds of years and tens of thousands of users but are confronted, rather, by instant "transition." With MUSIC V, an outlook that inevitably bounded the useful area within which one can work had been created by a small group of persons in a short period of time. The limits of their musical experience, the equipment available to them, as well as their financial and temporal resources all influenced their choices and the compromises they saw fit to make. Mathews emphasized three principles by means of which he and his collaborators tried to solve the primary restrictions on computer synthesis (unmanageable amounts of information and the difficulty of addressing the computer conveniently).[13]

First was the notion of *stored functions*. Since, as will be seen below, a staggering amount of information is necessary in order to produce sound output of satisfactory quality, it was virtually impossible for even a very fast computer to generate sound in "real time." That is, computers were not capable of generating control numbers fast enough to keep a sound output going continuously. Instead, it was necessary to store in a computer's core memory all functions that could be stated as repetitive expressions and to call them at a later time in the order and with the modification specified. It was understandably tempting, considering ease and economy, to use repetitive functions in sound synthesis. They can be stored and easily read out at the proper moment, rather than having to be recomputed. As we have seen, however, perfect repeatability in sound material is unacceptable, and the computer programmer had to find ways of imposing the necessary quality of irregularity or directed randomness onto any regular signal. In any case, stored functions were a basic aspect of MUSIC V and must be carefully considered not only as a source of ease but as a basic assumption.

Secondly, MUSIC V included the concept of *unit generators*. These function almost directly analogously to the electronic devices used in analog studio sound synthesis: oscillators, adders (mixers), noise generators, attack generators, modulators, and so on. The difference was that no analog electronic signals were processed in the case of the computer, only digital (DC electronical) pulses that result in a series of stored numbers. The computer's unit generators are actually computational devices that shadow-process sounds, predicting the results rather than actually instigating the physical operations. Again, although the concept of the unit generator is quite general, examination of actual practice revealed the need for more imaginative use of the concept, and this began to occur. We are perhaps not yet in a position to know whether this concept will be sufficiently flexible as musical ideals pass beyond the more static concepts of Western tradition.

The final principle prominently assumed by MUSIC V was the *note concept* that postulated that musical flow be broken up into discrete segments,

---

13. See M.V. Mathews, *et al. The Technology of Computer Music*, Cambridge, Mass., 1969, for a thorough treatment of this approach.

however complex, that need only be turned on and off at the right instant. This was perhaps the most limiting concept. For example, Mathews observed that the computer's ability to automatically synchronize notes or voices (in his chosen terms) means that "the tyranny of time, which so harasses the performing musician, is almost completely eliminated." Our earlier discussion has made clear that this is a deceptive oversimplification. The tyranny of time is as much a matter of attitude and perceptual capacities as it is of objective synchrony.

MUSIC V was an extraordinary achievement by any measure. In suggesting the need for careful consideration of the assumptions and limiting mechanisms of this approach, one hopes to increase its flexibility rather than to deprecate its use. Working with technology commonly produces a certain failing of perspective. As one becomes more and more involved and invests very considerable amounts of energy in trying to overcome the unnatural barriers that technology so often throws up, one begins to understand and cherish the *relative* excellence or implication of one's results. It is imperative to step back occasionally, and listen with some detachment, to reconsider the boundaries one has accepted.

It has been observed previously that computers deal in integral numbers, in discrete, digital representations of phenomena. Since sound inevitably involves analog (AC) electrical and pressure fluctuations, experiments in analysis and synthesis necessitate conversion in both directions: from analog to digital and from digital to analog. A schematic representation of the D-to-A, of the numeric-to-pressure conversion, is given in Figure 13. The graph indicates how amplitude varies with time. It is a familiar wave shape representation. As a result of some program-directed operations, the computer has stored a sequence of numbers.[14] The digital-to-analog converter represents each number in sequence by a pulse whose voltage (amplitude) is proportional to the size of the stored number. The curve is then approximated by a succession of small rectangles that correspond to the size and shape of the

---

14. The methods by which a computer stores information are beyond the scope of this discussion, but one should take note of the form in which items are stored. As instructions to a computer must be translated into the more efficient machine or programming languages available now in order to be understood by the computer, arabic numerals also are coded differently. This is done according to a *binary* system that is ideally suited to digital operations. A binary number can have only two representations—0 or 1—as opposed to ten choices in the arabic system. The binary system enables one to represent any integral number by the correct sequence of 0's and 1's. Each 0 or 1 is called a *bit*. The pattern can be understood intuitively on the basis of a few examples: 0=0, 1=1, 2=10, 3=11, 4=100, 5=101, 6=110, 7=111, and so on. Each column in the binary system represents a power of two as opposed to a power of ten in arabic representation. To store or transmit numerical information for calculations, the computer needs only a sufficient number of storage cells, each of which is either off (0) or on (1), and the knowledge of the correct order in which they must be addressed. A computer traffics, them, in gross, easily transmitted, and easily detected electrical states: a signal is present or is not, a voltage appears or does not. Small fluctuations are of no importance to the system so long as a broad range of limits is observed.

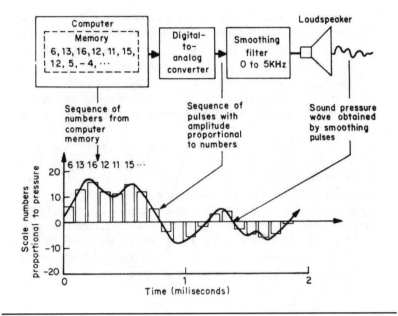

Figure 13. A schematic representation of computer-numbers-to-pressure (or digital-to-analog) conversion.

volume enclosed by the smooth curve. A smoothing filter removes the abrupt edges of the component rectangles, allowing a more continuous movement of the speaker cone, generating a smoothly and periodically varying pressure. The more complex the wave shape, or the more precisely refined one wishes the approximation to be, the more pulse samples will be required.

This raises a matter of great importance. As we have seen previously, a naturally occurring sound wave, although periodic, is subject to unexpectedly subtle and incessant alteration. This is particularly true of the attack transient (approximately the first tenth of a second of any sound), for this is the moment during which the auditory cortex is cued to recognize the uniqueness and hence identity of the sound. It is a sound's most distinctive moment. In addition, we have seen that not only the fundamental but generally the first dozen or so harmonics as well can be essential to full sonic experience. These facts indicate the importance of an extremely detailed representation of the wave form, an ability to follow or generate minutiae to the limits of the ear's response. Since, in the normal adult, such responsiveness extends to approximately 16,000 variations per second, it is necessary that the computer generate details at that pace. This requirement is compounded by a phenomenon basic to the design and operation of the computer, an inevitable result of the process of sampling by which measurements are taken for storage. The phenomenon is "foldover" and it necessitates a sampling rate twice that of the frequency of detail one wishes to exist in the final analog output.[15]

To maintain a frequency range of 16,000 cps from one speaker requires the computation of samples at a minimum rate of 32,000 samples per second. If, in addition, one is preparing a two-channel representation, normal stereo sound, twice as many samples per second are required. The facts are formidable even in light of the great capacity of computers for calculating. Assuming that 512 points per period give an adequate description of a 500 cps tone, a brief five-minute segment in four-channel sound (four channels are necessary for the creation of fully satisfying spatial effects as discussed below) demands that a staggering 614,400,000 12-bit numbers be calculated and stored. The practical implications of this situation are all detrimental to the production of interesting musical output. The high cost of computer time means that only segments of limited length can be calculated at one pass and that compositions of substantial length are exorbitantly expensive. Compromise again enters the picture, with consequent loss of frequency range (up to perhaps 8,000 cps instead of 16,000) and monaural (single-channel) reproduction, as well as less complex and hence excessively symmetrical, regular patterns.[16]

As the speed of computers increases, as the quality of digital-to-analog conversion—the smoothing operation—improves, it seems certain that computer-generated sound will become a readily available and manageable resource. The limits, again, are defined by incomplete knowledge of what qualities a resultant sound should possess and how these can be physically achieved. In particular, we need to understand the nature of the irregular fluctuations introduced by human beings performing on naturally vibrating instruments. Assuming theoretically that the computer can introduce perturbations with far more ease than the component analog devices around which most electronic studios have been built, we still need to know more about temporal flexibility, synchrony, form, and continuity. The interim step while self-sufficient computer systems mature involves hybrid systems: analog or digital modules that generate materials while a computer issues control signals. This allows a much more complex range of constructed patterns than simple sequencing procedures can achieve. Several break-through developments, like John Chowning's frequency-modulation approach to computer sound synthesis at Stanford's pioneering CCRMA installation, may change

---

15. *Foldover* involves the reflection in the direction of lower pitch of any desired frequency exceeding one-half the sampling rate. As a result, requested higher harmonics may be reflected back down in such a way as to produce unwanted complexity or dissonance in the analog result.

16. In a 1972 letter to the author, Mathews wrote, "I would tend to add one more basic limitation to direct digital synthesis … it can't operate in real time. This means that it is really impossible to 'perform' on a computer and hence to introduce the human variations that the traditional performer adds to almost all existing music."

this picture and elevate direct computer generation to a prominent position. Human variability remains the focal point and it generates barriers impossible to circumvent with utilitarian compromise. Now that the need to understand and take into consideration psychoacoustic facts is accepted by researchers, it is possible that more inventive forms of simplification will be devised. Chowning's method suggests so.

The computer's strength has resided in stored functions and operations, in the capacity to issue extremely rapid control commands. For these reasons, electronic studios with large numbers of analog devices are now being equipped with small computers. By such means, a composer may store indefinitely a particularly attractive array of settings and interconnections between the devices of the studio. Having achieved an allover studio state that may involve hundreds of dials and connecting cables, he is now frequently required to tear it all down so that the next scheduled studio user can proceed with his work. The computer, however, can remember the exact condition of every item and reestablish them upon command in an instant.

Not only a vastly increased level of access to natural sounds now exists but also virtually unlimited potential to create, directly by enhanced means, whole sets of new and as yet unexperienced sounds. The expanse of material is sobering in its dimension. And one should not dispose easily of a further possibility: non-electronic synthesis, as suggested by sculptural and aerodynamic work with a growing number of new fabrication materials.

The Last Dimension: Space

The preceding discussion of the mechanisms of musical effect, and almost any other basic discussion one is likely to encounter, has concentrated on the characteristics commonly assigned to sounds, without formally announcing them as pitch, loudness, and timbre. Although at root pitch and timbre are functions of time, the temporally important factors—duration, rhythm, tempo, and succession—may be said to belong more properly to organization rather than to the material itself. There is another independent physical quality that a sound can have, and it too can be continuously manipulated and perceived with some accuracy: *location*. This represents, it would seem, the final frontier in the expansion of the perceptual dimensions of music. There is no other evident category of quality that sound can have. Although musicians have paid little formal attention to location, to the physical disposition of instrumental or choral groups, it was a dramatic and structural factor in early church music, as a result of divided performance groups, and in the massed experiments through the late nineteenth century, particularly those of Berlioz. Since the middle of this century, experimental composers have been intrigued with the possibilities of spatially disposed groupings, but have found them awkward due to an absence of suitable spaces and inconvenience in rehearsal. Divided groups, however, still produced essentially antiphonal music, although with added complexity. What was needed was a more flexible method of moving sound sources or the means to produce such illusions.

During the past twenty years, electronic developments have provided the means, by implication at least, and are now able to produce a stunning repertoire of convincing illusions of spatial movement. Again, although commercially available high fidelity equipment has made us aware of the possibility of sound location, especially through demonstration records and popular albums with exaggerated stereophonic separation, it was theoretical and experimental work that laid the foundation. Those investigators concerned with deafness and psychoacoustics as well as cognition have had particular interest in the localization mechanism since it has implications for both the specialization of cochlear cells and the temporal acuity of the cortex, especially its ability to act as a comparator for minute temporal distinctions between messages to the two halves of the brain.

Curiously, the pitch area where positional discrimination is most weak, 3,000 cps, is the same area in which we are maximally sensitive to quiet sounds. Above this frequency, localization seems to occur as a result of amplitude differences, and below it because of temporal differences. The mechanisms are as follows: a sound source that is, for example, at some distance, 45 degrees to the left and in front of a plane running through the middle of a stationary subject's head, will be heard in darkness as being partially to the left. There is some tendency to confuse this position with a similar angular displacement in the left rear quadrant, but this will disappear if the subject is allowed to move his head, as we all do as a matter of course when visual clues are lacking. In fact, if one is free to move his head in all planes, sound sources anywhere in three-dimensional space can be quite accurately placed. (We are also aware of the relative spatial extent of the sound-emitting surface; we easily differentiate between a point source and a radiating area.) At higher frequencies, the period or wave length is so short that the skull acts as an effective barrier, lowering the amplitude of the signal that arrives at the right ear relative to the left (in the case of our example). At lower frequencies, the more prominent factor is the difference in time of arrival of a wave front. That is to say, there will be discernible time intervals separating the arrival of transient components or of maxima in a continuous wave front. Complex tones are more readily localized than pure tones because of the fact that their perception will probably involve both factors more complexly: interaural time of arrival interval and amplitude difference.

Position is cued not only by relative amplitude differences and distinctions in time of arrival, but also by at least three other factors. In almost all spaces, save a deliberately constructed anechoic chamber, there is some element of *reverberation* (sound waves that emanate from the same source that transmits sound along a direct path, but arrive at the ears by way of reflection and therefore longer paths, creating very slight but perceptible delays). The distance of a source from an observer can be partially described in terms of a ratio of directly received sound to that which is reverberant or indirect. In general, the higher the reverberant content, the further away a sound will seem to originate. Prominent high-frequency components are sufficient for stationary or very slowly moving sources, but one more, Doppler shift, must be added when more rapid motion is introduced. Anyone who has been close to a passing train with its whistle sounding knows how the pitch of the whistle rises continuously as the train approaches and how it falls abruptly when the locomotive passes. The speed of the train is added to the normal velocity of sound propagation as it approaches and is abruptly subtractive as it passes. Moving-source illusions, then, must take Doppler shift into effect, especially if they are to traverse convincingly spacious and wide-range patterns of movement.

Experiment with spatially distributed but stationary instrumental groups became relatively common during the second half of this century, though it was by no means unknown before this.[17] Composers also began trying to evoke the illusion of smooth movement between these stationary groups by having spatially separated but identical instruments pass a matched tone from one to the other, the second swelling as the first fades. The advent of high fidelity and sophisticated public-address equipment encouraged experiments aimed at producing similar effects more economically and under better electronic control. It is a simple matter to fade gradually between two outlets with only one manual control. Moving it smoothly among four speakers placed at the corners of a rectangular space is somewhat more difficult to accomplish through mechanical controls, but still simple electronically. Now both computer programs and independent analog devices have been developed by means of which all relevant functions can be accomplished economically and conveniently. Using an early control device, the "joystick," moving in two dimensions, as does an airplane pilot's control stick, one could move a single source in two-dimensional space, describing abrupt, angular motions, wide arcs, or figure-eight paths. Reverberant content, amplitude, Doppler shift, and high-frequency attenuation would all have to be controlled automatically by electronically adjusting the signal transmitted from each speaker in a constantly integrated way. The sound could swoop and dart as the operator desired, entirely as a result of which proportions and properties of a sound source emanated from each of four stationary speakers.

---

17. The spatial separation of independent sound materials in a complex musical context increases the clarity of the perceptual whole. Our selective abilities in listening are not fully understood, but spatial location plays a major role. It is, for example, far easier for a secretary to transcribe a conversation recorded stereophonically—retaining directional information—than monaurally.

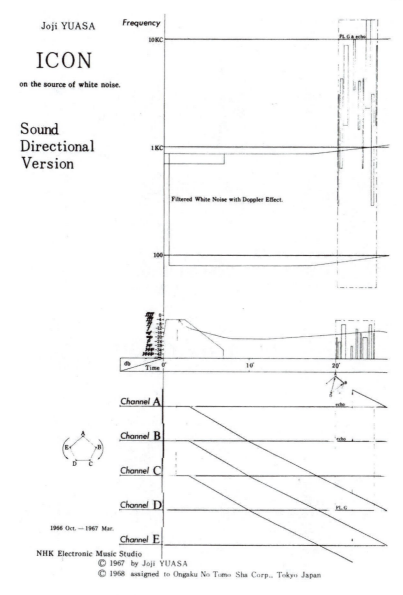

Figure 14. Opening minute from the score of Yuasa's *Icon*, showing (from top to bottom) frequency ranges from 10,000 to 1,000 to 100 cps; dynamic level from *ffff* or 0 dB to *pppp* or −42 dB; time passage; and distribution of the sounds among five channels, A to E, which correspond to five loudspeakers.

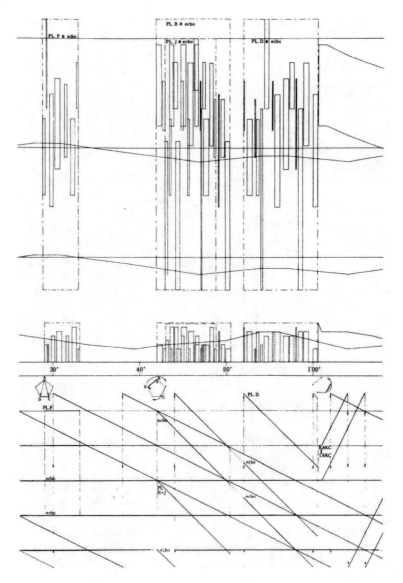

Fig. 14. (continued) Note the slow, circular motion of the continuous low band and stationary positioning of the origin and echo for each group of brief exclamatory sound shapes.

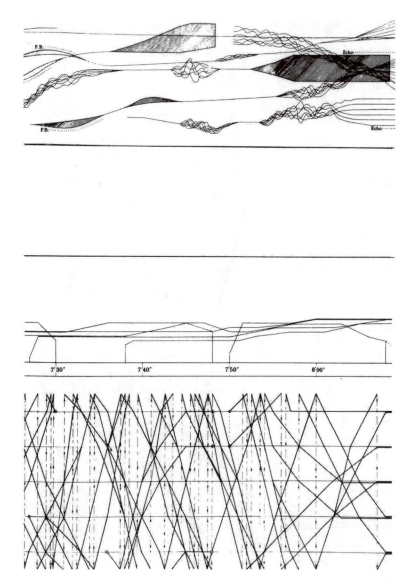

Figure. 15. Passage of high lyrical section of *Icon* just preceding the initial thunderclap: narrow, complex, constantly inflected noise bands; relatively constant and high dynamic level; rapid, complexly interlocked and opposing rotationally patterns.

Not only one but multiple sources can now be moved independently through space, although this requires either preprogrammed pathways or the use of several performers, one for each signal. Less has been done with the

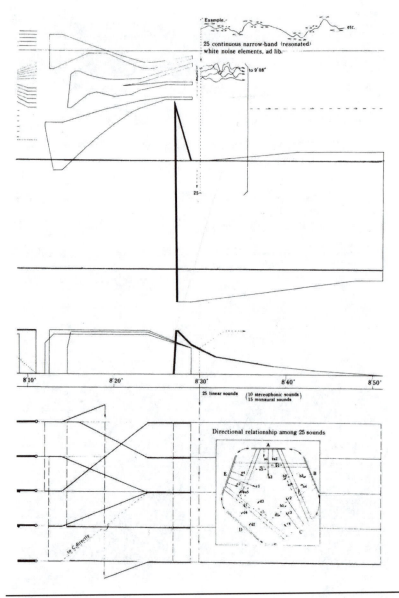

Figure. 16. Passage from *Icon*, showing the first of three stunning thunderclaps that define the work's remembered shape. Note the detail of this representation: high frequencies precede the lows slightly and amplitude builds sharply, and then both fall away from the initial transient rather rapidly.

possibilities for increasing and shrinking the effective size of the resonating surface, however. One looks forward to the time when complete control of this sort is available, when focused trajectories, broad fronts, or masses of radiant sound may be positioned precisely and moved in independent patterns as the composer desires. There is no question about the feasibility of these concepts. We have the ability to discriminate position more accurately than dynamics, for example, and there is no reason why available technology cannot allow us to begin working with location and trajectories within musical structure for affective ends. This would not represent an unprecedented flowering of a neglected musical characteristic but would be, rather, analogous to the sudden outburst of experimentation with dynamic contrasts, crescendos, and sforzandos that occurred during the middle of the eighteenth century in Europe. Previous to that time, dynamic indications of any kind had been rare and some staple instruments were without the capacity to vary their dynamic levels widely or with subtlety. The expressive and structural power of dynamic growth, contrast, and accent in the middle to late decades of the eighteenth century laid the foundation for the dramatic force and depth of Mozart, Haydn, and Beethoven. Perhaps the exploration of a new and deeply affective dimension may again spur new levels of aesthetic imagery.

Jōji Yuasa: Icon (1966–67)

The first effort to produce a fully controlled and elaborately gestural electronic music in space was completed by the Japanese composer Jōji Yuasa (b. 1929) in the Electronic Music Studio of the Japan Broadcasting Corporation during 1966–67. The title refers to the composer's intention of producing an aural icon, a piece with a clear and forceful outline, that could be apprehended easily and directly. The score of the work raises directionality and position to a level equal with that of pitch or dynamic shape, and this diagrammatic representation of the sound structure of *Icon* was achieved, *composed*, before actual work in the electronic studio began. The sole sound material for this five-channel tape composition is filtered white noise. Bands of colored noise take on altered timbric dimension depending on their width (the narrower, the more pitch-centered and strongly characterized) and other factors including reverberation and microstructure. The two basic aspects of *Icon*—form and timbre—change in opposing directions during a performance. The forms of individual sound elements, initially distinct, gradually lose definition, become shapeless, and dissolve. Timbre, on the other hand, is at first simple and thin to the ear, consisting only of wide-band filtered white noise, but as the piece progresses, the sounds become richer in timbre; instead of continuous, internally monochromatic noise bands, composite bands are constructed. The composer employs as many as twenty-five narrow-band filtered-noise components simultaneously, each resonated and possessed of individually characteristic pitch inflection and dynamic microstructure. From these he makes up larger conglomerates of greater timbral richness.

As one can see by examining the score examples, the materials—sometimes stationary, sometimes slowly or rapidly passing from one speaker to another—are given spatial treatment fully as detailed as the more traditionally recognized elements of musical composition. Slowly rotating bands and stationary exclamations at the outset give way to more diffuse, slowly shifting whistles in a high register that are rapidly flashed about the performance space. In performance, members of the audience are surrounded by sounds in a manner analogous to daily situations in life. A *total* musical space is achieved. Individual bands of colored noise shift to the right or left, behind or in front of the listener. As they shift, band width and dynamic level may also be gradually changed, slowly reduced, or increased, along with altered reverberant characteristics, to create the aural illusion of an expanding or contracting spatial horizon. One complete revolution in the low register may take as much as forty seconds, the material changing all the time. Not only do single sources move, but a number of separate stereophonic axes may rotate simultaneously, at different speeds and in opposing directions.

Approximately two-thirds of the way through the work, the first of a series of three tremendous thunderclaps occurs. It is a stationary event, issuing from all five speakers simultaneously, and is the first sound item to be so treated. Examination of the score reveals the maximal dynamic force (ffff or 0 dB) and an unprecedentedly broad frequency band (from the bottom limit of audibility up to approximately the high *F-sharp* of a coloratura soprano). The sharp spike at the front edge of the frequency representation (top heavy outline), in combination with the at first steeply and then rather more slowly sloping dynamic envelope (lower heavy outline), produces the effect of initial transient complexity discussed earlier. This combination of simultaneous attention to transient frequency components and dynamic envelope is unique to the three thunderclaps, giving them a particular, visceral memorability.

The cuing factors mentioned earlier are here employed by the composer to produce an event-profile of truly iconic power. The entire work is masterful, operating as the best art should, on emotive and intellectual levels with equal success. The spatial factor is used by Yuasa in structural and gesturally affective ways, becoming an undeniably major element of the work's effect. Recorded on tape, the signal levels at each of five speaker outlets are continuously controlled so that the listener perceives dramatically convincing spatial illusions not only of position and movement but also of the *size* of auditory space. *Icon* is a work of the first rank, suggestive of exactly the wider and deeper musical horizons that one has a right to expect of this newly available dimension of musical sounds.[18]

---

18. The score of *Icon* is published by Ongaku N Tomo Sha, Tokyo, 1968.

PART V
Time

Preliminary Remarks

We begin with a brief look at two views on the problem of evaluating temporal experience:

> It is perfectly accurate to say that a sense of time can only exist where there is submission to reality

> **—Paul Fraisse**
> *The Psychology of Time*

This statement by an eminent French researcher in time perception—an author who legitimatized fresh consideration of this long-neglected subject—rests on a variety of assumptions that merit our scrutiny. One could, of course, debate the existence and nature of a uniform "reality" which we are all presumed to share during the normal course of normal days. In the grip of a compelling musical performance, though, what does any reality have to do with our experience? We are, evidently, somewhere else, in a place which may be shared to some degree by others at the concert but is necessarily unrelated to the passage of mundane events outside the auditorium. From our vantage point, the implied uniformity of both "submission" and "sense of time" is also troublesome.

> The old notion of an internal "time keeper" rooted in a periodic biological process is not a *useful* concept for an analysis of *duration* experience. [There has been] a confusion of the experience of time either with ordinary clock or with biological time.

> **—Robert E. Ornstein**
> *On the Experience of Time*

This statement by a research worker in the Langley Porter Neuropsychiatric Institute of the University of California suggests a basic and essential distinction: that temporal experience is a totally different thing from subsequent evaluations of it. In subsequent evaluations, whether subjective (after-the-fact) or based on "objective" standards of measurement on a scale appropriate to daily existence, the process is not disturbed by the fact that we are inhabiting the physical frame that is being explored. Evaluating the dimensions of time from within its stream is a different affair. We have no way of effectively storing the extent of experienced durations other than by the recollection of corresponding numbers indicated on the face of an often irrelevant clock. The freshness of the peculiar mix of factors determining our in-process response will have been permanently, irrevocably, expended by the time we reach the end of an episode. The evaluation or reconsideration of a temporal experience is entirely distinct from the experiencing of it. The complete impossibility of an experiential replay becomes clear as soon as we consider the disruptive effects of self-consciousness and the inevitable disruptions of memory upon direct experience.

We become spontaneously aware of time *in media res* only when we are dissatisfied in some sense. Fraisse cites two primary factors: *waiting* (as in the conscious interval between the emergence of a need and its fulfillment) and the *effort of continuity* (the obstacle to be overcome in order to complete a task once the initial impulse has been exhausted). What sort of "time" are we becoming conscious of in such cases? It is not a quantized variety of temporal experience, not that sort we might refer to as "real." The latter variety would probably have a more objective, measured quality, based on the rate of some reliable clock. Most of the experiments performed on time have gone in this direction, toward evaluation of how accurately human beings are able to make judgments relative to objective clocks; toward the discovery of physiologically based clocks in the individual body that might support such judgments.

But composers are far more concerned with the individual's experience than with a hard-won "objective" synchrony. They seek *extra*ordinary manipulation of the time sense—the evocation of temporal expanses, for example, or the attentive immersion that comes from absorption in streams of commanding detail. They are concerned, as well, with the development of skills of perception, and hope that the rewards of aesthetic experience will argue for skill enhancement. The psychologist, on the other hand, has frequently excluded any experimental subject with experience (since it might prejudice the subject's naïveté).[1] This is not to reject experimental psychology's results. Quite the opposite. A responsible attitude toward innovation demands that the creator inform himself about perceptual capacities and the procedures by which cognition develops. In doing so, however, extreme caution is in order.

---

1. Others have undertaken studies in perceptual limits only with highly trained subjects, recognizing that it is important to establish a knowledge of human capacities, not our restrictions.

In considering the following materials, one should always bear in mind the artificially restrictive conditions under which the data were collected. The stimulus array in the psychological laboratory is no more than a small part of what we subjectively experience in daily life. In any case, even that portion of our physical experience that actually enters and is processed by the nervous system is still subject to as yet poorly understood workings of memory and recall. Disregarding the primary temporal content of that constant flux made up of our momentary impressions—units of which may be termed a "perceptual present"—one might even indulge in unexpected reversals, as in the following view of Heinz Von Foerster:

> It is clear that it is due to memory that temporal abstracts can be computed and stored. Although memories may have charming aspects, their crucial test lies in their efficacy to anticipate sequences of events, in other words, to permit inductive inferences. The conceptual construction of "time" is, so far as I see it, just a by-product of our memory.[2]

Musicians have been remarkably slow to assume what would seem even a decent level of interest in time; it is, more than they apparently realize, their proper concern. With a minimum latent period of 30–70 milliseconds, the ear is far better suited to the discrimination of temporal successions than the eye, with a latent period of 70–110 milliseconds. The latent period measures only the time necessary for a signal to reach the proper threshold, the necessary strength for triggering a response. Below this point, the nervous system will fail in detection. The difference in capacity of the ear and the eye for detecting discontinuities is more striking: a ten-millisecond gap is recognized by the ear, but another factor of ten is necessary before the eye achieves a similar impression. As the early French experimenter Guyau noted:

> Hearing only locates stimuli very vaguely in space, but it locates them with admirable precision in time. It is par excellence the sense that appreciates time, succession, rhythm and tempo.[3*]

Thus music—streams of events apprehended aurally—is preeminently the temporal art.

Short Intervals, Duration, and Temporal Perspective

It will be useful to enumerate the categories into which temporal experience is divided for experimental purposes. *Short intervals* (those events

---

2. In Von Foerster, "Time and Memory," *Annals of the New York Academy of Sciences*, Vol. 138, 1967.

3*. Quoted in Fraisse, *The Psychology of Time*, London, 1964.

consuming up to approximately 8–10 seconds) include (1) the perceptual apprehension of short durations; (2) the motor responses involved in their production (this production process has been termed "timing" by J.A. Michon); and (3) the problem of the meaning of simultaneity. Factors affecting one of these phenomena may not influence the others; for example, a rise in a subject's body temperature speeds a tapping rate while leaving verbal estimation of interval length unaffected.[4]

Fraisse discusses the "perceived present" in detail. Its duration, he writes, "like the richness of its contents, depends on the possibilities for the organization of successive elements into one unit."[5*] The field of the perceived present has upper limits determined by the following consideration: the temporal interval between stimuli (as this interval approaches two seconds, the possibility of perceptual integration based on a rhythmic sense begins to disappear); the number of stimuli (varying from 3.3 for an interstice of 1.8 seconds to the 5.7 that can be apprehended as a unit for a separation of 0.17 seconds); and, lastly, the pattern of organization for the stimuli. The last factor is particularly important because of its dependence on our pattern-organizing or *encoding* skill. If sufficiently similar sounds are grouped in two's, three's, four's, or even five's, we can hear four or five groups of these in one perceptual present, making, in all, a unity of twenty to twenty-five sounds in less than five seconds. "As our perception of succession is dependent on the possibilities of organization," writes Fraisse, "everything which facilitates this—the attitude of the subject, grouping by proximity, structure, meaning—increases the richness of what constitutes the present."

Motor response is usually studied using sequential stimuli, and often involves the rhythmic impulses of key-tapping. It is the physical response or replication dimension of short-interval perception. *Simultaneity* is an intriguing subject. Its specification depends on the operational definition of "at the same time." The base of temporal reference, the fineness of temporal grain in use, is the direct determinant of "simultaneity," and this grain changes with the circumstances. The distance the observer is from an event and the effects this distance has on the information transmission times for various sense modalities are also crucial. In view of what we know about the speed of light and sound in air, why do we persist in waiting for the thunderclap which "follows" the flash of lightning when we *know* they are simultaneous?

A recurring term in the literature of time psychology is "indifference interval." When asked to make verbal estimates of the duration of small time intervals, subjects tend to overestimate durations of less than

---

4. "Tapping rate" and "verbal estimation" are among the methods psychologists use to measure temporal response (*cf.* following section).

5*. Fraisse, *The Psychology of Time*

0.75 seconds and underestimate those that are larger. Though there is a considerable variety of experimental data, it seems generally agreed upon that 0.75 is the vicinity in which subjects tend to be most accurate, the zone in which there is no systematic tendency to err. There are three important related psychological factors, however: the *central tendency* (the bias we show in weighting judgments toward our experience with some preestablished or gradually detected average); the *anchoring effect* (where we fall under the influence of a reference value by means of which we are gauging our estimations of other stimuli); and the *order effect* (a weighted presentation of intervals; for example, a long series of short intervals followed by a relatively longer interval will increase the latter's apparent length). As a result, the "indifference interval" can be manipulated by widening or narrowing the range of test intervals used, thereby providing a cunningly divergent reference, or by the sort of order and degree randomization we employ in the overall presentation. Naturally, all of these factors are at work in aesthetic situations and could be employed with greater tactical skill if the composer had a clear understanding of them.

The second temporal category is the longer experience of *duration*, those periods in excess of ten seconds. In this domain, the possibility of achieving accurate estimations (again, bearing in mind that the very idea of "accuracy" may be spurious) will necessarily involve some form of clock, biological or man-made. Long intervals simply are not directly apprehended. Prominent divisions of this category include *endogenous, exogenous, external,* and *circadian* rhythms. Theoretically, the first of these would be present in the organism even in the absence of all external influences. Endogenous rhythms are biologically based and reflect the usually spontaneous operation of internal physiological periodicities (chemical concentrations, fatigue, *etc.*). Exogenous rhythms are those biological rhythms that are forced or *entrained* by external rhythms acting on the individual as synchronizers. The most prominent synchronizing rhythms or agents of entrainment external to an organism are light, temperature, and the regimen of the surrounding environment.

Circadian (*circa,* about, and *die,* day) rhythms are those which, though endogenous, have periods closely approaching those of external, naturally occurring phenomena with 24-hour cycles. In general, notes J.E. Orme, the period of greatest sensitivity in the human circadian cycle is approximately 4 A.M., as can be seen by the peak incidence of cardiac and asthmatic attacks, births, and deaths occurring at that time. Of course, these data are dependent on time zone (*i.e.,* cluster at 4 A.M. in each time zone). This class of biological rhythms is the most populous and powerful. It would certainly seem traceable to the planet's imposition of 24-hour clocking on all its subjects. Not only internal biological rhythms, but also external clocks can serve as references. We can judge the ordering and spacing of events by matching their sequence with any externally generated series that we choose to accept as a reference. Still, it is inherently less exciting to evaluate one's temporal experience by matching it against the objectively generated units of man-made clocks. The fascination of experimenters remains with the vagaries of biological clocks, although hope of discovering any single oscillator that might serve this purpose is by now very slight indeed. Botanist Karl Hamner sums up the situation nicely:

> If, as most biologists do, we accept the theory that the [biological] clock is truly endogenous, we are still faced with additional problems. Since uni-cellular organisms exhibit circadian rhythms and presumably possess a clock, does every cell of the larger multicellular organism also possess an individual clock? And if this is so, how are these clocks synchronized? A still more difficult question is how such a clock can be temperature com-pensated. If the running of the clock depends on metabolic energy, as it must if it is truly endogenous, how is the energy supplied and why is it that treatments which affect the rate of metabolism do not affect the functioning of the clock? Is the oscillator involved of the relaxation or the pendulum type or are there, perhaps, several oscillators involved which are coupled together in some fashion?[6]

The third category, *temporal perspective*, is dependent on context to an even greater degree than the other two. In relative contrast to *short intervals* and *duration, temporal perspective* alters radically with age, social context, and personality make-up. It is a measure of the way in which the individual integrates his temporal experience, developing, in the process, an attitude toward the past and future—determining to what extent they will impinge upon the experience of his present moments.

Experimental Approaches to Measurement

A knowledge of the methods by which psychologists attempt to test human apprehension of time is basic to any evaluation of their results. There are four primary approaches: direct verbal estimation, production, reproduction, and comparison. *Verbal estimation* requires the subject to state (retrospec-tively, of course) how long he felt the interval was (using either unself-conscious approach or by trying to keep accurate track during the test interval by referring to some internal clock). *Production* tests ask the subject to define an interval on command by activating a buzzer or some such signal; this is a noncomparative technique. In *reproduction*, the subject's response is based not on a quantitative, measured preevaluation but on a reflexive

---

6. From "Experimental Evidence for the Biological Clock," in J.T. Fraser (ed.), *The Voices of Time*, New York, 1966.

attempt to reproduce the durational phenomenon he has just experienced by means of a buzzer or light. *Comparison* involves the retention of two or three durations and their subsequent evaluation by comparative recall. As might be expected, the last is the least reliable method. There is considerable disagreement about the value of the others as well, and, in the end, the results from each must be understood independently and accepted or rejected on the basis of their utility. Most serious for the unwary reader is the possibility that he or the writer—or both—will confound verbal reports with physical responses.

> Case in point: if a subject listens to an interval delineated by a short burst of noise that is objectively 2 seconds long and then reports his impression that it lasted 3 seconds, he will be said to have "overestimated" the interval. This would appear to demonstrate that the subject's internal clock is running *fast*—that is to say, that the number of units of his time passed during the experimental interval was greater than the number recorded on an objective time scale. But if this is so, and if the subject had been asked to make a physical representation of 2 seconds by pressing a buzzer, his proposed matching event would then have been *shorter* than the test signal, and could have been described as an "underestimation."

The experimental literature abounds with this sinister variety of flora.

Commentators on time share a further and perhaps more distressing tendency: to extrapolate the results of *retrospective evaluations* to the domain of *in-process experience*. It is generally true that a temporal interval which seems long as we traverse it (*i.e.*, one that dissatisfies us by its scant or lackluster detail) will, in retrospect, appear brief. On the other hand, an engrossing experience in time will appear brief if artificially interrupted (*i.e.*, if no consciousness of the passage of time arises spontaneously) and long in retrospect, due to the richness of variegated detail retained in memory. The most frequently promulgated view of time has been clock-based. Research has concentrated on our "sense of time" and judged its quality on the basis of how accurately we are able to measure intervals or place ourselves in the stream of objective chronology. The theories of Einstein uncovered certain curiosities in the operation of clocks moving at extravagant speeds, but this did little to ruffle the outwardly calm reliance of experimenters on the value of "objective reality." While accepting a largely uncritical view of this approach, Paul Fraisse's *The Psychology of Time* is an extraordinary achievement and a serviceable shore from which anyone curious to wade into these treacherous waters can set out.[7]

---

7. Two other useful, if more general, compilations are Leonard Doob's *Patterning of Time*, New Haven, 1971, and J.T. Fraser's *The Voices of Time*. Each contains, as does Fraisse, an extensive bibliography.

Fraisse's book is divided into three major sections. "Conditioning to Time" is concerned with man's ability to adapt his behavior to external influences that have some measure of regularity. "Perception of Time" discusses the admittedly narrow range of temporal durations within which we can actually *perceive* change. In some cases, it is possible to say that a change has taken place only after the fact, while in others one can actually perceive the process. But process itself can only be defined if it is possible to organize successive stimuli among themselves. For example, to reproduce separately—out of rhythmic context—the durational intervals in even a simple rhythm is far more difficult than reproducing the unified sequence.

For a musician the thresholds of duration and succession are critical aspects of hearing. Beginning with a continuous stimulus and gradually increasing the rate at which it is interrupted, one can gain insight into the relative precision with which aural, tactile, and visual receptors cope with inputs:

> At the moment when stimuli cease to be confused and appear successive and distinct, we cannot yet actually perceive an interval which is like a gap between them. At this point the sensations appear to be distinct, but *contiguous*. When the interval is a little longer, we perceive an *integrated pair* of stimuli. Thus we do not spontaneously perceive a gap. We perceive two more or less closely linked stimuli. The interval is not perceived in itself, although it is discernible if we fix our attention on it. When the gap between the stimuli reaches about 0.6 seconds we have spontaneous perception of an interval, but this is not dissociable from its limits. When the gap is greater than 1 second, the interval becomes the dominant feature and it requires an increasing effort to regard the two stimuli which delimit it as one unit defining the duration of the interval. Finally, when the gap reaches 1.8 to 2 seconds, the two stimuli cease to belong to the same present.[8]

It is worth interpolating here that subjective judgments about the experience of time are affected by so many factors that generalizations can do no more than indicate tendencies. For example, is the duration to be judged *filled* (by a continuous sound or homogeneous collection of sounds) or *empty* (its extremes marked by solitary impulses)? In the latter case, are the limits marked by events in the same sense modality (visual, aural, tactile, olfactory) or in different ones? Stimuli from different sense modalities are difficult to integrate and therefore disrupt the formation of objectively accurate judgments. Is the sound heard against a background of noise and reproduced in silence or vice versa? What of the listener's *set* (formed by his experience, present expectation, *etc.*) and the voluntary exercise of

---

8. Fraisse, *The Psychology of Time.*

attention? If two signals arrive at the cortex simultaneously, the one that receives attention will appear to precede the other.

Change is the basis of all perceptual mechanisms. The ear quickly detects any change in auditory stimulation, including cessations, and routinely ignores the sameness of monotonous signals. During experiments with a totally uniform visual field, one-third of the subjects experienced a complete cessation of visual experience: not a "blackout" but a void, an absence. The experimenter conjectured that perceptual mechanisms, evolved to cope with a differentiated field, experience a temporary breakdown when they encounter total uniformity. Those who lose their hearing relatively late in life complain not only of the lack of communication but that life seems to have lost its "ongoing" character.

The final major section in Fraisse's book, "Control over Time," explores a more subjective level. Once we accumulate data and impressions regarding our temporal life, how do we use them? This discussion is concerned with a scale too large to be of immediate value in a treatment of aesthetic experience and the performance arts. However, his treatment of "The Estimation of Time" is important in establishing the relativity of temporal judgments.

> We are not spontaneously aware of duration when we give our whole attention to the present situation, that is when we are not made to turn to any other time of action through our needs or through social necessity. In other words, we are not conscious of time when we are fully satisfied with the present situation.

Implied here is a distinction between an awareness of succession and an awareness of duration; at a musical performance, the listener, however engrossed in the moment-to-moment absorption of detail, is certainly constantly aware, at some level, of the passage of one idea as it evolves into the next. Without such a retrospective frame in constant operation, even the sensuous dimension of the listening experience would be depleted. Apparently duration is a sensation that comes beyond the level of information necessary to inform us of succession.

Robert Ornstein develops an alternative view in his book *On the Experience of Time*. It is summarized in the following quote:

> The idea of a 'sense' of time may be useful in ordinary experience when one might want to compare experience to the clock—in cases when someone is habitually not 'on' time for instance—but as a scientific metaphor, the time 'sense' leads to a search for a nonexistent organ of time experience and has not proven a useful guiding principle.
>
> We replace the 'time sense' metaphor with a 'concept of time' similar to our concepts of order or of chaos, one formed out of the immediate data of experience. Duration may then be studied without reference to any sort of

external clock, 'biological,' 'chemical,' or the ordinary mechanical clock. The experience of duration of a given interval may be meaningfully compared only with other experiences. If duration is considered solely as a dimension of experience it is then unnecessary to determine whether this experience is 'accurate' or not with respect to the clock. Lumping time experience into two simple categories of 'accurate' and 'inaccurate' has seriously impeded the flow of work on time.

As distinct from *short intervals* and *time perspective*, duration can be approached using the computer as a reference: "If information is input to a computer and instructions are given to store that information, *in a certain way*, we can check the size of the array or the number of spaces or number of words necessary to store the input information."[9] A more complex input will require more space, as will one consisting of more varied items. The phrase "in a certain way" is critical to Ornstein's approach because one is obliged to deal at length with the question of storage by *encoding* (the systematic translations of language or other information that are usable by the computer). Inefficient coding or *resistance* to coding will increase the required storage space, producing a concomitant increase in the subjective duration attributed to an experience.

The key to Ornstein's metaphor is that retrospective duration is a function of the amount of information from a given interval remaining in mental storage, not a direct function of the initial input. As will be explained below, it is possible to increase or decrease the amount of information remaining in storage *after the fact*. But, of course, larger inputs suggest the *likelihood* of more expansive memories. In their book *The Varieties of Psychedelic Experience*, Masters and Houston state that:

> ... *for consciousness* a heightening of sense perception definitely occurs: but it may not occur in such a way as to be measurable by the tests now in use. We do doubt that the eye is absolutely seeing more, ... or that the nose is smelling more. Rather, it seems likely that more of what the eye sees and more of what the nose smells is getting into the consciousness. Some of this *more* doubtless results from the subject's paying greater and more prolonged attention than he usually does, but deinhibiting factors may be involved.[10]

The practical result of the *storage size* idea appears to be this: the search for details of a supposed biological clock base within the organism should

---

9. Without understanding the complete mechanism of computer information storage, it is enough to know that this capacity is measured by the number of coded "words" of a given complexity it can store magnetically and retrieve as needed. The "words" may be, for example, 8, 12, or 16 bits in length.

10. From R. Masters and J. Houston, *The Varieties of Psychedelic Experience*, New York, 1966.

be replaced by the examination of mechanisms that underlie registration and encoding along with the subsequent storing of information. Although the approach Fraisse adopts with small intervals is functionally useful, Ornstein's suggestions for investigating duration seem more hopeful.

Several partial models of temporal experience offered by other investigators are provocative. J.E. Orme proposes the concept of "extensive time." He asks us to imagine that space is a plane moving at right angles across time: that the intersection of the two planes represents the present, that above and below are future and past.[11*] (See Figure 17.)

Now suppose, Orme continues, that it is a property of organisms that they possess an extension in time covering their entire life spans, so that memory can be seen as simply a communication from the past part of this organization and prerecognition a communication from the future area of the plane. From this base, a number of interesting inferences follow. (See Figure 18.)

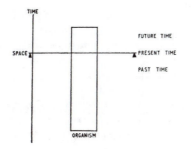

Figure 17. The life history of the organism in extensive time. Future above the line, past below.

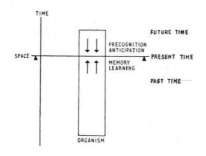

Figure 18. The organism's channels of memory and precognition in extensive time.

11*. J.E. Orme, *Time, Experience, and Behaviour*, New York, 1969.

Roland Fischer's stimulating and discursive treatment of biological time includes the idea that evolution might be regarded as the stretching out of life into time. A spiral becomes a graphic representation for the view that life on earth may be regarded historically as a single event, with evolution, learning, perception, hallucinations, and dreaming differing from each other only in their time rates of change. Each category represents an increasing efficiency in the use of energy. In the case of the most advanced state characterized, one can understand this by considering how little of hallucinating or dreaming experience is dependent on outside stimulus, how much on internal attention, expectation, and experience.[12] Using this scheme, he explores the relativity of our reference points and the restricted range of our consciousness, ending with this passage:

> The frequency ranges for this co-occurrence (the speed at which sucessively presented images will cease to be separate and will fuse) are varied in the various species as well as in the various sense modalities ... four tactile stimulations per second with a rod on the snail's belly compel it to crawl upon a nonexisting coherent surface which it perceives as a simultaneity. This attempt is an illustration of the transduction of his simultaneity into our duration. In human terms, this could be expressed in a reformulation of Descarte's *cogito ergo sum*: I am aware of perceiving rhythmical sequences of simultaneities as metabolic rate variant durations: therefore, I am. From that point of view, perception and learning are processes involved in the production of simultaneities; the cardinal difference between them is the speed with which we perceive simultaneities and the slowness with which we learn them.

With this discussion, we have moved from the experimental literature far afield into the world of speculation. The excursion may help to indicate the vastness and fascination of the subject. In following chapters, we shall cover both cautionary and predictive materials: in a discussion, first, of the inherent experimental barriers in testing temporal perception or experience and, secondly, of the extreme relativity of our reference points as individuals with highly differentiated personal histories. It will then be possible to evaluate some current efforts at utilizing aberrations or extensions of temporal experiences in the arts and to venture a few predictions as to what the future may well hold.

Some Pitfalls

Having completed a survey of the categories, terminology, and biases of various approaches to the study of time, we are in a position to examine more

---

12. Roland Fischer, "Biological Time," in Fraser, *The Voices of Time.*

carefully some of the factors influencing testing and the interpretation of experimental results. The complications are considerable, the footing uncertain. The complexities of test procedure have been mentioned previously, but here four will be treated in more detail: the importance of ambient conditions; the illusiveness of the "biological clock"; the complex nature of attention; and the mechanism of memory. A review of this sort may aid in sharpening the insight of the lay reader as he approaches the professional literature. It is, of course, very much to his advantage to cultivate a guarded approach while retaining a favored position for utility. The creative artist or speculative layman is, after all, in search of new and rewarding experiences. They are not dependent on proof.

Ambient Conditions
In 1956, led by I.J. Hirsch, investigators at The Central Institute for the Deaf published a paper entitled "The Effect of Auditory and Visual Background on Apparent Duration." They claimed that while physical referents for vision were objects, the physical referents for hearing were events. They postulated a basic interdependency of temporal sense and aural stimulation. Using the

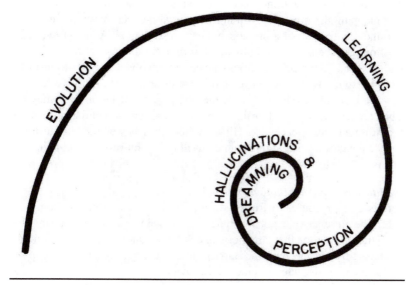

Figure 19. The *exponential (logarithmic) life spiral of time* symbolizes the unity of evolution, learning, perception-hallucination, and dreaming as adaptive event of increasingly efficient utilization of energy as well as increasingly rapid time rate of change. The origin of our spiral is the logarithmic spiral as first considered in 1638 by Descartes and then by Torricelli. John Bernoulli found all the "reproductive" properties of the "wonderful" spiral and wished to have the curve incised on his tomb, *Eadem mutata resurgo.*

technique of reproduction to measure short intervals, they discovered that psychological time runs at quite different rates during noise than it does in relative silence. The comparatively high level of aural stimulation during noise apparently speeds the flow of subjective time (no actual mechanism is proposed in the paper), and the subjective reproduction in silence of a durational interval heard in noise will be considerably longer, objectively measured, than the original. These tests were made with a white-noise background; in closing, the authors speculate that quite different results might be expected if a patterned ground were used. This suggests the more complex question of what constitutes back- and foreground in sound experience and implies, as well, that auditory background may somehow act as a calibrating monitor for our temporal experience.

The perception of aural "figures" (rhythmic motives) is sharply distinguished, in terms of clarity, from characteristics of the gaps separating them. At what level of definition do we receive and process the ambient aural background? Is its effect based upon the high incidence of aural events—some kind of priming excitation—or might the temporal influence of background relate rather to a division of the attentive capacities? One might simply be able to pay better attention to his task in silence, to become more absorbed with mapping the time flow within the interval he is currently reproducing onto the recollection of a previously heard test interval. Although we may question the mechanism of ambient aural impact on temporal flow, there is no doubt that laboratory conditions invariably involve the effort to insulate subjects from any distraction. If aural ambience *is* crucial in its effect on the speed of subjective time flow, the entire array of test results may be subject to modification or translation by some constant or nonlinear function to a different numerical plane. Hirsch's theorizing is weighted because his complementary investigation of ambient illumination revealed no temporal effects.

The Illusiveness of the Biological Clock
Here is a major source of frustration for observers, and no resolution is in sight. The presence of cyclical behavior even in single-celled organisms has led to the assumption that larger organisms must somehow draw on a similar cell-based timing mechanism. Barriers to the acceptance of most proposals for locating the internal clock are provided by the endogenous clock's considerable insensitivity to temperature and chemical influences. (This is particularly true of rhythms on a circadian scale.) At this time, the most likely source of a biological reference appears to be diffusion within the cell, a cyclical variation in concentrations caused by variations in membrane permeability. But, not only must a stable internal oscillator be identified; questions of cell rhythm synchrony and how the overall clock is consulted by the organism have yet to be answered. There is, in short, no secure

information as to what mechanism underlies the variety of an individual's time experience; hence, the formulation of revealing experiments is an ambiguous pursuit.

The Complex Nature of Attention

Since the number of events we observe during an interval is at least one basic determinant of our temporal judgments, attention is crucial. What actually happens in physical space, what stimuli impinge upon the organism, may correspond rather poorly to the pattern of signals that actually arrive at the cortex.[13] A "pattern," then, develops in the brain by means of its integration of the origin and rate of many identical incoming signals. We are unable to maintain a constant level of activity, and fluctuations in our efficiency are frequently observed, particularly in the realm of perception. Fatigue affects all biological systems. The visual phenomenon of reversible figures (such as that based on a diagrammatic representation of a cube) is complemented in the auditory mode by the fact that a regular, rapid repetition of "say" is alternately heard as "say" or "ace." Although words appear before you on this page as discrete units, they are an almost unbroken flow of phonemes in the spoken sentence. The involuntary perceptual flip-flop results from imperfect pattern recognition by the nervous system, probably as the result of fatigue. It is but one area of the complex landscape of attentive phenomena that includes the subliminal rejection of or defense against "improper" or distasteful stimuli and the conscious direction of attentive capacities. Because of limitations on our nervous system's capacity for handling information, the second process involves not only special attention to one set of stimuli but also a corresponding *repression* of nonattended streams of events which are only subjected to a minimal level of monitoring. In addition, it has been shown that it can take appreciable periods of time to "switch" from attending one stream of messages to the like processing of another. In the case of differing languages, for example, the changeover time for a multilingual person may be a matter of seconds.

One needs to inquire both how rapidly it is possible to switch back and forth among several messages and how long it will take to change from the complete processing of one message to fixing on another. As Moray observes, this is equivalent to studying the rate of cycling of the attentive mechanism and whether there is a "dead time" in the switch, a period between messages

---

13. By "pattern," the identification of receptor cells stimulated (and, hence, firing—transmitting—impulses up afferent nerve fibers toward the cortex), their order and rate of firing is meant.

No matter how they are stimulated, nerve fibers carry only one kind of message, an electrical impulse of similar strength and length. The "message" derives from 1) the point of origin (eye, ear, arm, nose, *etc.*) and point of arrival in the brain (visual cortex, auditory cortex, *etc.*), and 2) the frequency with which they transmit their sole impulse. The more intense the stimuli, the more rapidly the nerve fires.

when no input is processed.[14] Both of these *directly concern our capacities for admitting and retaining events and hence the evaluation of our musical experience.* Moray observes that all the models of the attention mechanism are deficient, in that

> ... they concentrate entirely upon competition between inputs. There is growing evidence that we may need to take into account competition among outputs, and between inputs and outputs" ... listeners who were shadowing non-redundant prose (statistical approximations of English) omitted many of the words but claimed that they had heard of them, as if the problem of receiving a difficult message prevented them from generating an output.

But the mechanism of attention is not so vague as common-sense ruminations might suggest. Not only can the sensory receptor cell signal receipt of excitation; it can also receive, by way of efferent nerve fibers, inhibitory signals from higher levels of the nervous system. In effect, these can turn the receptor cell off, forcing it to refrain from signaling.

Before temporal experience can be understood with any security, much more complete and accurate data on the functions of memory are needed. This is an area of research that has been strongly stimulated by advancements in computer technology and particularly in programming strategies, so that a considerable quantity of interesting material is now available. There is apparently an architectonic structure, and in *Models of Human Memory* (New York, 1970) UCSD psychologist Donald Norman postulates a mechanism for storing perceptual information before *naming* or *encoding* occurs and, in addition, both a short-term and long-term memory system. But, although it is of considerable interest to understand how and in what form information is stored in some form of mnemonic system, it is still necessary to describe its retrieval and use.

The importance of memory is multilayered, concerned not only with storage of the salient stimuli from a particular temporal duration, but also with the suggestions that might have accompanied it during its occurrence (the contributions of resonances struck in memory). Further, there are the new referents that this combined set of features (the real stimuli and the original memory traces) gives rise to during the process of recall and regeneration that accompanies its retrieval for report: "I remember that it felt like. ..." Of course, if the whole or part of an experience is privately recalled or rehearsed—and hence layered with referents—before its public dissemination, intradurational stretchings and imbalances can easily be introduced.

---

14. Neville Moray, *Listening and Attention*, Baltimore, 1970. Another, more critically revealing study is Donald Norman's *Memory and Attention*, New York, 1969.

An example of a potential pitfall in discussing the process of encoding perceived items: if an experiential item can be identified as already "known," it might take up less storage space (to adopt Ornstein's metaphor) as a reoccurrence in a fresh context. Still, the identity of the original coded form must be stored elsewhere in the memory, necessitating some form of cue indicating the need to refer elsewhere and the "address" of the relevant definition. The necessary mnemonic rules—the procedures necessarily involved in both recognition and recall—will require fairly extensive excavation. How much time will such a translational process take? Will it not interfere with the reception or reporting of items immediately following it in the stream of actual events or of memory traces?

The Relativity of References

The trend of the preceding discussion leads to another major perspective on time studies: consideration of the sometimes extreme relativity of our reference points, of our psychological "set." At no time in history have individuals and nations been barraged with such a welter of contrasting cultural perspectives, faced, at the same time, with the necessity of dealing with them on a practical level. Each culture (and subculture, one might add) has some form of "basic unit" upon which its temporal judgments are based. What happens at an intersection of the American culture's devotion to the second and to an Indian culture's traditional reliance upon the time required to boil rice?

Variety of psychological make-up affects the evaluation of temporal experience in profound ways. For example, a less authoritarian childhood seems to result in what might be called, from some points of view, an "underdeveloped" sense of conventional time scales (whatever the local culture may reward). In McClelland's The Achieving Society (Princeton, 1961), distinctions which he attempts to draw between subjects with a "high need for achievement" and those that were "low need achievers" are listed as follows. The former had a longer future time perspective; used more anticipatory tenses; were able to tolerate delay better as a function of increased reward; tended to recall past events as nearer to the present; and were more conscious of time as fleeting and valuable, thus tending to give more accurate time estimates than the "low need achiever." Children with a greater ability to fantasize have a greater ability to wait, reported J.L. Singer, and attempts have been made to contrast introvert and extrovert on the basis of their temporal responses. These are statements of coexistence, not necessarily of cause and effect pairings.

It has been suggested earlier that the suitability of an experience to concise encoding will influence the way in which it is temporally evaluated; a brief, concise trace leaves a correspondingly slight durational impression. One might speculate on the implications of this, for example, in the case of

Japanese grammar, where the well-defined Western system of subtle tenses is paralleled by two basic modes of describing completed and incompleted actions. Perhaps the preponderance of incomplete formulation (imperfective modes) in a Japanese-speaking person's mental life could incline him away from completed, easily circumscribed, and encoded experience into a sea of undulating, undirected contingencies. This might explain, then, the development of what a Westerner views as "patience" and the Japanese see as a sort of unemotional resignation.

What are we to think of a culture whose language does not make a distinction between the verbs "to exist" and "to become," where the same adverb indicates both "yesterday" and "tomorrow"? This is India. As Hajime Nakamura in *Ways of Thinking of Eastern Peoples* (Honolulu, 1969) observes, when one's life is seen as an infinitely repeating cycle, it loses urgency, and the value of acquiring a quantitative sense of time—for example, to write chronologically accurate history—is slight.

> The persistent Indian conception of a transcendent reality as more important than the phenomenal world it underlies and sustains results in a kind of paralysis of the individual's sensitivity to time, if we understand "time" to mean the passage and flow of specific events in our experience. This paralysis manifests itself in a characteristic lack of time concepts which non-Indians regard as common sense.

Although we Americans are comfortable with the idea that time can be possessed, bought, borrowed, stolen, and wasted, it is well to remember that *these are not inherent properties but culturally established.*

Altered Time Frames

How might investigations into the dimensions of time be practically useful to artists? In spite of the concern with which the wisdom of caution has been argued here, it would be regrettable not to explore and test the many extraordinary paths that wind off into indistinct but undeniably intriguing hollows. And although the foregoing discussion is an exhaustingly qualified treatment, what follows is even more frankly speculative. In defending these excursions, it is not out of place to reemphasize that the composer is presently in the undesirable position of having been for some time far in arrears of the implications of his available materials. There has been too feeble a level of translation or response between the patterns of daily life and the forms and potentially radiant expanse of aesthetic acts. Historically, composers and sculptors have moved rather easily to develop and master the influx of new ideas and technical developments, for the pace of their eras was moderate. This is no longer the case. In the past few decades, the range of *potential* has spread almost virulently. Many artists have been left helpless before the complexity of unfamiliar perspectives and technologies, ignorant of their promise. It is imperative for artist and audience alike to increase their awareness of current possibilities, to resist the temptation to indulge only in more or less novel collages of pretested ideas—ideas that have their origins in synchrony with times of far more leisurely pace and limited resource than our own. The examples that follow are meant only to suggest the sort of trains of thought which could lead to innovative applications with genuine impact.

In 1959, a report by Lettvin, Maturana, McCulloch, and Pitts, "What the Frog's Eye Tells the Frog's Brain," announced the startling discovery that different classes of receptors in the frog's eye responded to different geometrically defined object motions in physical space.[15] These fibers respond only if appropriate patterns are present in their field: for example, local sharp edges and contrast, the curved edge of a dark object, vertical edges moving, vertical edges only, vertical edges moving right only, vertical edges moving left only, and so on.

If tiny frames supporting basic geometric figures are attached directly to the surface of the eye, they negate the unavoidable tendency of the eye to scan rapidly, minutely. The basic figures will then engage continuously the same retinal cells, forestalling the normal constant realignment of object, lens, and retina. In this way, the effects of visual fatigue can be studied. As expected, figures tend to fade after prolong exposure if the eye is unable to vary the affected receptors. Of particular interest and related to the above picture of cell specialization is the fact that figures fade in very orderly ways, so that what remains is still quite definite, possessed of a strong and orderly configuration.

In *The Auditory Pathway* (London, 1967), I.C. Whitfield discussed the presence of similar nerve specialization in the cochlea, the center for the processing of aural information. He has isolated groups of cochlear cells, some that respond only to ascending sound glides, some only to descending glides, and others that fire only if the stimulus glides down in the high-frequency part of the response area and upward in the low-frequency range. Experiments related to this recent knowledge have already been carried out, though they originated from a quite remote set of circumstances. John Lilly and his associates discovered the phenomenon of "alternate words" in 1967 while engaged in studying the intelligence of dolphins. If a multisyllabic word such as "cogitate" or "kettle" is clearly and regularly repeated for periods ranging from fifteen minutes to an hour, under varying circumstances, subjects will hear, unambiguously literally dozens of other words and phrases. In the case of "cogitate," for example, the following are representative of the "alternates": agitate, brevity, cachet, can't you see, can't you stay, can't you take, Cape Cod you say, casualty, catch a tape,

---

15. In *Proceedings of the Institute of Radio Engineers*, Vol. 47, 1959.

caught your tape, cavity, cognitive, computate, concentrate, conscious state, count your tape, God did take, gravity, quantity, and start her please.

The prospects inherent in this phenomenon are abundant, depending, as all realistically planned musical works should, on the mental experience of the individual listener, automatically rewarding his searchings in the direction for which experience has fitted him. When the classes of auditory receptors have been completely characterized, and their properties catalogued, it would be possible to construct aural fabrics that—by virtue of anticipated fatigue patterns—continuously change as perceived facts in foreseen ways. The composer should be able to anticipate and allow for desired sequences of ellipsis and recombination. As fatigued receptors temporarily become inoperative, certain elements of the objective sound pattern are deleted, opening the way for new—no less "real" or precise—identities. The more general and nonredundant the verbal context, the more freely the mind's associative properties may be engaged.

What is a fact, one might ask? Do you know when you encounter one? Though not yet employed in the prestructured context described above, the principle of fatigue-produced shifts in apparent content has been a prominent component of the avant-garde field for the past decade. In 1963, John Cage produced the first New York performance of Erik Satie's outrageous *Vexations*. The composer decreed 840 repetitions of an eight-bar study in irresolution. At a properly slow tempo, full performance takes around fifteen hours. As a performance wears on, arguments flag over the question of how appropriate shifting the mood, accent, and tempo is to the substance of the experience. In a performance that I arranged, it was generally agreed that perfect uniformity was the correct goal. After eight or ten hours as a listener, one came to regard as heretics those members of the rotating team of performers who indulged in the slightest deviation. One literally basked in the security, the relentless *presence* of those few mournful chords lurching through the night. The performer—bearing the strain of an hour-long stint during the latter stages of the performance—would find himself plagued by a host of fears that were preposterous and yet unavoidable: of omission, losing his place, playing wrong notes, and so on. Only afterwards did it become clear that patterns of attentive and perceptual fatigue were constantly suggesting to the numbed mind unreal, disorienting "facts."

Composer Steve Reich (b. 1936) began a series of "phase pieces" in the mid-1960's. He studied philosophy before music and has gradually moved from realizations of his ideas achieved with tape machines to instrumentalists and finally electronic phase-shifting devices. The basic principle, as in his *Piano Phase* (1967), depends on a gradually more severe misalignment of identical or nearly identical sound fragments. Short segments—in one work, the words "come out to show them" spoken by an accused murder suspect in

Harlem—"looped."[16] Using multiple-track tape machines and mechanical or electronic speed change, a second (or third, or fourth ...) layer can be added, very gradually moving out of synchrony with the first. The result is at first an echo-like effect, then multiplication, and, eventually, as fatigue and the complexity of the aural fabric increase, an excitingly rich array of unexpected aural illusions—all from the simplest of materials.

Though the identity, even the existence, of a biological clock is still shrouded in doubt, this is not the case so far as the measured periodicities of the body are concerned. The accompanying table gives some notion of the range involved, in excess of 1,000:1. Experiments into more than the obviously visceral facet of rock music's appeal have been undertaken as a result of concern over possible hearing loss due to sustained high listening levels. Apparently the preponderance of dangerous sound pressure levels occurs below 500 Hz in a range where the muscles of the inner ear provide maximum damping protection and prevent pain. The simple vibratory coupling with the environment and between bodies achieved by amplification may be the foremost agent in the pleasure attached to rock events. One might investigate the effects of coincidental or deliberate synchrony of vibratory peaks with bodily periodicities or their harmonics.

A constant tremor of slight amplitude underlies the activity of all muscles in our bodies. Shivering would appear to be an amplification of the normally unobserved periodicity that results from the constant counterbalancing of muscles to achieve apparent stability. The amplification of slight sounds, now so easy electronically, would make it feasible for performers to utilize tremor impulses consciously, expanding elements of the technique. If both the aim of matching the body's natural rhythms and the conscious harnessing of normally inaccessible impulse speeds are practicable, it might be fruitful to examine the possibilities inherent in muscular entrainment or conditioning. One might employ consciously amplified bodily responses synchronized with, or in patterns of controlled deviation from, externally applied rhythms. After all, in examining the sources of sound, we saw that periodicity is central to pitch, that when the speed of replication was not sufficient for our hearing mechanism (as is the case with brain waves), it could be translated up into the audible range. For centuries respiratory and circulatory rhythms have been cited as tempo referents as has our bipedal construction been for meter. It is not beyond imagination that it would be possible in performance to tap other periodicities resident in the body, though this would require new sophistication in transduction.

---

16. In other words, they are copied several times and spliced together so as to form a tape loop that can be played continuously for any desired length of time. *Come Out* has been reissued on Nonesuch records 9 79169-2; it was originally issued on Odyssey records 32 16 0160.

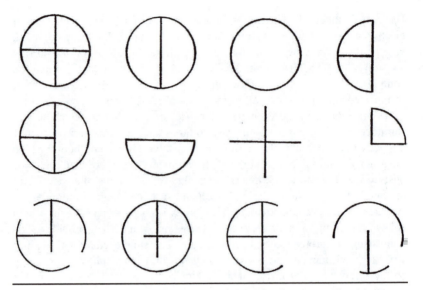

Figure 20. Some typical fragmentations reported when a target (in this case a circle with an inscribed cross) is viewed in stabilized vision, and also under conditions of rigid fixation.

Figure 21. Opening segment from Steve Reich's *Piano Phase.*

It would be imprudent at this time to speculate too elaborately on the impact of fuller and clearer descriptions of our attentive and mnemonic mechanisms. For reasons described above, though, it will surely be extensive. Consider:

Table 1. Scale of Biological Rhythms in Humans

200 Hz	Pulse transmission on nerve fibers (upper theoretical limit might go as high as 500–1,000 Hz
20–60 Hz	EEG gamma waves
5–50 Hz	Flicker fusion depending on intensity of light stimuli
14–18 Hz	EEG beta waves
10 Hz	Small amplitude tremor accompanying contraction of voluntary muscles
8–13 Hz	EEG alpha waves (2 Hz amplitude variation superimposed)
7 Hz	maximum speed for voluntary actions (tapping, chewing, *etc.*)
4–7 Hz	EEG theta waves
6–0.3 Hz	Uterus contractions
4–5 Hz	Contractions of the small intestine
3.5–0.5 Hz	EEG delta waves
2 Hz	Spontaneously satisfactory speed for voluntary actions
1–2 Hz	Contractions of the large intestine
1–2 Hz	Penis and scrotal contractions
1–2 Hz	Heart auricle contractions
1 Hz	Pulse rate (superimposed variations at intervals of 15, (0.6–1.7) 30 and 60 seconds may occur)
0.3 Hz	Heart apex contractions
0.2–0.3 Hz	Respiration rate (with superimposed variations at intervals of 1, 4, 9, 20, 40, 150 minutes)

- The receptor cell may be inhibited from any response, by internally originated directives. Attentiveness can be sought but it is normally bestowed, not commanded. It would seem, however, that certain drugs greatly enhance our absorptive capacities, in part by blocking inhibitory messages from traveling on the efferent nerve fibers. The individual loses, at some levels, the ability to censor and select his experience—less focus of attention, perhaps, but far more detailed content.
- Control of environment, like that undertaken in studies of sensory deprivation, is relevant for what it may tell us about the influences on experience that accrue from depriving the attentive mechanism of a normally paced train of stimulant events.
- Fischer speculates that hallucinations and dreams are characterized by an apparently more efficient use of energy and a more rapid time rate of change. Hypnosis has been used with some success in attempts to

improve performance in problem-solving tasks by suggesting to the subject an artifical elongation, expansion, of time. A minute becomes the subjective equivalent of an hour.

- The hypothesized relationship between alpha rhythms and pattern discrimination—proposed over two decades ago by Grey Walter—also involves preferred instants and periods of sensor reaction that shape the limits of our possible experience. If some physical or physi-ological system does monitor the speed with which we scan our world and this system were subjected to control, drastic shifts in the nature of our experiences might be induced.

This all leads in the direction of private art as discussed in earlier chapters. There can be no question about the potential for manipulation of experience that now exists. We can only hope that it is harnessed by beneficent spirits. One can postulate controlled environments with deci-sive impacts on their inhabitants. The necessity of referent chains of events, against which one is able to make estimates, remains a central factor in any scheme to obtain altered temporal experience. Without some "clocking," in other words, there is no way that an individual, let alone the distinct members of an audience together, can inhabit novel sorts of time. Our use of reference tempos has been traditionally rather limited: only one at a time, uniform speed, rates ranging from just below that of the heart to a factor of four greater. Music in the several decades has begun to invade purposefully both far slower and more rapid pacing, accelerative and retarding rates, mul-tiple references occurring simultaneously. Although the experience fostered by the rethinking of habits is unquestionably interesting, occasionally mani-festing striking results, it has not gone far enough. Indeed, our tethering to dance or ritualized labor for temporal references is unnecessarily timid. If the ear is the organ of time, music the temporal art, there is certainly much it has not yet ventured. It is known that both the mind and the senses can accommodate more subtle manipulations than the hand is capable of, and it is the composer's opportunity to foresee, to utilize these arenas in his peculiarly nonutilitarian but uniquely valuable way.

PART VI
Notation

New Whats (.) Require (.) Hows (.)
Possibilities (.) (?) Endlessly (.)
Demand (.) (:) Explanation (.)
Process (.) Replaces (.) Listening (.) Isn't (.)
Enough (.) (!) (...)[1]

Preliminary Remarks

In the limited context within which notation is usually discussed, it is characterized as a means of transmitting the composer's intent. Its task is to make possible a faithful aesthetic representation in performance without the personal guidance of the creator. A successful score, then, presents and explains materials accurately. It can never duplicate a second function served by the actual presence of the creator: the correction of misinterpretations and the modifications of divergences that are too extreme. An inert score is unable to accomplish the feedback that a responsive human being can. In placing on paper a representation of his intentions, the composer inherits an obligation to anticipate possible misunderstandings and to insert suitable admonitions into the score.

Notation is not expected to serve the second, corrective function, and it supplies only the special instructions related to the event envisaged. Here I do not refer to what is traditionally called the "message" of the composition. Particular classes of events and/or processes are requested, and thus certain sequences of actions necessary to produce them are anticipated by the composer: a particular embouchure, certain breath pressures, bow angles and drawing speeds, a sequence of fingerings, levels of effort, coincidences, reactions, *etc.* Content is expected to follow naturally from the sounds and relationships specified and manifested. But this is only true because of a large and powerful second source of information, which might be called the "understood" information imposed by a social and historical, not to mention professional, context. In short, information comes to a performer

---

1. The author's contribution to John Cage's *Notations*, New York, 1969.

in two ways, assuming the absence of the creator's guiding hand during rehearsals. As a rule, notation deals directly only with the first.

How is it, then, that we recognize a "correct" performance or think we do? Psychologist G.A. Miller comments that our search for the solution to a problem "is guided by our conception of the form a solution must take or by the form we want it to take."

> The contextual, or syntactic, patterns of the language impose constraints upon the configuration the answer can assume. The answer must come out in a sequence of words that seems probable against the background of our habitual intraverbal connections. Transformations of the problem materials that produce an improbable configuration are distrusted and are often disregarded as opposed to common sense.[2]

Extending this will suggest the degree to which our concepts are dependent on preestablished values and experience. The composer not only needs to give special instructions called for by his concept; he may also need to neutralize, even to combat, the "understood" preconceptions of the performer and predispositions of the performance space if they are in conflict with his intentions. Even in the ideal case, however, the notational document is rooted in and circumscribed by its own historical context.

In the section on notation in his book *Twentieth Century Music* (New York, 1967), Peter Yates broadly illuminates the ways in which the meaning of notational symbols and conventions alters with the passage of time. Actual practice—often quite distinct from the avowed reverence for urtext testaments—negates the idea that the substance of the composer's intent is always inherent in the score's printed symbols. It does so by constantly embracing the encroachments of technical and social modifications. We play music of earlier centuries and remote environments with different tunings, altered pitch standards, and revised conventions of instrumental ensemble, tone quality, and projection than were practiced originally. What, then, do notational symbols actually convey? What are the varieties of notation and what are its values?

The Creative Continuum

This examination of the extraordinarily flexible and powerful concept of notation in music begins with a survey of the processes to which it may be applied, in which it may be imbedded. There are at least three *continua* worth observing and characterizing for their value as references. First, we might note that between the creator's idea and the listener's response stretches a path along which a continuous process of decision-making occurs. It might

---

2. This discussion is contained in G.A. Miller, *Language and Communication*, New York, 1951.

be plausibly divided into seven regions: idea, crystallization, storage, study, performance, hearing, and interpretation.

An idea—something observed, an unlikely coincidence of events, an unexplained resonance in the mind—suggests itself and one begins to explore allied implications. One seeks ways of making the attractive essence more concrete, more manageable, more communicable. The process of crystallization is succeeded by some form of storage; the idea is encoded in the memory, on paper, or on tape. It is fixed sufficiently so that it may be considered and *re*considered at will. After enough rehearsal (internal or external), a public presentation may be attempted and the results heard. This is not the end of the sequence, however. Interpretation, intellectual and affective response, is still pending and can be radically different for two persons absorbing essentially the same patterns of stimuli.

A second, five-term continuum might be hesitantly borrowed from Information Theory: source, transmitter, channel, receiver, and destination. Much that is inappropriate to musical applications accompanies this model, however, not the least of which is the fact that aesthetic information is not easily quantified. That is to say, it is difficult to represent with sufficient fidelity when broken up into a series of blocks that are characterized by short-term averaging. The rate of subtle change on which the substance of aesthetic experience normally depends is so rapid as to require staggering speeds of measurement and storage if a successful representation is to be sent and received. We have seen this in the discussion of the computer generation of sound. Under these circumstances, simple encoding procedures like Morse code or narrow-band telephone voice communications are patently impractical. Further, knowledge of the limitations of human perceptual and attentive capacities tempts one to argue that precise identification of items is less crucial in aesthetic situations than in most scientific or linguistic communications. It might be debated, of course, but I suspect that our response to music involves a far lower level of stress at decision-making moments than more practically contingent aspects of our lives. Musical response therefore implies a wider concern for trends and accumulations, for the *values* we have learned to associate with particular sound patterns rather than for the unambiguous recognition and assessment of each component event.

As listeners, our responsibilities have tended to be evaluative (passive) rather than participatory. Nothing critical or public hinges on a "right" or "wrong" decision. Nothing but the inherent fascination of the moment obliges us to make a decision, to identify or understand an aesthetic event at all. We tolerate, even thrive on, high levels of macroscopic redundancy in sonic forms (*e.g.*, verse songs), at the same time finding a microcosmic redundancy (the incessant vibrato of an electronic organ) insupportably annoying in aesthetic situations. Consider the gestural and harmonic repetitiveness of much of the operatic literature and, further, the differences in our attentiveness if an aria is realized on a Hammond organ or by an intelligent baritone. Communication theory does not involve value judgments. It is essentially unconcerned with the nature of the materials transmitted. Musicians are unavoidably tethered to operations taking place within the *source* (the composer) and the *destination* (the listener) and, in particular, to their attitudes regarding the nature of the materials they transmit and receive. In the communication model, the *transmitter* and *receiver* are simply concerned with encoding and decoding the information to be passed—in convenient from—across the *channel* that spans space and/or time.

The third continuum I wish to cite is implicit in a page from Paul Klee's *Pedagogical Sketchbook*, shown below. Here there is a reductive generalization that is more compact than the views described before. Klee's trichotomy comprises a *listing* of brain as active organ, muscle as medial, and bone as passive; a *pictorial representation* delineating function by purely graphic means (arrows and flow patterns implying the desired progression); and a *verbal scheme* including waterfall (active), wheels-transmission belts (medial), and hammer (passive). One of the interesting dimensions of this representation is its architectonic implication. The moving bone, in turn, becomes active and, like the falling hammer, delivers an impulse.

The compositional idea might be seen as *active*, notated materials as *medial*, and the performance as the *passive* result; the same triadic relationship could be applied to the performer's preparation as active stimulant, the physical actions he performs in concert as medial, and the sounds produced as passive. Again, however, the listener has prepared, and heard, and responded. It is worth commenting on Klee's multileveled presentation. There is a useful but not disturbing level of redundancy. The picture deals with affective specifics and includes engaging ornamentation while the word schematic is coolly categorical. Several distinct forms are taken by an organizational idea, several forms of presentation used at once. The ways in which they overlap communicate a whole collection of insights suggesting a broad principle and its dimensions. This process, at work within one of our explored continua, itself serves as an example of notational skill. Consider the relative value of the three contributing factors separately and how they are made to coexist.

Exercises

(based on the Trichotomy):

First organ active (brain).	Second organ medial (muscle).	Third organ passive (bones).

a) Waterwheel and Hammer

I The Waterfall (active).	II Wheels (medial).	III Hammer (passive).
Drums of the big wheel.	Spokes of the small wheel.	Transmission belt.

Figure 22. A page from Paul Klee's Pedagogical Sketch Book.

The first of the above three processes is the continuum most directly relevant to us. Most contemporary approaches to musical composition can be seen in relation to it if one asks at what stage in the continuum the major concentration of decision-making occurs and takes note of which decisions are of major importance. Normally, the concentration is greatest in the crystallization region where the task of ordering and working out one's materials is faced. Such a convention as the Baroque figured bass[3] required a large number of lesser decisions to be made during the act of performance. So, also, does the music of indeterminacy, although here the impact and hence the importance of these far less stylized choices is greater. A similar mapping of *notational* emphasis can be made as one views the process between the idea and response, and might reveal other-than-normal roles for notation.

The Function of Notation

Transmission of Intent

All regions of the continuum between idea and interpretation involve storage, internal or external, of items unconsciously or consciously coded. The most familiar notational function is, of course, *transmission of intent*. In previous eras, when transportation of already rehearsed performing groups, their instruments and leader was impractical, there was a clear and urgent function served by printed music. It is no longer impractical for those who are the actual source of an idea or a technique to travel from place to place, directly demonstrating and coaching others. There is also no difficulty in sending a

---

3. The *figured bass* convention allowed composers to indicate in a standard notational form only the notes of the bass line. Accompanying these indications were various standardized numerical signs that indicated the harmonic function of the given notes and, thereby, those additional pitches upon which the performer could improvise further contrapuntal materials.

more or less faithful representation of the sound result desired by recording it in some form. Notation is no longer restricted to paper now that tape, film, digital storage, and video are available.

Storage

Storage is the process by which the composer's intentions are made available for examination at some distance in time and space. But this is a practice rooted in economic structure. For a variety of reasons, this function of traditionally practiced notation is likely to undergo continuous deemphasization. The composer now moves with and to his outlets. Increasingly accurate documentation of performances may be made through technology to serve as models for others. Not only is paper itself becoming less essential, but technologically involved conceptions such as mixed-media events are not easily trimmed and packaged for representation by neat sets of symbols. When each work stretches the restraints of tradition in its own way, a composer cannot hope to foresee crucial aspects of the performance situation that, with more commonly practiced forms, used to be assured by professional standardization. He must be there, dealing directly with matters still too vaguely defined to have emerged much beyond a need to "get the feel of things."

Abstract Representation

More fundamental and less likely to fade is the importance of *abstract representation*, essential in the economical manipulation of materials, the trial and rejection or acceptance that materials undergo in the regions of *idea* and *crystallization* (*cf.* the seven-term continuum). As Alfred North Whitehead observed:

> By relieving the brain of all unnecessary work, a good notation sets it free to concentrate on more advanced problems, and in effect increases the mental powers of the race. ... It is a profoundly erroneous truism, repeated by all copybooks and by eminent people when they are making speeches, that we should cultivate the habit of thinking of what we are doing. The precise opposite is the case. Civilization advances by extending the number of important operations which we can perform without thinking about them. Operations of thought are like cavalry charges in a battle—they are strictly limited in number, they require fresh horses, and must only be made at decisive moments.

Entities—ideas, images, effects—are stored in memory and therefore available for our consideration only after they have been encoded and "rehearsed" properly. Researchers in mnemonics tell us the number of individual items we can retain depends on the efficiency of our encoding mechanisms. The better one is at finding manageable classifications, the more one can grasp and store. The more information in convenient forms that is available, the wider the range of possible connections that can be achieved by the thoughtful mind. As an example of the ways in which encoding mechanisms allow us to reform and store a category of basic items, consider the twenty-six individual letters of the alphabet. In a random series of letters, roughly seven members of a rapidly presented sequence can be recalled. (Interestingly enough, the retained list commences from the beginning of the sequence, rather than the end which is closer in time to the moment of recall.) By enlarging the classification to familiar *words* (and, hence, encoding the individual letters) we might store five times seven letters, or, again, if dealing with common collections of words or *phrases*, four times five times seven letters. If we find ways of encoding, of schematically or graphically representing complex entities, we ease the restrictiveness of the chains of retrieval and collation normally required.

An exercise undertaken in a graduate notation seminar of mine was revealing. After listening to a three-minute tape recording of Buckminster Fuller discussing the continuity of personality, students were asked to make a response within five minutes. The response could take one of two forms: either two complete sentences or one sentence and a single one-line drawing. The papers were collected but not discussed. Ten weeks later, the same persons were asked to recreate their impressions of Fuller's remarks as precisely as possible. It became immediately clear that those who had used words alone were able to reconstruct their impressions far less accurately. (It was not simply a question of different word choices, but of altered perspective and content.) The graphic notations were not only more clearly reproduced but also, it was reported, aided in recalling the accompanying sentence. In the following discussion, all were impressed by the degree to which their brief attention to storage had focused impressions that might otherwise have been transient and had subjected them to more ready recall weeks later.

Once a valued experience has been grasped in some way, it is to our advantage to find an effective external notation for it. We have all had the experience of finding how a thought, only recently comprehended, can slip into vagueness or even total eclipse, leaving only an annoying, elusive trace. The value of symbolic representation is, of course, not just mnemonic in the sense mentioned above. More important, it allows us to rearrange, combine, order, and modify ideas or conditions in our own time to a degree and with an ease otherwise totally unmanageable.

Liberating Reference

Notation has another function that operates in the region of performance: as a *liberating reference*. Recent professional practice has required a soloist to memorize the music he plays. The value of this is questionable, even in traditional cases, but when a player is faced with the necessity of ordering his materials or altering his responses *during* performance, memorization unnecessarily compounds the difficulties of the task. During any activity in which a larger awareness and responsiveness is appropriate, simple representations of materials, roles, and so on liberate the mind to concentrate on more significant dimensions. During performance, the quality of an individual player's attention to inflection, to shadings of tempo, color, rhythms, and intonation is crucial; the instructions represented as visual materials, then, should be clearly fixed and easily discriminated. Such performance notation should be as simple as the learning process and performance situation for a given piece will allow. Wherever possible, it should be *no more than a reference.* Complex information about techniques and tasks is better presented elsewhere in the creative continuum. One might well consider the advantages of different notational modes in complex situations: one for physical mastery of material, one for the exploration of relationships, and still another for reference in performance.

Generation of Richness

In the tradition of Western music, the practice of notation has been an extraordinary vehicle for the *generation of richness.* What, for example, if the art of painting had evolved a system whereby famous artists provided maps for line, mass, and color designation? What if their works were not fully realized proposals on canvas that remain inaccessible to reconsideration? There might have developed a tradition of performing artists devoted to realizing" the maps of the master painter/planners. One of the most virile and profound dimensions of Western music has been the fact that compositions maintain an existence beyond the score. The printed document is a respected aid but hardly capable of total specification. As a result, the substantial intellectual and emotional resource of generations of musicians has been brought to bear on the notated representation of concepts whose original form remains essentially unknowable. This resource continually adapts and may possibly enlarge the musical substance to meet changing social, educational, technical, and acoustical facts. Such processes go on, of course, not only in the case of incompletely specified music which depends in part upon the knowledge current in performers' minds. They also operate subtly in what we imagine to be completely written-out compositions. Yates observes that many composers, including those of early keyboard music, baroque continuo accompaniments, and written-out jazz compositions, never expected the music to be played as it looks. To some degree, the same is probably true of almost every composer who has ever used notation.

The value of historical accumulation, of recycling and adaptation, is inestimable, and its loss—even in the short term—would be severely damaging to the size of musical experience available to us. For this reason the idea of recording difficult compositions to serve as models for other performance attempts strikes me as undesirable. Recordings are useful to sample unfamiliar sound materials or demonstrate performance techniques, certainly, but not to reveal (and thereby cement us into) a particular mold for eventuation. Commercial recordings of more popular repertory pieces maintain a balance through multiple treatment, but audiences learning the work of young or infrequently played composers often fall prey to the impression that the single extant recording of a work *is* the work, rather than one manifestation of a larger ideal.

Communication with the Self

Finally, the usefulness of notation in the private world, the *communication with the self*, grows more substantial with each new increment of acceleration in the pace at which we live. We change; in fact, those of us active in almost any professional capacity are under an increasing obligation to alter and redirect our abilities and opinions, to increase our capacity for absorbing the change going on around us. It is hardly likely that each new piece of information or that each position adopted will be superior to or more productive than that it postdates, so change is by no means synonymous with progress. We are forced to consume information and vicarious experience rapidly, with little time for rehearsal and, hence, accurate and complete enough storage. Neither is there opportunity for that essential, arbitrary play of idly made associations. Events slip by, imbedded in and softened by the processes they populate. Selective storage of experiences or viewpoints can provide valuable counterbalances to an otherwise unidirectional motion almost devoid of the enrichment of feedback and *re*consideration. Psychologist G.A. Miller points out in his study *Language and Communication* that "When a person writes himself a note on his memorandum pad, the writer at one time is the source, the process of writing is the transmitter, the permanence of the pad is the channel that spans intervening time, the reader's eyes are the receiver, and the same person at a later time is the destination." Notebooks, tapes, photos, or intriguing bits of information revisited in odd moments generate and deeply root ideas. They help an artist to develop the effect of a powerful economy in generating materials. They help to insure that initially vague, unfamiliar ideas are developed fully, that their fabric of implications has been densely and coherently woven over a sufficient period of time at some perhaps unconscious level of the mind. Such development *can* come about only when suggestive bits of information and the stances they imply are available for later scrutiny.

Symbols: Graphic and Verbal

Assuming a desire to note something, with what does one work? Most generally with graphic symbols, secondarily with written words. Graphic symbols stand either for events (a particular form corresponding to a generally agreed upon and well-defined sound) or actions (the graphic indication comprising a signal that implies a certain physical action or chain of closely synchronized movements). Symbols, however, seem more suited to one-to-one correspondence with singular events than to the description of extended processes or attitudes. In the latter case, words or flow charts using brackets, arrows, or other indications of groupings and gradients are common.

It is important to bear in mind the increase in potential power that a symbol gains by corresponding to an inclusive classification; at the same time, there must be a balance between breadth of meaning and the necessity for precise application. Usually, several sets of information overlap and the redundancy inherent in the representation fixes the precise meaning. Compare a fortissimo marking for flute on low *B* with a pianissimo for oboe on the same pitch. A trained musician knows that physical realities of instrumental range dictate the likelihood that, even with the oboist's most repressive effort, his sound will not fail to emerge above the flutist's fortissimo.

A common technique of mapping sound events with relative precision onto paper is to consider the page as a two-dimensional space, with pitch determined top (high) to bottom (low) and time flowing left to right. In the score for *The Emperor of Ice Cream* (1962, C.F. Peters), I retained the horizontal time representation but used normal music staves to indicate pitch. This allowed the vertical dimension of the page (top to bottom) to stand for position left to right on the stage. Hence, the score was able to indicate not only what sounds were being made, but the relative positions of the musicians with respect to each other as a constant function of time.

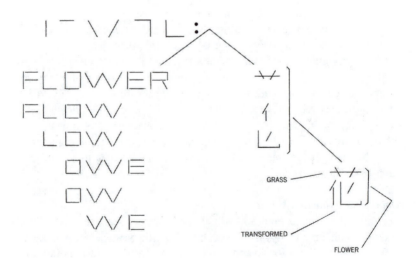

Differing language systems provide clear evidence of the effects that various notational options bring about. Let us begin with a repertoire of simple, angular strokes, as shown here. With them we can approximate the word for "flower" in English and Chinese/Japanese:

An examination of the elements in these two representations clarifies an important distinction between them. In English, the marks (1) are used to create letters (2) which combine into the correct phonemes (3) to make up a word (4) that represents an unambiguous class of objects (or a process). If we note the possible linearly consistent combinations of phonemes that can be extracted from the whole word "flower," however, we see that they have no necessary connection to each other: flower, flow, lower, low, owe, ow, we.

The Chinese/Japanese form moves from marks (1) to radicals (2) with particular and specific meanings, to ideographs (3) that complete a composite and unambiguous concept. The same radicals can, of course, combine with others into new compounds but they do not lose their basic significance.[4] The ideographic representation corresponding to our printed word "flower" is a composite meaning, literally, "changed or bewitched grass." Its meaning resonates, even includes a certain graphically suggestive aura.

Good Notational Practice

Difficulties

Frequently, in first attempts at notating unprecedented events or systems, composers misjudge. Stravinsky admitted his inability to write down the "sacrificial dance" episode in *The Rite of Spring* at a time when he was quite able to perform it. More recently, composers are often frustrated in their attempts to describe either the quality of or the actions necessary to produce some new aural phenomenon. Occasionally, in larger-scale divergences from traditional means, one will find an unsettling tendency for the number of sound parameters under description to exceed the number of dimensions of the notation, creating unsolvable logical dilemmas. It is easy to overlook the amount of basic restriction/definition that the traditional notational system provides. John Cage's incomparably elegant "The performance will last an agreed upon length of time" has spawned far less well-considered evasions.

But the most demanding requirement is not usually the symbolic representation of events or actions but the description of processes and attitudes: saying enough to stimulate without inhibiting. Cage is, of course, the master of verbal formulations. Robert Ashley is another composer skilled

---

4. Because of the complexity with which the written forms have evolved, this is not as neat as suggested. To the degree that the radical has a meaning, it is constant, but radicals are often used as determinants of pronunciation or in other contingent combinations.

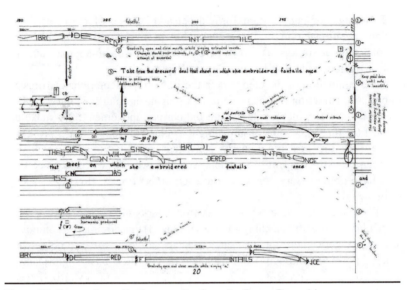

Figure 23. A page from *The Emperor of Ice Cream* by Roger Reynolds

at describing, within the confines of a few short paragraphs, processes with massive potential and firm identity. The definition of processes and relationships is relatively new terrain, however, and this explains the frequency of resort to words—actually an intermediary stage.

It is well to bear in mind that the finest notational achievements remain at the mercy of the prejudices and distractions of the interpreter. "Understood" information is an invaluable facilitation in a time of common practice but a formidable adversary to one attempting to fashion a genuinely fresh experience. We absorb, at least in part, through pattern recognition, and its power of generating details to fill sensory elisions is great, indeed. *In Kinesics and Context* (Philadelphia, 1970), Ray Birdwhistell writes:

> When we take a tape recording and turn it over to a secretary for typing, her patterned memory, her belief that human beings speak in turn and her belief that most human beings, on paper at least, speak in complete sentences, leads to a situation in which she hears this kind of material on tape. By actual count, even skilled secretaries working from unstructured interviews make about one mistake every five words. ... Utilizing the ears of some of the best linguists in America has shown that even these experts, when working with shapes of material larger than a word or simple sentence, give us records with errors every ten to fifteen words.

(We could choose to look at the positive side here and maintain that these "errors" represent the intrusion of "common sense" or an exercise in initiative that should be viewed positively.)

Further psychological studies such as that reported by J.S. Bruner and L. Postman in *Experiments in Visual Perception* (M. Veron, ed., Baltimore, 1966) are dismaying. Testing a subject's abilities to discern perceptual incongruities, they came to the decision that "for as long as possible and by whatever means available, the organism will ward off perception of the unexpected." They tested subjects by means of rapid presentation of cards where an incorrect color had been applied to a suit (*e.g.*, red clubs). Reports fell into one of four categories: *dominance* (the subject denied the incongruity); *compromise* (a purplish combination of red and black was reported); disruption (no report at all could be made, even after relatively long exposure); and, rarely, *recognition* (a red club was seen). These responses were, of course, relative to experimental conditions but they nevertheless suggest caution when speaking of accuracy and dependability in the notation of new ideas.

The preceding discussion will serve to underscore the importance of careful consideration regarding the form and level of redundancy a notational effort requires relative to its addressee. We all labor under what psychologists call "limited channel capacity." We encode and store—*we comprehend*—by no means all of what we see; the less easily a symbol or idea is mapped onto the inner fields of our previous experience, the less likely we are to register it accurately. Unfortunately, we are only rarely made aware of the changes we make in incoming information during the process of acquiring it. The passive score is ill-equipped to catch a momentarily clouded brow and retrace its argument.

Whatever material we use, graphic symbols or words, a context must be clearly defined. Context is, at a convenient level, the small-scale formalization of "understood" information. It allows us to indulge in virtuosity of implication. If I write on the blackboard, "'That' is an extraordinary word," and then, stepping back, say in a normal voice, "I am now demonstrating that that that that that sentence contains is, indeed, a remarkable set of symbols," few listeners will react immediately to the presence of a string of five "that"s. The importance of context to content is easily stressed by observing the effect of recasting the above commentary: "I am now demonstrating why the word 'that' contained in the sentence I previously wrote on the board is a remarkable set of symbols."

The following chart suggests one means of ordering the possible approaches to notation:

One might explore various combinations of these approaches, one from each column, depending upon the particular confluence of ideas, materials, and performers anticipated.

After the discursive path we have just completed, how might the elements of a good (which is to say effective) notation be summed up? Five points discussed below seem to me essential: economy, scope, generality, appropriateness, and definition of terms.

SOUND MATERIALS	COMBINATION: PLACEMENT IN TIME/ARTICULATION
SPECIFICATION OF "KNOWN" ELEMENTS	SYNCHRONIZED SPECIFICATION OF/IN TIME FRAME
(Nothing is assumed—everyone knows what is expected, composers and performers alike, for all share an unambiguous experience with a set of musical materials) traditional systems of notes, clefs, *etc.*	(Nothing is assumed, everything is delineated)
SPECIFICATION OF NECESSARY ACTIONS	SPECIFICATION OF GENERAL RULES DEFINING PROCESSES AND THEIR INTERACTIONS
(Resultant qualities assumed—the products of specified actions correctly performed are assumed to be acceptable) tablature as in guitar music	(The details of intersection are not fixed)
SPECIFICATION OF SOUNDS (QUALITIES)	SPECIFICATION OF TEMPORAL OR TEXTURAL RESULTS: EFFECTS/SUCCESSIONS
(Necessary action assumed—achieve the specified sounds in any way you wish)	(There is no specification of what processes or synchronics might produce desired result)

Economy

Economy implies the presentation of information in accurate and compact form. To quote Whitehead again:

> When the initial statements are vague and slipshod, at every subsequent stage of thought, common sense has to step in to limit applications and to explain meanings. Now in creative thought common sense is a bad master. Its sole criterion for judgment is that the new ideas shall look like the old ones. In other words it can only act by suppressing originality.

With this in mind, consider the following points. Deviate from standard forms of notation no more than your idea actually requires. Explain only as much as is necessary to achieve the special conditions under which the piece can be realized. Reinforce key factors by several statements in different form, for such strategic redundancy can prevent basic errors in conception or procedure.

Scope

Scope suggests attention to the depth of variance in architectonic level to which a system of notation and its components can apply. In a provocative volume called *The Image of the City* (Cambridge, Mass., 1960), Kevin Lynch reports on his investigation of a set of basic elements that may be said to establish urban environments for their inhabitants. He discusses in detail paths, edges, districts, nodes, and landmarks, indicating along the way impressions gleaned from interviews with persons having a variety of experience with identical environments. Those who were unfamiliar with an area, who lacked experience in traversing it, depended almost entirely on large-scale factors such as the continuity and identity of paths and districts for orientation. In contrast, the more familiar one became with a district, the more one began to notice, to place, and to guide oneself by means of small-scale local landmarks.

It is tempting to draw an analogy between the acclimatization process for environments and for musical works. It immediately suggests that an imbalance of attention by the performer during a presentation to either intimate detail or to the large outline and surface will result in dissatisfaction at some point, as the listener attempts to experience and understand a work. Therefore, notational approaches must include means of handling effectively the entire range of implication in a composition (or, better, a series of works). A successful approach must provide not only for an arresting sequence of detail but also for the coherent overlay of implication—the context—that allows detail to make its effect in sympathetic performance.

By scope, I do not mean the compounding of inference that arises from overlaying the symbols of a particular notational system. In the 1950's, some implausibly strained notational practices developed, including the idea of proportions within proportions:

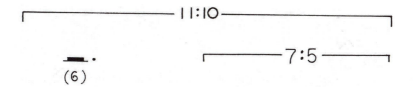

Combined with extensive elision and constant reference shifts, this led to detractive despair in even the most earnest performers, who projected, as a result, more anxiety than rhythmic precision. Scope concerns the applicability of a convention to a range of uses significantly larger than those required by any one occasion.

Generality

Generality is achieved *by* abstraction, usually in terms of classes of symbols and an appropriate matrix described verbally, and *for* broad utility. To become a part of a successful *system*, a symbol must be sufficiently nonspecific to accommodate a variety of situations and materials. Generality of the individual symbol or phrase and of the scope of the notational system comprised of such symbols represents the other side of economy. Generality insures that the symbol is sufficiently suggestive without being restrictively precise. It implies, as well, an ability to intuit or anticipate the various lives that an idea might manage. For example, if a composer sets several processes in motion and does not wish to define their interaction at every point, then he should try to forecast *possible* modes of interaction and allow for these. A good notational element is general enough to suggest new varieties of events in and of itself. Thus a notational procedure that defines such vocal factors as lip shape (open, pursed, drawn) and vowel shape (ah, ee, oh, *etc.*) as continuously variable, independent factors may result in previously unsuspected vocal timbres.

Appropriateness

Appropriateness is a criterion applied to the overall appearance of a notational presentation. The form and manner of a composer's notational means should imply the quality of his compositional position and, by extension, the nature of the expected result for a given piece. Delicacy and precision in notation will argue differently, though perhaps no more powerfully, to the performer than does a bold, sketchy broadside of a score. With thought, it is frequently possible to devise symbols capable of suggesting at once the means (hands, forearm, *etc.*) and the approach (open fingers, side of hand, *etc.*), as in these devised by Mauricio Kagel:[5]

Definition of Terms

Without clear *definition of terms*, there is little point in the rest. One must decide how much to assume about the knowledge, ability, or good will of the performer (normally, suspicion is directly proportional to the size and age of the performance group). Each symbol or word not a part of the average performer's vocabulary should be clarified, and each component

5. Discussed in "Tone, Cluster, Attacks, Transitions," in *Die Reihe 5*, Reports Analyses, Bryn Mawr, 1961.

of the average performer's experience or of the normal performance space layout *not* wanted should be specifically ruled out.

Clearly, most of these factors are routinely taken care of by the innovator out of experience and in self-defense. If the composer chooses to neglect formal scoring in favor of personal appearances, he will most certainly have easier and more immediately excellent representation. The question remains as to whether the dimension of his ideas will be explored in the way that it would be within the traditional framework, by the exercise of various outside minds and needs; and further, whether he will as fully plumb the reaches of his own inspiration without facing the task of focusing it, uncovering the deeper reality of his personal tastes and concerns, and committing them to some form of storage.

There can, however, be no avoidance of the impact of economic and social realities on notational practices. Whereas Schoenberg was able to demand of professional players—without fear of committal—eighty hours or more of rehearsal, such a privilege is more than unlikely for contemporary composers. An overly complex notational approach is almost certain to fail in most professional ensemble situations because of the degree to which economic realities curtail rehearsals. Socially, on the other hand, we are all habituated to change and a constant influx of new information and experience. It may be that the traditional function of art as providing occasions for reflection will be radically reshaped. Perhaps the possibility of revisiting the materials of an experience will continue to decline, and more of the brunt of creative effort will fall on the sensory quality of material in unrepeatable and provocative process. If so, graphic conventions bound primarily to specifying events and ordering actions (as I have suggested) may give way to a less obviously expressive symbology, to languages of words or other indications by means of which newly evolving yet consistent streams of events can be continuously generated without repetition.

PART VII
Morphology in Music

Computers: The Necessity of Foresight

Having undertaken an inquiry into the materials of music, how they have been and may be enlarged, a treatment of our responsive capacities, and various comments on the transmission of intent, an overview may be possible. Is the availability of an unprecedented range of sounds and a more comprehensive insight into the mechanism of human response leading us toward new structures for aesthetic experience, or does form remain somehow above influence? At first thought, it is easy to see how analogous, if not identical, forms and functions can be served by substances that differ as radically as do the stylistic allegiances of the artist. The clay of the ancient jmon potters of Japan, Michelangelo's marble, and the welded metal that served Giacometti all illuminate the individual human condition, although occasion, perspective, and scale are widely divergent. What serves to divert one age may be approached reverently by the next, or conversely. In examining morphology—the patterns of formation and structure in aesthetic experience—my intent is to uncover any fundamental shifts in attitudes towards the forming process as well as changes in the resulting form.

An evident discontinuity with traditional Western ideals is upon us the moment we begin seeking contemporary forms in the traditional "closed" sense. Artists in all fields now seem less concerned with the production of contained, finished objects that reflect well-established structural models. The formalized nicety of clearly defined beginnings and endings, of announcing unambiguously that one was about to do something, was now doing it, and had now finished, has been widely questioned. Experiences tend to evolve gradually (or sometimes commence arbitrarily), to end by simply fading away. The experiential implication is that one has, as a listener, sampled a process that existed before and will continue to exist after the immediate occasion has passed. The notion of clearly packaged forms of experience seems suddenly arbitrary to many artists who opt instead for a less constraining mode of presentation: the sample adroitly selected. The influence of biological process on contemporary thought; the acceptance of change as a norm (and the consequent alteration in our evaluation of permanence versus transience, of process versus object); and a more contingent concept of morality—these have alerted all, and the artist in particular, to the futility of adopting and depending on fixed models or positions. But form in its experienced detail has perhaps never been so demonstrable as supposed by some observers. Although it is difficult to find a sonata movement of the mature Beethoven that corresponds to the classic analytical model of the sonata form as established by theorists, there is no doubt that such a formal pattern existed in some sense as a conceptual or procedural model. About such an image, the work of almost all composers of the later eighteenth and early nineteenth centuries revolved more or less tightly. Actually, it would be of no great moment whether such a basic mold— introduction, exposition, development, recapitulation, coda (and their associated tonal levels)—was recognized as such during this period or was overlaid upon its practice after the fact. By a consensus of individual actions, composers established the sense of such a general scheme in response to the musical materials and socio-aesthetic needs of their time. Publicly concrete or not, such a scheme was in the air, and the paucity of invention or genius of the individual creator guided his adherence or resistance to it.

The sonata pattern suggested, if generally, how conflict between opposing (contrasted) themes—in a broader than melodic sense—could be stated (exposition), elaborated (development), and resolved by a transformed return (recapitulation). This package was based in part on the assumption that there existed a capacity for resolution, that resolution was possible and desirable. There were accepted ways in which musical statements could be made (including on the local level conventions of phrase length) as well as assumptions about the containment of dramatic conflict in formal terms, and thus on both micro and macro levels symmetry was primary. In classical sonatas, exposition and recapitulation tended to correspond closely in terms of the number of bars of music and the order in which materials reappeared. What I wish to emphasize here is that the habit of mind in those times suggested orderly resolution of contrasts (potential or realized) and a certain architectural perspective towards form. It was the habit to repeat, without extensive alteration, save in transitional passages, entire sections within the total form. Thus "architectural" symmetry was emphasized *where*, as the above discussion of time perception has indicated, *it could not have been actually experienced.*

The possibility of decisive action in *any* arena now seems a much more remote and arbitrary idea. Where a sensitivity to events once bred a decisive response, our awareness of the primacy of processes leads to *deflection* and *redirection*. Resolution is likely to mean, in practical terms, disengagement accompanied by some often temporary accommodation. In the presence of an enormously expanded range of considerations and physical scale, victory and defeat may now be recognized as nostalgic concepts. They were suited to more restricted contexts than those we now inhabit. The larger the number of factors known to exert compelling influence or provide illumination, the larger the corresponding obligation to foresight. One can excuse indifference only on the basis of ignorance. Once one has knowledge of what is involved in our realities (as contrasted with those of earlier times), how then can one justifiably neglect the obligation to consider and to weigh the primary sources of influence upon, for example, one's child, communal concerns, business, or humane growth?

Indeed, such consideration has not been absent from art and from music in particular. In the early decades of this century, Western musical language had grown dense and complex to a degree that seriously weakened the viability of traditional systems of organization, in the eyes of the major creative figures. In earlier eras, the twelve available tempered scale tones within the octave had been, for practical purposes, restricted to use of seven at a time. By the twentieth century, such sub-ordering restraints had been stretched to virtual uselessness. Although, from our perspective, the musical situation during the first few decades of the twentieth century looks turbulent but exhilarating, it was profoundly agonizing for some of the strongest musical personalities of the time, including Debussy, Stravinsky, Schoenberg, and Busoni. A wide variety of paths were tried, and the basic necessity for escape from an over-grown and unhealthily extended edifice, from the elaborate chromaticism of the German Romantics, was generally recognized. Many were concerned with a return to simpler values in some form. Neoclassic or folk-inspired models attracted some, while others sought new ordering principles.

In the early 1920's, Arnold Schoenberg began to employ the principle now called *serialism*. It was necessary, he felt, for pitch materials to be under some overall constraint. The distended traditional tonal system had come to tolerate a virtually free usage of all twelve pitches; it was now necessary to reestablish some form of primacy, of hierarchy. Schoenberg proposed and began to employ an organizational principle based on maximizing the already existing pitch variety, saying that no tone could reappear in the overall musical texture until all the other eleven had been introduced. He further structured the enlarged palette with the condition that the twelve available pitches were to be ordered in a *series*. Such a sequence became the generative substance of each musical composition. In practice, a series was defined not so much by twelve pitch classes represented by the notes of a series as by the eleven intervals separating them. In keeping with his passionate commitment to tradition, from the outset Schoenberg retained elements of contrapuntal technique and traditional formal schemes with his serial method.[1]

---

1. The little-known but major composer Roberto Gerhard, one of Schoenberg's students in Vienna at the time that the latter was first employing the serial method, has observed that it is impossible for any of us now to understand, at a sufficiently real level, how painful the adoption of this new technique was for Schoenberg, how much he and Webern and Berg *suffered* in pulling away even so short a distance from the canons of tradition in which their training had steeped them.

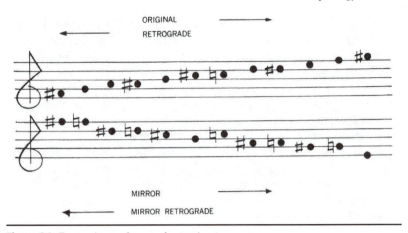

Figure 24. Four primary forms of a twelve-tone row.

The series could take four forms: *original*; *retrograde*, the same series reversed in order; *mirror*, the original intervallic structure in mirror image; and *mirror retrograde*, the mirrored series of intervals taken backwards. There is, of course, no way that a pitch can be mirrored since it is no more than a frequency designation. Melodic intervals, on the other hand, can be described by the number of half-steps separating the two defining notes and whether these are to be taken ascending or descending. It is worth stating that, even before the many refinements and elaborations of the serial method were introduced over the next forty years, one was by no means obliged to make every melody consist of twelve different tones (as has so often been charged by critics of dubious purpose and intelligence). The serial idea involves a few basic principles: *select a number of items* from an array defined by measurement against some reference scale (in the case of pitches, a set of twelve defined by a particular division of the octave, which is itself defined by a doubling of frequency); *put these items in a series* (define an order for the items which at the same time defines an order of inter-item measurements—"intervals" in the case of pitches); and *determine rules for systematically reordering* the items in the series as compositional imperatives require. These insure a minimum level of motivic and harmonic variety as well as consistency. The thoroughgoing classicism of Schoenberg's early efforts with this new technique is evident. They are conservative in every dimension other than pitch. It was only later that he and other began to see the wider implications of this first step.

Of primary long-term importance has been the fact that the serial idea implies the necessity of foreseeing the impact of organizational decisions. The pitch series is resistant. Once a particular pattern is chosen, it cannot be bent to every purpose (though such a wide range of ancillary techniques has by now evolved that this is a less meaningful constraint). In the beginning, at least, one had to consider carefully before committing oneself. Row (series) selection was made on the basis of what sort of materials and musical effect the composer sought. Like all general techniques, serialism can accommodate any number of intentions and personal styles. As the larger implications of the serial principle came to be recognized, it was natural that composers should conceive the idea of applying it to other musical characteristics, to rhythm and dynamics or to formal proportions. The more extensively it was applied—and, of course, any dimension of music that can be quantized can be ordered serially—the more essential it became to understand the properties of the series and to use them as helpful stimuli to musical invention. The danger was in taking on more predisposed dimensions than one was prepared to handle. Just as a particular pitch series defined and restricted, to a degree, the musical results one could obtain, so, too, did a rhythmic or dynamic or timbric series. With "totally serial" music, the precompositional decision-making stage consumes a markedly more demanding portion of the overall compositional process. A multidimensional serial matrix can easily become a convenient source of justification. It is a tempting theoretical apologia for the perhaps experientially unwelcome events that result from the intersection of predetermined processes as they unfold in more or less automatic ways. Still, even in the most complex matrixes, one deals with specified elements, not shifting sample populations or processes, and the length of the normal series is—albeit arbitrarily—set at twelve.

Computer programming has opened up involved speculative horizons and, concurrently, more sobering responsibilities. With the computational resources of the computer and the speeds at which it can characterize the broad effects of varying assumptions, one is in a position to try out ideas that were previously impractical to test. One can immediately go beyond series to more general processes. One can postulate a particular repertoire of materials, set several organizational processes in motion, and obtain with relative convenience a picture of the ways in which they will interact. One is able, that is, to extend considerably the range of one's predictive facility. Not only the ordering of events but also patterns of change (the introduction of deviation from any given norm), degrees of divergence (the relative size of such deviation), and such a basic matter as so-called "continuity can be readily investigated. The computer not only accommodates such inquiry, it tends to demand it. As has been frequently observed, the computer is unable to assist us by making basic decisions that the human programmer has overlooked. It is not in possession of what I have called "understood information," in the discussion of notation; hence, no matter is too basic for definition.

At first, as I have indicated, the programmer and engineer, although forced to make fundamental decisions as a regular course, tended to avoid the radical implications of the fact. They tended to make assumptions that were

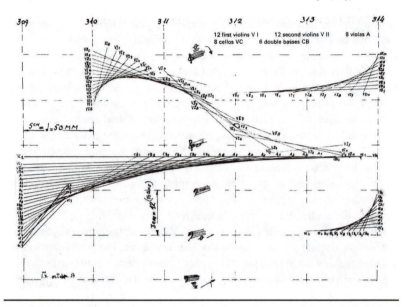

Figure 25. Xenakis' graphic plan for string "sound-masses," bars 309–314 of *Metastasis* (1953–54).

convenient to handle, to adopt patterns that facilitated economical results. If a particular factor required scaling in some way—for example, as in the proper amplitude for successively higher harmonic components of a complex wave form—the assumption was that some constant decrement, say 3 dB per step, would be sufficiently real to serve. A gradually declining series of numerical measurements might be assumed to be exponential quite simply because mathematics has established means for dealing with such orderly models. Hence the suspect nature of all "facilitating assumptions" to the serious musician. One must constantly ask exactly what is being discarded when one allows a particular, well-behaved assumption to define a broad spectrum of what one wishes to be a richly rewarding aesthetic experience. The artist is disquieting to the scientist because of his unwillingness to accept utilitarian compromise.

One composer who has, from the beginning, faced basic questions directly is Iannis Xenakis (b. 1922). Variously active as an engineer, a resistance fighter, and a mathematician, he has struggled to instill in his work a radical reconsideration of musical structure. To him, music is "catalytic: its mere presence permits internal psychic or mental transformations in the same way as the crystal ball of the hypnotist." Music, he feels, includes "a world of sound-masses, vast groups of sound-events, clouds and galaxies governed by new characteristics such as density, degree of order, and rate of change, which require definitions and calculations using probability theory." The diverse roots of Xenakis's energies emerge in his references to "the gratuitous play of a child" and "a mystical (but atheistic) asceticism" as well as to his experiences as a member of the underground and his studies in the essence of Greek historical thought. To my ear, his music is radiant and lean,

Figure 26. Score of *Metastasis*, bars 309–314.

remarkably clear of traditional allegiances to harmonic substance and melodic gesture. His works are compelling samples of previously unknown event-worlds. One can objectify them by virtue of their image-making, formative strength. They stand not on arguments made but on materials revealed. They are above pleading.

One of Xenakis's most basic concerns, most prominent sources of dissatisfaction, is the notion of scaler resources, the organized pitch systems, that is, that have underlaid Western music for centuries. In his seminal book *Formalized Music*[2] he draws three categorical distinctions in musical architecture: "outside-time," "temporal," and "in-time." He draws them with a typically uncompromising severity, reproduced here intact:

> A given pitch scale, for example, is an *outside-time* architecture, for no "horizontal" or "vertical" combinations of its elements can alter it. The event in itself, that is its actual occurrence, belongs to the *temporal* category. Finally a melody or a chord on a given scale is produced by relating the *outside-time* category to a *temporal* category. Both are realizations *in-time* of *outside-time* constructions.

He argues that the "outside-time" category, that which concerns structures set up before and apart from their actual use in a developing musical process, is the most fundamental and least attended-to domain of music:

> ... the tempered diatonic system—the musical "terra firma" upon which all our [*Western*] music is founded—seems not to have been reached either by reflection or by music itself. This is where the next stage [of musical development] will come. The exploration and transformations of this system will herald a new and immensely promising era.

Although one might explore the historical grounds for this argument, there is no denying the provocative effect of his emphasis upon the fundamental importance of distinguishing "structures, architectures, and sound organisms from their temporal manifestations." He is pointing out the clear but often ignored fact that one can distinguish between the structural ordering of the musical materials themselves (a scale, for example) and the actual living sound event as well as the manner in which these living sound events are patterned for an actual, musical purpose (a phrase, for example). A focus of musical concern prior to and thus more fundamental than the stage of sonic realization is essential if composers are to expand the useful scope of their activities, Xenakis thinks.

Some of the strength of this viewpoint derives from its unexpected perspective. But the unfamiliar viewpoint is by no means a rarity now. It is an almost unavoidable by-product of the major new investigative tool of

---

2. *Formalized Music*, Bloomington, 1971; revised edition, Pendragon Press, 1992.

the twentieth century, the computer, with its capacity for trend exploration. Musicians with the intellectual astuteness of Xenakis are beginning to undertake the consideration of form-giving factors that may be employed in directing any temporal flow of sound events. Composer Yuji Takahashi (b. 1938) uses computer programs to define morphological worlds, trying several compositional realizations of one program and then modifying the program so as to achieve more unique and interesting structures. He holds the view that the time proportions of sections within a musical work are of only incidental importance. Duration defines only the width of the experiential window through which we gain access to an arbitrary segment of some statistically defined texture. The length of a section is significantly limited only by the condition that materials be sufficiently exposed so that one may comprehend the nature of the population, the collection of defining conditions. Contrast, says Takahashi, tends to focus attention on time, upon proportions. Consideration of higher levels of continuity—of sameness from one area of a piece to the next—better suits his aims. Distinctions between one segment and another continue to exist but not on the basis of dramatic opposition or arrival, as after the accumulation of a tendency to speed, volume, or density, for example. Rather, identity is based on prearranged conditions (playing technique, pitch registers, degree of overlap between one sound and the next, *etc.*) that may be realized in a statistically large number of ways while still fulfilling the program's basic restrictions. Of course, the composer may prefer certain realizations over others and can still select and reject on the basis of taste.

If one thinks of music as a language—in a technical as well as a metaphorical sense—then one must be concerned with the identity of individual elements (what they represent) and the probability with which one thing follows another. One will necessarily be immersed in a process of considerable sequential complexity. Takahashi regards the computer as a powerful ally in countering such a daunting perspective. Consider music as a world defined by *spaces*—in the mathematical sense of a particular aggregate of items inhabiting a situation that can alter according to a certain number of variables—rather than as, traditionally, a discursive argument drawn from narrative images. This repositioning would help us return to the abstract, "spatial" condition of earlier and also of some non-Western music, he feels. The computer is ideally suited to applying rules of restraint upon aggregates of events that might themselves be generated by statistical rules; it is, in short, good at playing games. Again, as argued in Part II, it is objectively obvious that we risk little in encouraging this and other forms of genuinely radical experiment.

Takahashi has not yet been involved to a large extent with computer-generated sound. Writing his own programs, he has used the machine as a compiler of numerical data which he then translates into musical notation.

The results are played by live musicians—incorporating, not incidentally, the benefits of human variability—and one hears in the results the engaging clarity of the composer's morphological radicalism. One should, optimally, enjoy Takahashi's advantage, hearing multiple realizations of a given program in order to fully appreciate the significance of each considered step in his effort to devise altered frames for musical experience.

Working in a different manner and toward different ends, composer Robert Ashley has nevertheless been equally concerned with revealing particular moments that are possessed of unique quality. He, too, has sought to achieve special musical experiences not by specifying events but by establishing a net of interactive processes that may invite the catch but cannot ensure it.

> I can describe any particular event in terms of what makes up its beauty. But the performer can't recreate from this description. You can take a piece and say that this is a very beautiful moment, but there is no way you can recreate that moment. The moment is the result of a peculiar, ensemble situation that you are listening to. As a composer, I feel, naturally, that I must try to create these social relationships that make music.[3]

Ashley's remarks are premised on his belief that *social relationships*, the particular dynamics of an interactive human situation, generate the special moments with which he is concerned. This stance is as original as Xenakis's focus on the structure of materials that exist before they are subjected to temporal display, but it is totally distinct. Ashley's exploratory work is aided by his relaxed, American pragmatism. He works with what is at hand and consequently his music over the last decade exists apart from a need for standard forms of performance skill. This is not to say, however, that the performance problems are less formidable or that the work lacks effect. By no means. Although it may be erroneous to assume that skill can derive only from practice, and that it therefore belongs primarily to those privileged with certain approved forms of education, we adopt such a position with respect to the performance of art quite routinely. If we assume a slightly different view, one that concentrates on innate capacities or, as the dictionary would have it, "aptitude," then the composer's task might be to provide proper frames within which this *form* of skill could be rewardingly exercised. He attempts to draw forth the natural aptitudes existing in the sympathetic persons or the environmental conditions he finds, for it is virtually axiomatic that traditionally trained musicians will object to putting aside their laboriously acquired, practiced skills and depending for a while on less obvious and automatic functions. Even more basically, they may object to entering into a process that requires a reconstructed view of the performer's function and relationship to his fellows.

---

3. Robert Ashley, with Larry Austin and Karlheinz Stockhausen, in "Conversation," *Source*, Vol. 1, No. 1, 1967.

I interviewed John Cage in 1961, and Robert Ashley, who was also present, made the following extraordinary remarks:

> It seems to me that [Cage's] influence on contemporary music, on "musicians," is such that the entire metaphor of music could change to an extent that—time being uppermost as a definition of music—the ultimate result would be a music that wouldn't necessarily involve anything but the presence of people "would be one that defines "music" without reference to sound. If our awareness of time increased to such a degree that it didn't require that we be informed of time through the medium of sound—if our awareness of time became enlarged or changed to a really radical degree— then it's conceivable that we could do away with sound.[4]

Contrast this with Takahashi's view of the passage of time as no more than an opportunity for getting at a certain distribution of events. Ashley is saying that the substance—in a less weighted word, the *matter*—of a musical experience comes from the participants and the particular environment housing the performance or event. The confluence of natural processes is foremost: some internal to the human interactants and some, perhaps normally unnoticed, generated by the surroundings. Ashley would seem, then, to be more concerned with enlarging the individual's capacity for accepting and processing his experiences than with the sensuous substance itself or the degree and type of order it possesses. His interest is in fostering situations that are remarkable in ways that transcend materials. Fascination with complex, "mysterious" events leads to a concern with the processes that might serve to generate them, and this, in turn, allows an open attitude towards the component sounds and skills themselves.

Ashley's project "The Place Where the Earth Stood Still" is a study of the computer's impact upon the structure of possible ideas. Without direct involvement, the computer, both by its actual and its rumored capacities, stimulates repertoires of ideas that might otherwise remain too unreal to command attention. An instance: If one is in the center of a completely dark room with speakers placed in each of the four corners, and an identical sound program issues simultaneously from each, the sound level will be evenly balanced. Normally, one could determine by means of the human capacity for sound localization one's own relative position as one moved about. Instead, assume that position sensors monitor one's movements and a computer calculates continuously and almost instantaneously what adjustment in levels from the four speakers is necessary to maintain the balance of the center position, regardless of where one stands in the room. Only a collision with one of the walls—an abrupt transfer from one sensory mode to another—would serve to reorient one, and even then one could not know

---

4. This interview is included in Elliott Schwartz and Barney Childs (eds.), *Contemporary Composers on Contemporary Music*, New York, 1967.

relative position within the space, only that one had reached a boundary. In this example, the computer's ability to make extremely rapid and numerous calculations is fundamental to the idea. There are a wide variety of ways in which the computer, even without direct intervention, has altered our concept of forming and the manipulation of processes, and will continue to do so. It is likely that, because of the press of essentially clerical functions requiring its attentions, the computer has not yet been used with appropriate imagination.

Robert Ashley in memoriam ... ESTEBAN GÓMEZ (quartet) (1964)[5]
In the early 1960's, Robert Ashley (b. 1930) wrote a series of four works, "*in memoriam.*" They were addressed not only to the personal and social implications underlying traditional musical institutions (the quartet, concerto, symphony, and opera) but also to a subtle analysis of the kinds of procedures used in establishing their musical repertoires.

He was asking about and revealing the actual meaning of these affiliations to the life of the individual musician and, on another milder level, the meaning of these institutional conventions to the listener. The *quartet* explores the notion of agreement by means of an exquisitely defined concept of *reference sonority.* "Prepare a sonority within which the individual components cannot

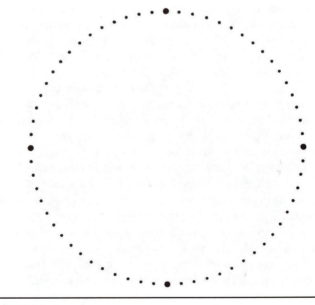

Figure 27. Ashley's score.

5. Published in *source*, Vol. 1, No. 1, 1967.

be distinguished," admonishes the one-page score, continuing with similarly concise yet provocative conditions. The composer at once establishes the requirement of complete apparent homogeneity. (The judgment is made on the basis of the listener's perspective.) The dimensions of the problem are not stated and will depend upon the instrumental and personal make-up of the quartet. One can adjust the size of the task to any convenient level. Four identical instruments will provide less challenge; a group including percussion, bassoon, trombone, and violin would prove more formidable. The concept of reference sonority will absorb perceptive, inventive, and interactive skill on any imaginable level, though it is *not* exclusively dependent upon traditional instrumental skill.

The structure of the work, of the processes that form a given performance, resides in a series of covert deviations from the reference sonority and in the responsibility of each performer to reorder his pattern of four allowed departures (pitch, dynamic, timbre, and density) each time he notices a deviant element other than his own. The pulse that performers establish individually is heard only indirectly through its establishment of the outer temporal limits that a deviant process can consume. Assuming a continuous wind instrument sound, for example, the sixteen beats marking off a single deviation could not take more than the duration allowed by the capacity of one full breath. The pulse functions as a self-imposed guide to the performer, increasing his ability to restrain and therefore render subtle the pace of his deviation, as with a gradual upward glissando in pitch.

Concentration upon the control of one's own departure from the reference sonority (which may occasionally be reduced to the status of a concept during performance if all four performers are deviating simultaneously) will lessen the likelihood of one's noticing another deviant element. With even the finest performances, a considerable inner world of subtly gauged activity results: an affective, graded dissonance. Ashley has noted that *ESTEBAN GÓMEZ* is "a rather 'fast' piece. That is, in the only realm that counts, things happen fairly quickly around the players' decisions, and a lot of things are going on for them." The truth of this observation from the performer's perspective is unquestionable, but the listener is dependent upon his ability to grasp the nature of the forming activity. Even in the score, the composer has resisted indicating the importance of covert alterations, so that the discovery of this fundamental aspect of the work must also, in a sense, be composed by the performance group. For the listener, in a properly extended performance, gradual awakening to the substance of the *quartet* will be tenuous if his listening habits have been confined to event-centered music. Also significantly vague, and therefore demanding for the performers, are the definitions of "timbre" and "density." By implication, Ashley requires a unanimity from his performance group, both on a conceptual and physical plane. He leads them necessarily to the mechanical and conceptual exploration of their instruments and their roles as performers and participants in a group. *ESTEBAN GÓMEZ* is a remarkable achievement and one that should help to make us aware of the restrictive ways in which musical experience has traditionally been defined. An arresting performance can arise not only out of the specification of events or performance techniques in exhaustive chronology as has been our tradition, but from a description of attitudes and forms of activity as well. This work achieves an identity that is retained from one realization to another if one listens on its terms, in spite of the vast variance in sound materials and performance styles it can accommodate.

The Implications of Abundance

All that we have spoken of thus far implies the making of what critic Peter Yates has called "aesthetic instances" by *composition*, the putting together of materials, events, processes, and so on. Historically, composers have achieved by additive construction. Their training has centered on the control of clearly characterized relationships that were built up according to prevailing values and techniques. It is no longer inconvenient to venture several steps beyond the use of a limited repertoire of given items. We can now begin with a surfeit. Our technological capacity for storing, synthesizing, and rapid sampling from diverse sources makes it possible to start off with a practically unlimited store of individual sound items or patterns, a selection as structured or random as one wishes. Such abundance is perhaps the most genuinely new resource with which we are faced. Now, in a demanding, clangorous environment, one may *select rather than construct, sample differently rather than develop*. In short, the composer's function might become essentially subtractive, rather than additive. Working in this way, one could seek an enlarged sensitivity to trends and concurrent streams of eventuation. One could learn to be adaptive and persuasive rather than deterministic and manipulative. The implications of a selective posture are practically and philosophically large, involving the whole notion of art as a message-bearing medium. What distinctions will be meaningful between messages given and selected?

Nobel Prize-winning neurologist Sir John Eccles has underscored the growing attention that is being accorded to inhibitory processes within the human nervous system. No longer does *excitation*, the stimulation of sensory receptors, dominate the experimental physiologist's work. The prevention of sensory overload, the selective and protective mechanisms, operate in part through efferent *inhibition*. Appropriate sensory receptors are, in effect, turned off upon command from the higher centers of the nervous system. Speaking about the importance of subtractive or *decremental* measurements, Eccles invokes the example of sculpture. It is, he notes, what you cut away from the block of stone that produces the statue.

Artists in the 1950's were concerned with abundance in a slightly different sense than here described. Although an interest in Oriental attitudes toward spontaneity might have led to the refinement of descriptive or manipulative techniques, it became instead a rationale for license. Whether an author's unrevised outpourings, as with Ginsberg or Kerouac, artist Jackson Pollock's abundant drippings and spatterings that comprised a total record of the painter's actions, or the endless and decisively exhausting improvisation of jazz's John Coltrane, the impulse was unrestrained genera-tion: total documentation. Spontaneity is, perhaps, outside of the primary thread under discussion here, but it is worth observing that one cannot have it simply by relaxing conscious control. Particularly in the case of such con-tinuous, rapid, and, therefore, necessarily patterned or roughly automated procedures as those employed by the artists mentioned above, this word can have only very limited meaning. The significance of spontaneity here will converge closely on accident, and accidents of a narrowly confined sort. The inertia of subconsciously governed process is not so easily disrupted. We are, perhaps more than we would like to admit, composite records of habits developed and indulged.

Although "complexity" does not inevitably go with "contemporary," their pairing would presently seem almost unavoidable. Composer Ben Johnston has observed that we "have more use today for the ability to concentrate in the midst of distraction than for the intellectual ability to follow intri-cate formal patterns." Value could well accrue, then, not to the production of detailed and crowded textures but to the human selective capacity. We all need to sort, to extract meaningful elements or trends from a confusion of information and experience. The artist has always been particularly selective, but the array from which he drew his materials was always quite manage-able, and aesthetic structures could be conveniently reassembled. Technique, economics, taste, and the practical barriers to rapid information transfer and large-scale retention all served to limit the composer. They do so less now.

The development of computers and powerful analog synthesizing equipment at first generated the obvious meta-organ. As discussed in previous chapters, this has given way to devices that generate not only a variety of sound materials but also relatively complex, self-perpetuating, endlessly permuting arrays of pitches, of temporal and spatial event-patterns. With engineering assistance, Salvatore Martirano has developed a marvelously ambitious, individually sponsored, real-time synthesis capacity. Digitally controlled, the sixteen oscillators of his Sal-Mar construction have continuously variable wave shaping and may be distributed through a twenty-seven-channel system, according to numerous automated and independent routings. The elaborate, touch-sensitive control panel allows rapid but definitely quantized alterations to be imposed in real time upon preestablished (automated) streams of events. Statistically defined pitch and/or timbric arrays are generated within whatever limits of speed and randomness the composer/performer wishes. He is then able to apply—somewhat in the manner of a computer program but with much greater immediacy of feedback—new levels of limitation, more attractive boundary conditions, as he thinks appropriate. Martirano's concept allows him to go beyond the synthesis of desired sound events or more or less orderly progressions to the direct exploration of chains of contingency. Having established a particular "patch" (a pattern of electrical connections between the independent elements or modules of such a synthesizing device), the composer explores it in the way that a variety of scored realizations allows one to explore the morphological assumptions inherent in a particular computer program. The stress here, however, is upon during-the-fact evaluation. One has the invaluable capacity to deflect trends and restructure references *in medias res* by practiced use of the digital control panel. To date, the computer is still used constructively, but Martirano's extended synthesizer deals in real time with preestablished fabrics of aural abundance. There are, of course, other ways that such basic arrays could be established and subjected to filtering and directing. Storage of any desired, naturally occurring, or instrumental materials as a readily available, massed resource might prove sonically richer than a digitally achieved selection, although harder to shape at the level of trend or process. Nevertheless, the essential reorientation involved here is of profound significance.

The traditional "given" material for composition has included particular groupings of instruments, each with inherent limitations, and a certain repertoire of generative and accompanimental figurations defined by the prevailing common practice. This need no longer be the case. One may, by electronic means, select almost any human or environmental factor as the basis for an independently established continuity—an extracompositional given. Through its prior and disinterested existence, this continuity becomes the passive side of a dialogue whose active compositional element is reactive/selective. Gordon Mumma has been exploring the application of electronic circuitry to musical purposes since the mid-1950's. His design expertise allows him to build electronic devices that are integral to his compositional aims and has led him to explore the potential for several pregnant forms of dialogue: man with circuits, a man with himself. This may be accomplished by giving separate attention to the physical or mental process necessary to produce an event and to its actual sound. In a work entitled *Beam* (1969), the movements of the string-playing performers are registered by what the composer calls "bow-arm coordinate sleeves." These sense the spatial orientation of the arm at every instant, and signals so derived become the basis for controlling the electronic processing of the basic instrumental sound.

When control signals are automatically derived from the sound materials themselves or the actions necessary to produce them, Mumma characterizes the process and the music as "cybersonic." Of very considerable significance is the fact that his approach allows the derivation of numerous streams of information from the overall range of physical and mental activity of only one performer. The individual becomes an effectively larger resource than previously. In other works, Mumma's electronic circuitry, as in the case of Martirano's extended synthesizer, establishes an automatic flow of events so that, in performance, the composer is engaged selectively instead of constructively; it provides the composer with textured fabrics rather than individual items. It is, after all, not necessary to restrict the nature of extra-compositional "given" materials. Given a sufficiently inventive perspective and the means to achieve an appropriately large physical control, the flow of traffic, the flight trajectories of birds, or the pattern of activity in an actual team-sport contest might conceivably become the material tapped and abstracted for aesthetic ends.

Gordon Mumma: Hornpipe (1967)[6]
According to the composer (b. 1935) this work is a musical interface between the Machine Age and the Electronic Era. Mumma provides basic sound material acoustically by playing a French horn, often substituting a double reed for the normal mouthpiece. This method produces a considerably more complex spectral distribution than is normal to the horn. Two miniature microphones are used to feed the live sound into analog control circuits. Acoustical and electronic feedback loops are combined into a resonant system which is balanced at the beginning of a performance, and therefore silent.[7] The first sounds of the horn during a performance unbalance the electronic circuits of the resonant system. In the process of rebalancing itself, the electronic array produces sound heard through loudspeakers.

Hornpipe involves the storage of results from a systematic aural probing of the performance environment by the performer. The horn sounds continually unbalance the associated electronic circuits, thereby triggering critically resonant amplifiers which reinforce the acoustical resonances of the performance space. These amplifiers can, in turn, be reinforced or overridden by sounds from the horn. As indicated, the innovative power of Mumma's concept derives from his use of preexistent or self-generating

---

6. Recorded, as realized by Mumma in an abridged performance, on *Mainstream* MS 5010.

7. *Feedback* is a principle of great importance in the control of processes of any sort. It was, for example, employed to govern the build-up of steam pressure in the first Fulton engines. A system acts upon and transforms material in some way. There is, in other words, an *input* and an *output* corresponding to the subject material before and after its alteration. In the simplest terms, feedback indicates the recycling of a portion of the output from any system back to the input for the purpose of controlling its further activity. In the case of a resonant system, the output fed back into the input can be used to reinforce the natural mode of oscillation, thereby strengthening its stability, or such reinforcement can be withheld.

materials rather than from large numbers of musicians following detailed instructions and depending upon conventions of tempo and meter in order to achieve rough unanimity. He avoids the inconvenience of dealing with unwieldy and often uncooperative masses of performers and is nevertheless able to achieve large-scale and abundantly detailed musical results.

Hornpipe is of variable length and is derived from several earlier compositions, including *Horn and Second Horn* of 1965. *Horn* involves three persons: the composer/performer and two assistants who influence the potentially automatic circuitry by adjusting its limits and biases. In *Hornpipe*, Mumma performs the work entirely without assistance, with the electronic control and sound generation devices neatly packaged in a metal box strapped to his waist. What remains is a characteristic process of acoustical probing (sounding a horn call, evaluating the result, reorienting oneself, lobbing another sustained sound into the environment, and so on); the gradual emergence of characteristic electronic sound components, generated by Mumma's equipment and serving as a powerful reactive element; and the developed dialogue between this omnipresent synthesized ambience and the corrective/selective prowess of the horn's unnatural cries. The actual sounds of the work change, of course, from performance to performance, as will be true of any process-oriented work. The dominant sonority in *Hornpipe*, however, curiously and characteristically straddles a canyon between two apparently incompatible sonic realms: the edgy, buzzing presence of the electronic signals and the double reed, on the one hand, and the predictably mellow resonance of the natural French horn on the other.

Mumma has now come to know the essential work—that is to say, the total configuration of acoustic and electronic elements—so intimately that the solo form is definitive. Simultaneous, independent and overlapping ostinato oscillations are often employed; the periodic slurring back and forth between two component elements of the pieces's basic harmonic set results in a complex set of rocking pitch exchanges. The speed of these hypnotic, rocking ostinatos can be adjusted by electronic and acoustical means, producing a sonorous fabric that is both abrasively assertive and resonantly appropriate to the performance space. There is an almost total absence of what might be called gestural content or dramatic eventfulness. Mumma's music is undeniably strong, phenomenalistic rather than relational. It rejects any taint of the seductive. It is theatrical in that the sound resulting from the composer's restrained and rather proper movements in performance is grandly out of proportion to one's expectations. On another plane, *Hornpipe's* combination of breath-limited brass sounds and inhuman durational capacities of the electronically reinforced resonances evokes a contradictory lyricism, suggests a transformed and only painfully maintained human strand in a context of potentially unlimited, automated power.

The man-machine dialogues present in Mumma's music have been based primarily upon signals derived from external, physical movements—the mouth-hand coordination involved in playing the horn or the bow-arm movements of string players. More intimate sources of information have been tapped by others, including David Rosenboom (b. 1947) and Alvin Lucier. An autonomic process (minute patterns of electrical excitation associated with muscular movements, for example) may, by means of appropriate detection devices, be made to influence other external equipment or mental and physical outputs from the same body. As in the case of biofeedback training for medical purposes, the establishment of feedback loops is the key to gaining conscious control; the definition of such abilities and their resolving power is in most cases still quite limited. Normally, the utilization of brain potentials or other internal bodily functions as sources of information or control are limited to presence or absence, a simple off-on relationship, though amplitude factors may also be involved. It will no doubt be possible to go beyond these restricted dimensions relatively soon, as the work of Manfred Clynes suggests through demonstrations of the potential for increased analytic definitions of the electrical activity in the brain.

Alvin Lucier: Music for Solo Performer (1965)
The path-breaking effort in the use of internally derived, nonmuscular control functions was made by Lucier (b. 1931) in collaboration with Edmand Dewan, Gordon Mumma, and William Ribbens.[8] A performer and assistant come onstage, and the latter affixes electrodes to the soloist's scalp. Subsequently, the performer attempts to generate and suppress the occurrence of alpha activity in his brain and, thus, to guide the presence and absence of sound issuing from auxiliary sources. The approximately ten-cycle-per-second alpha signals from the soloist's brain are detected and amplified to drive a number of loudspeakers deployed throughout the performance area. The ten-cycle signal is not frequency-multiplied but, rather, is used to drive the speakers directly so that the physical excursion (movement in and out) of their cones occurs at this same rate. Large speaker cones directly face suitable resonant sound sources—gongs, bass drums, or the undamped strings of a piano—and the air currents generated by the cones will drive them, producing sound. The electrical signals entering the speakers, then, are not directly audible but serve to stimulate the production of sounds from other resonating surfaces by mechanically generated air pressures.

Of course, longer bursts of alpha activity will result in growing loudness for certain of the freely resonating instruments, short bursts in very slight responses. The limited range of actual sonic variety—all on, all off—is

---

8. Much of the factual detail for the following discussion is drawn from Gordon Mumma's article "Alvin Lucier's Music for Solo Performer 1965" in *Source*, Vol. 1, No. 2, 1967.

mitigated in some versions of the work by the addition of previously recorded alpha activity stored on tape and frequency-translated into the audio range. This serves as a ghostly obbligato to the real-time control functions generated by the performer's efforts. Conscious decisions on the part of the performer, the desire to continue or terminate activity, may or may not be directly enacted, since even well-trained subjects have only a limited ability to define consciously such usually autonomic functions. The real drama of the performance, then, is obscured by the fact that the listener, although aware of the strange drama of electrodes being affixed to the soloist's head and of the curious mix of medical, ritualistic, scientific, religious, and musical elements, is still in essential ignorance as to where difficulties are encountered and when success is achieved.

The work is bounded by the performer's limited capacity to act decisively in response to his judgments and by the digital (on-off) nature of the control signals he can produce. (Another view might find this quintessentially human, systematically derived indeterminacy more than agreeable.) To a certain degree, an analog (continuous variation) element has been added by the use of resonant instruments that, being physical, can respond only in gradually accumulative or dissipative fashion to stimulating impulses of any sort. Variety in the sonic result can be introduced by the ways in which the assistant routes the performer's internally generated signals and by the audible addition of prerecorded and frequency-translated oscillations. Essentially, however, the more substantial elements of a performance would appear to derive from the topical, contextual dissonance—unexpected juxtapositions of circumstances, action, and response—and from the imposition of further decisions on the part of the assistant.

The provocative implications of this composition are considerable, however, as are those of many of Lucier's remarkably innovative works. As our understanding of the significance of cerebral potentials rises and as our abilities to detect with precision their frequency, origin, and amplitude become more reliable, one can foresee nonphysical generation of control on a more detailed and multifaceted level than now conceivable from a conductor who is necessarily encumbered by his body and the range of physical coordination it can manage. Further, as mentioned in earlier chapters, experiments have been done with deriving sound materials directly from the potentials of the brain through frequency translation. The first steps have already been taken.

In what amounts to a critical aside, let us examine the practical merit in proceeding with the sort of realignment of musico-aesthetic materials under discussion here. What immediate meaning will these restructurings have while knowledge of human perception, cognition, and emotional behavior remains as limited as it is today? Psychoacousticians and researchers in other branches of psychology are currently studying the interlocking domains of perception, attention, memory, cognition, and language in growing numbers and with apparent profit. Electronic instrumentation in the service of finemeasurement discrimination with computer sifting and analysis of data is largely responsible for present advances. One should, however, be circumspect about reversing the historical tendency to produce technical innovation on the basis of analyzing natural systems. Such a turnabout developed in the 1960's when digital systems and logic models which had proved workable in the context of computers were then used to explain the functioning of the human nervous system. Analogy is an honored investigative method, but its application merits some caution.

Given experimental evidence from psychoacousticians, for example, it is difficult to gauge its utility, to determine what contribution it makes to our understanding of the mechanisms of aesthetic response, and, thus, how it can aid us in enhancing experience. Experimental psychology operates within limitations of context and materials that are rigorously constrained (and therefore blatantly artificial) compared with those a listener faces. All the more so, it would seem, in the case of more recent experiments in musical presentation. But the adaptive capacity of human intelligence has proved itself equal to demands that appear objectively insurmountable even after the fact. One examines diverse new directions, then, well aware that not all will flower. There is no telling which will prove the genuine progenitor or a catalytic agent that deflects the aesthetic course in our divergently evolving day. That new and presently unnatural materials and experiential ideals will be used cannot be questioned. The enacted history of mankind repeatedly demonstrates our initial fear but subsequent absorption of whatever means are uncovered for enlarging and intensifying first the exploration of and later the control of experience.

Still, there are, as we have seen, human systemic limitations. One such is our capacity to pay attention. Only a limited number of sensory items can be attended to at one time. The full processing of the elements of one stream of information, that is, can only be accomplished at the cost of other information which arrives while such processing is going on. Conversely, the effort to attend equally to all incoming items of sensory information will necessarily result in a relatively less complete processing of any one item. Even under the assumption that biochemical means might be found for expanding our capacity to process information, there will still be necessary restrictions based upon time of nerve-pulse transmission, the latent period for receptor cells in various sense modalities, and so on. The limits referred to here are further narrowed (that is, more time is consumed) if one attempts to switch from one sense modality to another—from sight, for example, to sound, to touch.

Experiment in controlled mixed-media or with extraordinarily complex organizational-rational procedures should ideally proceed under an enlarged practical understanding of human abilities. Independently coherent strains of information can be effective in simultaneous presentation through rapid switching and sampling from one to another. The presence of multiple and even contrasted sources of internal experience is not excluded. The key is redundancy—the allowances the artist has made for the likelihood that a certain proportion of the information that the presentation provides will in effect be lost. Whatever methods the artist uses to expand our experience, to divert and deepen, will finally depend upon, first, the pattern of preexistent learned responses and, second, the degree to which the essence of the experience matches the observer's more basic internal mechanisms. If the breadth of relevance and detail of learned categories continue to shrink, as I believe they are now, better knowledge of the second area will become rapidly more imperative.

Krzysztof Penderecki: Threnody for the Victims of Hiroshima (1960)[9]
This work is representative of an essentially monophonic, texturally dense yet noncontrapuntal approach to music that focused international attention on Polish composers during the late 1950's.

— Highest tone of the instrument (no definite pitch)
— Play between bridge and tailpiece
— Arpeggio on 4 strings behind the bridge
— Percussion effect: strike the upper sounding board of the violin with the nut of bow or finger tips.
— Very rapid nonrhythmized tremelo

Figure 28. Symbols used in Penderecki's *Threnody.*

9. Penderecki's *Threnody* is recorded on RCA VICS-1239.

Written in 1960, it is uncommonly intense, its motivation certainly emotional and possibly political. In this work and others, Penderecki (b. 1935) relied on a severely limited gestural content that was direct, brutal, and elementally simple: a succession of vigorous, independent attacks. Fifty-two strings participate in the ten-minute *Threnody*, which explores idiomatically appropriate sonic areas. The players are repeatedly asked to produce the highest bowed sound possible on their instruments, sounds of considerable inherent tension. This effect, like the work's massed clusters that span varying but roughly specified ranges, has no clearly defined pitch content. The clusters are instrumentally realized analogs to electronically derived noise bands. Other atypical performance techniques are used as well, including knocking on the instrument's body and bowing the strings at unusual angles. Penderecki has admitted the influence of electronic models on his constructive procedures, both in method (the building up of dense, nonharmonic bands of sound from individual instrumental lines, as one might with electronic oscillators) and sonorous ideal.

Threnody is a work of undeniable immediacy. The bold focus upon sonic literalism, the screaming of massed high strings, the clatter of percussive knocks, and the cluster walls simulating the energy of explosions are viable as an occasional response, unlikely as a sustained psychic or physical condition. The importance of this work is limited compared, for example, with the more dimensional "noise" world of Michael von Biel's (b. 1937) *String Quartet No. 2* (1962)[10] or, in quite a different way, with the massed statistical detail of much of Xenakis's work. Penderecki established the potential force of raw sound not alone over the experimentalist but also over the unsophisticated individual listener. His work of this period demonstrates how directly an audience can be manipulated by the sheer force of the sounds themselves. Penderecki's utilization of timbric invention is limited, although perhaps intentionally so, focusing on those areas with expressionistic immediacy. His work also raises the question of how well an essentially one-dimensional stream of information can engage our attention and satisfy our aesthetic needs over the course of a more extended familiarity—or whether, in fact, a concern with the durability of aesthetic experience is relevant now.

The composer cannot have been unaware of the limitations of musical statement that remains so close to a single, though elaborated, line. At various moments in the work, unisons become not only the generative base for cluster expansion or the final focus of a narrowing pitch range, but suggest as well the functions of drone reference and fragmentary motivic structure. Classically, the scope of monophonic performance vehicles (solo string instruments, for example), has been expanded, by implication, to achieve a larger musical space. What is essentially a single succession of events can suggest "lines"

---

10. Published by Universal Edition.

by means of timbric and pitch range separations that characterize several discriminable classes. Archetypal examples here might be the solo violin or cello works of J.S. Bach. Physically, our perceptual capacities tend to support the effectiveness of such multidimensional illusions. We are disposed, for example, to separate pitch sequences that cover a sufficiently wide pitch range into several separate continuities, and our ability to discriminate order and timings in one or the other tends toward exclusiveness. If a listener attempts to track the upper components of a fairly rapid sequence, for example, he will lose the ability to report timing and even sequence properties of the lower pitches. In its simplest form, an alternation of two pitches, the point at which what has been heard as an alternation separates into two independent streams of repeated notes is called the *trill threshold*. It is dependent upon the rate of presentation as well as the width and ratio of the interval separating the two defining pitches. The trill threshold is one of many psychoacoustic phenomena that have yet to be fully explored in *musical* contexts. It has been amply demonstrated in traditional contexts that music dependent upon highly deflected single lines can sustain itself powerfully either through a strongly characterized sense of root or drone, from which and back to which the melodic inflection strays, as in some Eastern music, or from the illusory construction of multiple lines by sufficient differentiation of pitch, timbre, and timing.

Penderecki has forsworn these means in favor of the inherent force of sensory materials. It is conceivable that such a choice might prove reasonable as a general procedure, although the materials themselves would need more inner detail. They would need, that is, to accommodate continual search of their ongoing microstructure and reward moment-to-moment switches in attentiveness. The composite profile of the succession itself would have to be less elementally predictable. It is, perhaps, analogous, to individual oratorical skill: a continuous flow of imagery, of allusion and illusion commanding and variegated enough to engage continuously a public of diverse backgrounds. Penderecki's work is related to our earlier discussion of art that operates below the level of culturally established—and, therefore, to some degree relative—norms for values and response.

Changing Views of Experience

New morphological thought and practice need not necessarily be connected with technology. They may involve shifts in perspective—the role one is expected to play as a listener or a composer—or an interest in unexpected superpositions: medium upon medium, purpose upon purpose, even stacked cultural vantage points. New attitudes have developed regarding improvisational activity, the limits of active and passive involvement, of skilled or unskilled relationships to musical experience. To begin with, we might examine the notion of perspective shifting. Adopting a visual metaphor, one might be said to have a certain psychological proximity to the events he is experiencing. Of course there is a physical correlate musically: nonreverberance and enhanced high-frequency response imply physical proximity to the ear's position-sensing mechanism. But if one takes "perspective" more in the sense of a psychological distance—the norm being our attitude in receiving information during daily life—then less familiar states of proximity might be termed *close, multiple,* or *distant* perspectives.

In the visual metaphor, *close* perspective would involve the relative enlargement of event size and the consequent slowing down of the whole process of receiving and evaluating component items in a succession. The huge color-field canvases of painter Mark Rothko are often seen deliberately hung so that it is impossible to step back far enough to gain sufficient physical distance to take in the whole at one glance. Unable to register instantaneously the proportions or color balances of the whole in the way a painting is usually apprehended, the viewer is forced to search visually and store impressions in time with a perhaps capricious but nonetheless specific chronology. One has this feeling in La Monte Young's *The Tortoise, His Dreams and Journeys* and in some of the music of Terry Riley and Steve Reich where an extremely close perspective is used.[11] There is to this perspectival mode a certain obsessive quality, a consciousness of experiential texture as opposed to the articulation of detailed relationships. The pace of evolution in these works is slowed down to a degree that "events," as musicians normally think of them, do not seem important. If the listener accepts the experience of the magnified sonic stream, he can scan the aural fabric. Slight, normally "unimportant" deviations will assume a new status. The ability of such music to engross the cooperative listener may not be unlike the fascination one experiences in using a microscope or in observing, through microcinematic techniques, the course of minute events of which we normally remain unaware.

It would appear to be axiomatic that anything we can do to enlarge and generalize our overall perspective as individual human beings will consequently improve the flexibility and farsightedness of our thought. An occasion that offers us a convenient opportunity to observe in a new way should in itself be of value. The retarded flow of musical texture deprives one of the potential for discursive argument, for rhetoric or relational substance in a traditional Western mold. It undercuts the affective, anti-inertial quality of skewing in form, phrase, or gesture, Conversely, it removes the implied yet coercive obligation under which the listener normally functions; one is no longer bound to register significant events, characterizing them properly

---

11. See discussion of Reich's *Piano Phase*, pp. 164–166. Young is represented by a privately distributed recording, and Riley by several Columbia records, most notably *In C* on MS 7178.

for storage and later comparison. Meaning within the context of such radical slowdown does not come from logical trains of inference but from the freely evolving content of scanning procedures the individual follows without compulsion. The saturation of close perspective, then, is one of extent and it is *time*-dependent. Evaluations are privately achieved. They are inductively pursued on the basis of an individually extracted experience.

Multiple perspectives might be illuminated through a reconsideration of modulation. Recall that this process involves the superimposition of one stream or collection of information upon another, one becoming in some sense a stencil within the limits of which we view the substance of the other. Modulation increases our distance from the basic material and in extreme cases may completely overturn or transmute the original values or structure of the two combined continuities. One stream of events (in technical language, the *program*) need not be continuously applied to another (the constant component is termed the *carrier*), but there may be a series of changing influences, or programs, overlaid.

Los Angeles artist John Stehura (b. 1943) has evolved the notation of *fields* in cathode ray tube presentations.[12] He defines a "field" as an area in space having a certain effect upon anything entering it. The sun could be considered a point with such a field of influence. In practical, two-dimensional terms, as on the face of an electronic display tube, the basic image will change as it nears a field-defining point; it may get brighter or darker, enlarge, burst into points, or undergo axial distention.[13] * In visual terms, a basic image or pattern is moved about a screen, each area of which has been assigned a distinct modulating influence. Thus, at any given moment, the pattern may be under the influence of several different perspectives or modulating fields, the proportions of which will change continuously as the basic image moves.

Aural analogs to this process can be imagined. Basic sound continuities could be modified depending, for example, on spatial position or frequency-band discrimination. Numerous installations have been devised since the mid-1960's whereby the physical position of visitors in an environment, or the sounds they made, trigger other visual or aural events. Capacitive fields can be influenced by the presence of human bodies, increasing or slowing the flow of electrical current in a control circuit that activates audio

---

12. The cathode ray tube (CRT) has been basic to television receivers, oscilloscopes, and similar electronic display devices. A stream of electrons generated by a "gun" at the base of the tube is directed by electromagnetic fields so that it rapidly and completely scans the phosphorescent coating on the inner surface of the large end of the CRT. The patterns of darkness and florescence caused by this electron beam result in pictorial information that we can read on the outer tube face.

13*. For a more complete description of Stehura's and other experiments in new graphic, cinematic, holographic, and video presentation, see Gene Youngblood, *Expanded Cinema*, New York, 1970.

oscillators or a tape recorder, for example. Photoelectric cells paired with light-beam sources can establish light circuits that can be unknowingly broken by persons moving about an environment; pressure-sensitive switching devices can be simply implanted in the floor, registering the passage of spectators about a space. These or similar devices allow one to control programmed sound sources or simple synthesizing equipment so that casually occurring or performed movement in an environment can directly influence, even create, corresponding sonic events and successions.

One of the most serious drawbacks of such environmental-interaction constructs is their essentially *canonic* nature or, even more objectionably, the immediate, one-to-one correspondences between stimuli and the responses they generate. The difficulty in such a dependent exchange is to achieve a satisfactory balance between arbitrary results and transparently obvious relationships. One needs an interactive reciprocation rather than a simple reaction whose basis becomes quickly evident. Canon is a musical convention whereby a continuing and orderly relationship allows one sequence of events to generate others that will be compatible with the original within certain limits. This may involve a pitch sequence whose intervals are sequentially repeated at another pitch level and displaced in time, while retaining their rhythmic identity and not violating the rules of the harmonic practice concerned. The emotive and intellectual impact of canonic practice depends upon two general conditions, then: first, that there will be an orderly relationship inviolably maintained between the original and the translated copy or copies and, second, that the new structure will, in turn, conform to some further set of conditions. It is this further coherence and the foresight and inventiveness its fulfillment implies that stir the listener. In most of the sound environments mentioned above, this second condition is not fulfilled. The result is facile and sterile after initial curiosities are assuaged.

The above reservations do not preclude the possibility that fields of influence such as Stehura has imposed on representational visual images (faces, planetary representations, *etc.*) could be applied fruitfully in audio contexts. This is already paralleled by the manner in which computers can impose restraints of varying stringency upon ongoing calculations and, hence, upon the morphology of sounds synthesized or formal structures specified. To reemphasize: modulation or multiple perspective does not correspond to montaging techniques. The *superimposition* of several extracts from independently existing continuities—newspapers, television fare, filmed sequences, records—is not equivalent to the *confluence* of the forming properties or processes that characterize component continuities in modulation. In the second case, interaction is more profound, to some degree analogous to the way in which chemical compounds differ from simple mixtures. Multiple perspective depends on a saturation of distinct experiential perspectives concurrently held.

Cross-cultural influences are hard to meld without sacrifice, although it is evident that actual melds are imperative if the disappointments of translation are to be overcome. Now that the Japanese have mastered Western art forms there has arisen an opportunity for genuine, radical cross-cultural compounds. Foremost among those who have confronted this problem is Tru Takemitsu (b. 1929). A man with a keen ear and empathetic responsiveness both to the traditions of his own country and those of the West, Takemitsu has directly tested his capacity for resolving diverse roots without unreasonable loss in such works as *November Steps* and *Dorian Horizon*.[14] Here we can feel the profound sense of spaciousness and the unfamiliar attitude toward the pacing of events that characterize the Japanese traditions, while the language of the music remains basically Western and thoroughly elegant in its craftsmanship.

Salvatore Martirano: L.'s G.A., for gassed-masked politico,
helium bomb, two films, and two-channel tape (1970)[15]
A uniquely forceful mixed-media creation, this work was generated in 1968 by Martirano (b. 1927) in collaboration with filmmaker Ronald Nameth (b. 1942) and poet Michael Holloway, who performed the part of the "gassed-masked politico." In addition to this narrator's dramatic role, two other elements comprise a performance: Martirano's formative two-track tape composition and two Nameth films that are shown side by side. L.'s G.A. fractionates, inflects, and transforms, updating some revered American lines (Lincoln's Gettysburg Address). The politico postures in carefully prescribed ways, taking his action and recitation cues from a twenty-five-minute tape montage of concrete and electronic sounds. The tape is in seven sections ("Four score [*sic*] and seven ...") whose proportions are drawn from the Fibonacci series (1, 1, 2, 3, 5, 8, 13, *etc.*). The films generate a visual force that matches the aural power of the composer's music. The politico/narrator appears as an ominous, recurring motif, along with a multitude of other clothed and unclothed figures, images of atrocity and other manifestations of chaos. The live performer, dressed in helmet, gas mask, flight suit, boots, and black leather jacket, is dwarfed by his enormous, distorted, floating or strobed representations on film. The effect of the visual portion of L.'s G.A. is to underscore the implications in the text and music without ever lapsing into obvious illustration (the sort of predictable correspondences criticized above). The whole is an antiwar manifesto of howling, sledge-hammer force.

---

14. These and other Takemitsu works are available on RCA and Deutsche Grammophon Gesellschaft records.

15. *L.'s G.A.* is included on a Polydor record of Martirano's music, Pol. 245001.

Both montage and multiple perspective operate in this work, although the former appears almost exclusively in the filmed elements. Martirano has acted as a combiner and melder of materials in a far wider sense than has traditionally been the case with theatrical presentations. The music forms the processes of motion, speech, and imagery. The whole derives impetus from the aptness of the composer's transformational instinct. The text is one of the most basic documents that shape the American child's abstract image of his country. Lincoln's words are fixed in each of our minds, although their meaning probably resides very little in their literal content by now. His phrases are part of American mythology. Martirano has newly and ferociously etched Lincoln's words in the mind by modulating them with stereotypical accents as in the following passage from the score:

Tape:	sirens, everything very loud snap to attention, hold until 17:27	17:02–17:19
Tape:	animal howl	17:19–17:27
	raise fist—*DIE VOILD*—loud, distorted and punctuated with fist	17:27–17:32
Tape:	cock crow—	17:32–17:34
	VILL—voice distorts in high Nazi rage	17:34–17:35
Tape:	cock crow—*MMMM*—high squeak—	17:35–17:39
	sirens dying out—*WERY*—pause—*LITTLE*—	17:39–17:58
Tape:	silence clipped and loud, *NOTE—NOR LONG*—	
	REMEMBA—VAT VEE SAY HE-AH;—	
	BUT EET CAN NEV A FORGET—VAT—	
	DAY—DEED—HE-AH	

What horror these once reverent phrases exude under the influence not of the German language itself but of our affective response to the implications of the residual accent. At a later point in the work—specifically (and hilariously) with the words "That we here highly resolve"—another modulating influence is introduced. The composer directs that the helium bomb be turned on while the speaker enunciates with a mannered lisp. The effect of the helium is to raise the pitch of the speaker's voice approximately an octave since the gas is less dense than normal air and thereby allows the vocal cords to vibrate more rapidly. The effect is astonishing, an implausible yet undeniable transformation. It would appear to be the ultimate in outrageous modification of these hallowed materials but it is not. The text continues, incorporating Holloway's linguistic transformations and interpolating live imitations of the tape's animalistic shrieks:

THAT THE NATION SHALL, UNDER GOD, OINK-OINK, OINK-OINK, HAVE A NEW BIRTH—BLAH, BLAH, BLAH, BIRTH—OF FREEDOM—WAP, SMACK, SMICH, WOOP, sucked in lip, pushed out cheek noises, *AND THAT THE GOVERNMENT, EE-AW, EE-AW, EE-AW,* nasal donkey, *OF THE PEOPLE, HONK,* long voice chord like a donkey bray …

This continues at a frenzied pitch until the final two minutes when the tape begins a gross, drunken parody of "My Heart at Thy Sweet Voice" from *Samson et Delilah* by Saint-Saëns. During these final, withering moments the movie screens are filled with gorgeous, stop-action sequences of flower bloomings, as the politico gradually falls in exhausted disgust, repeating, "If it's sour, throw it out."

The levels of process operating here are almost too numerous involves a saturation of *quantity,* a profusion of samples from divergent sources. It is not, therefore, unrelated to the methods of *L.'s G.A.,* although in the present case rapid succession is a more prominent defining element than are overlaid influences. We hear an avalanche of brief bits of information—each coherent in itself—in such rapid succession that our ability to process or evaluate them is overreached. This kind of perspective has been more often exploited visually than aurally, as in the work of filmmaker Stan Brakhage. Dealing with images that cut every few frames, although maintaining a general thematic content, he may superimpose them on a second continuity where field is changing with great speed—a sequence filmed from a rapidly moving car, for example. The overall impression is dazzling, producing— if one makes an effort to comprehend—numbness and headache in rather short order. Or one can view from a certain distance, in which case it all becomes a textural blur. In order to involve themselves usefully in such an area, musicians, it would seem, will need to learn more about the nature of representational audio imagery, about the nature of aural and temporal information processing. For example, John Cage's rapid cut *Williams Mix* (1952) requires approximately 600 recordings to be made on tape and spliced together in very brief segments; the eight tape tracks so constructed are played simultaneously over a four-minute period. Faced with overload, one soon moves away to a more remote perspective, allowing the conglomerate to wash over one in a blur without attempting to register individual identities. As from any distant vantage point, the value of detail is sacrificed for coherence of larger shapes.

Ben Johnston: Knocking Piece (1963)[16]
Written for two players utilizing only the interior surfaces of a piano, this work by Ben Johnston (b. 1926) is a study in rapidly shifting perspectives. Although the most obvious patterns of rapid replacement or alternation

---

16. Published in *Source,* Vol. 1, No. 2, 1967.

Figure. 29. *Knocking Piece.* For two percussionists to play on the inside of a grand piano. The sustaining pedal can and should be used, *ad lib.* Pitch should be used only as color, if at all. Typical piano sounds should be avoided. The same sound should be used for successive notes which have the same speed, but contrasting sounds (to varying degrees) should enter with each change of note speed. The equal marks across bar lines mean that the same note speed should be maintained in spite of a change in notation. In general, specific kinds of sounds should predominate within a given phrase. All sounds should relate to knocking. A general dynamic level is given for each phrase (within boxes, at phrase beginnings). Changes of dynamic level are also indicated. The tempo of the opening is at performers' discretion; it is strict thereafter. Not all the notes must be played. Rests are permitted if rhythmic patterns are clear. [notes by the composer]

involve changing materials, there is a more subtle approach to what I have called distant perspective or the saturation of quantity implied in *Knocking Piece*. It is concerned with discrete, shifting reference, where the precise definition and comprehension of one moment (in terms of pitch, tempo, or irregular rhythms) is necessary to properly gauge one's reorientation during the next. The performance involves a series of contingent plateaus assumed in rapid, unrelenting sequence. The performer is obliged to command material based on an adjusted relationship to what has preceded while at the same time making preparations to abandon it. The process is extraordinarily demanding for performer and listener. The player cannot recover from an error since everything is constantly shifting and, if he falters, his partner will already have progressed to a stage beyond that which he needs as a reference. Each moment is nonetheless specific in each point. A detailed treatment of the first few bars of the work will make the general, braided evolution more evident. Though this description is made from the standpoint of player two, a similar interdependency obtains for player one. Player two is silent during the first two-beat bar. He begins in the second but must play three equal beats in the time of the two he has just heard from player one. Continuing in the third and fourth bars, he must readjust his response, performing a group of nine evenly spaced knocks whose tempo is derived from the materials of the first player's third bar. Specifically, player two must play five even beats within the time of four of player one's and then continue with this unit four more times to total nine. This process is repeated again in player two's fifth and sixth bars, except that this time the reference five against four is drawn from a new tempo first sounded in player one's fourth bar (and which player one has obtained previously from player two). The second player must detach himself from involvement with the tempo of his final four knocks in the first group of nine in order to register player one's new tempo.

Johnston's process is not directly parallel to the rhythmic practices of the early totally serial pieces, as, for example, in the piano pieces of Stockhausen published during the early 1950's. Here, one finds indications like:

This directive[17] requires the performer to *simultaneously* perform two levels of proportional abstraction, to form one relational construct and then, without physically enunciating it, to use it as reference for a second-level derivation which is actually performed. This second-order process can be directly achieved by human performers, I believe, only as an abstractly derived approximation. Johnston's proposal, however, *can be performed*, although the complications of interrelational demands as well as intrarelational assessments are formidable. The composer carefully admonishes the players:

---

17. From the opening of *Klavierstücke No. 2* by Karlheinz Stockhausen.

If the unity and simplicity of the knocking sounds are overemphasized, the realization will be monotonous. If the rationally controlled shifting *tempi* are not mastered, the realization will deteriorate into feigned vandalism. If the marathon ensemble cooperation and concentration required fail, the performance will be impossible to execute. A spirit of competitiveness between the performers will destroy the piece. The players must be friends; in quick alternation each must support the other.[18*]

Since *Knocking Piece*, the composer has extended this contingent reference system to more complex realms, making rehearsals taxing to a literally unprecedented degree. (This problem is being treated by the preparation of computer-generated "percussion" tapes that can be used either to facilitate learning or to replace the missing parts if a performer cannot rise to the challenge.) All process, of course, implies the idea of a reference against which its fluctuation may be measured. Reference is a very general idea, however, and the traditional concept in the West of "ensemble agreement" (not always shared by other cultures) is a far from inevitable commitment. Why should all members of an ensemble necessarily share identical tempo, tuning, and timbric ideals?

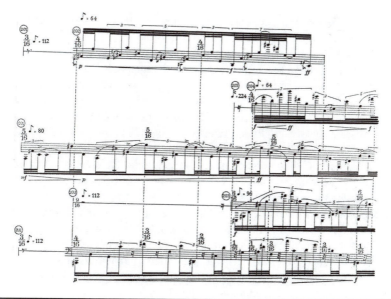

Figure 30. A page from Stockhausen's *Zeitmasse*. This example of extreme ensemble complexity shows the composer's concern with varied, simultaneous speeds and also the fact that his writing militates against the perception of any tempo.

18*. From the published version of *Knocking Piece* in *Source*, Vol. 1, No. 2, 1967.

Numerous composers including Charles Ives, Conlon Nancarrow, Karlheinz Stockhausen, and Elliott Carter have experimented in a limited way with simultaneous and independent tempi, but tempo is only one form of reference. Nancarrow has been working with player pianos since the late 1940's. Cutting his own paper rolls, he has been able to accurately reproduce such complex relations as 18:19:20:21 in canonic forms. The invincible precision of independent lines that results has an irresistible power and suggests the experiential dimensions that might arise from the experiment with temporal references proposed in Chapter 18, "Altered Time Frames."

The idea of ensemble balance involves a shared dynamic model among other common references. In Johnston's work, the references themselves are no longer constant and their discovery becomes part of an individual performer's deductive process. What this means for the listener is difficult to appraise at this early stage. Can one assume that a distant perspective can actually be maintained by the listener, that he can remain aware of successions of individual perspectives and accommodate them? If the rapid shifts of reference within the actions of one participant become the focus of a deductive effort, how will the definition of relationships by which the method of extraction is *known* to the second player be uncovered by the listener? *Knocking Piece* is, in any case, a revolutionary step in the redefinition of both performance and cognition-based activity.

Beneath the outlines of the general context within which performer and spectator enact their roles, fundamental to the materials upon which a spectator may impose the various receptive perspectives described above, there is another set of shaping influences. To what degree does the performer need to relate to his fellow performers? How does he do so? As stated above, in the Western musical tradition the idea of "ensemble" playing has a limited range of meaning. The larger the group, the more rigidly has regimentation been imposed. Conductors are necessary here, and the composer's musical ideas have been shaped so as to be not only artistically sound but practically (one might say *socially*) viable within the context of the large performing group. Members of smaller ensembles can act more autonomously, depending again on the nature of the musical materials. They can proceed without a conductor, although one of the group may be designated leader. The soloist is naturally the most flexible in his treatment of materials since he is not under obligation to synchronize his actions or compromise his conception with another player. The materials with which he deals have been inscribed by the composer with this knowledge in mind. Practices in other cultures and new approaches to group improvisation within our own show that the usual Western attitude toward the ensemble—the greatest possible human synchrony through common relation to a single reference thread—is by no means obligatory for satisfying effect.

Southeast Asian ensembles are often led from within by drummers who almost literally pull the entire group with them through accelerative tempo changes highlighted by the slight lag between leader and ensemble. The Japanese court music, *gagaku*, is performed by a body of musicians seated in parallel rows and facing straight ahead. General agreement is here obtained by the flexible, natural method of compatible respiration. They breathe and, hence, play, more or less as an organic unit, and the tensile synchrony with which we are familiar is simply not required.

To what degree, then, have other forms of interaction or interdependence between members of performing groups been explored by contemporary innovators? Most evident have been efforts at establishing new forms of improvisatory activity. Lukas Foss (b. 1927) originated a group in Los Angeles in the late 1950's (The Improvisational Chamber Ensemble) that attempted a "serious" counterpart to jazz improvisation on the basis of a notational system evolved through rehearsals and self-criticism. The group was concerned with delimiting useful frames within which interesting musical results could be assured to a degree. But this effort, like others in a similar vein, essentially resulted in group composition. The process of reaching performance included the gradual exclusion of risky elements and an at least tacit agreement about which devices and kinds of material were most likely to be effective. Far more radical in basic approach was the New Music Ensemble, developed at the University of California, Davis, in the early 1960's, primarily through the efforts of composer Larry Austin (b. 1930). This group actively avoided the normal safety mechanisms of the improvisatory ensemble. They even began public appearances with nothing more extensive than a general description of the size and spirit of the desired result. They did not decide the number or selection of performers involved until the actual moment of walking on stage, so that earlier decisions, plans, or desires were rendered virtually ineffectual. Naturally, the personal psychological balances within such a group are extraordinarily difficult to maintain, particularly since a very high degree of critical interplay is basic to any satisfying outcome. A further difficulty of this open, determinedly innocent approach to improvisational creativity is the necessity of forming a continuity of concept, an idiom of even the most general sort. Only then can the nature of an individual member's response to heard materials fall within usefully understood boundaries. Collective situations of this sort often result in a consensus of prohibition. The group finds and maintains an identity by reactive exclusion, a negative approach to a shared vocabulary of gestural, harmonic, and temporal—not to say overall emotive—shapes by means of which music can be generated with sufficient reliability. The importance of the New Music Ensemble (and the others to which it gave rise, such as Nuova Consonanza in Rome) was its combination of integrity in demanding high quality musical results and unwillingness to achieve this goal by overt planning (*i.e.*, predetermined rules of procedure). †Other efforts have been made to establish different kinds of performance matrixes within which performers can relate in new and hopefully discoverable patterns. There is finally, after all, little interest for the passive listener in observing a situation within which structured interplay takes place but does not result in changing the public face of the experience. Various reactive schemes have found their way into contemporary efforts, although generally not in a thoroughgoing sense. They have not, that is to say, been inclusive enough to shape the entire structure of the performance. Given a rapid flurry of events notated so as to appear equally spaced, a percussionist may be directed by a notational convention to exert maximum effort towards speed. Two strokes on neighboring keys of a xylophone will take much less time than two others involving drum heads as far as six feet apart. The attitude—maximum physical effort—is specified, but the actual result will vary according to the physical problems involved in completing the prescribed actions.[19] Instrumental entrances in a chamber ensemble situation may now be prescribed not by placement relative to a certain number of pulses at a given tempo but, rather, by the moment at which one performer judges that another's decrescendo has faded to an *mp* level, for example. In other cases, a notational system may be developed, as in some of the music of Earle Brown (b. 1926), in which performers gauge their entrances and relate according to graphic indications that *imply* certain linear melodic excursions or patterns of reciprocity. On still other occasions, composers have designated specific conditions governing the response of one performer to another, where each may be using precisely notated materials or one may be directed to respond to taped materials in more or less specific ways. In all such cases, the articulative structure and content of a performance depend heavily upon the tenor of performer interplay, as did improvisational practices common during earlier periods of Western music, when practice was thoroughly established by historical consensus. In our time, the "occasional" sets of conditions devised by a composer attempt to achieve, in effect, instant tradition. This process is certain to be unwieldy when attempts are made to go very far beyond normal conventions, for the number of hidden assumptions in anything so complex as cohesive ensemble performance is large.

Roger Reynolds: I/O: A Ritual for 23 Performers (1971)[20]*
The performance materials for this work include a generally descriptive conductor's score and a series of differing parts, one set for each active element in the performance: nine female vocalists, nine male mimes,

----

19. This sort of contingent procedure is discussed in some detail in Stockhausen's "... how time passes ..." which appears in *Die Reihe No. 3, Musical Craftsmanship*, Bryn Mawr, 1959.

20*. *I/O* is published by C.F. Peters Corporation.

three instrumentalists, two electronics technician/ performers, and two projectionists. With the exception of the director, who is responsible for rehearsals (there is no conductor), none of the participants is expected to understand the entire structure of interactions. The director may, in fact, also remainig norant of the details actually determining interactions among members of the ensemble. Taken as a whole, the separate parts describe the relationships and attitudes that should exist among a group of twenty-five persons during a performance. The directions for *I/O* are, in a sense, an invitation to collective expressiveness rather than a predetermined series of specific ensemble events intended to argue the composer's viewpoint. Based on Buckminster Fuller's concept of complementary opposites and, in particular, upon the wealth of relationships that exist between the phenomena male and female, this theatrical work involves an unusual level of inter-dependence, where each performer is responsible for several roles.

In an unpublished article, Fuller characterized male-female complementarity in the following schematic way:

Male	Female
I	O
singular	plural
discontinuous	continuous
compressive	tensile
hunter	consolidator
differentiator	integrator

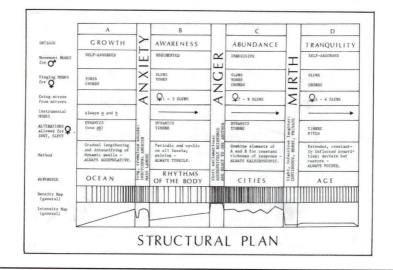

Figure 31. Structural plan from the study score of *I/O*.

I/O is an attempt to enact this relational pattern, enlarging the notion of complementarity to include social and logical/electronic implications. Nine female vocalists function as an expressive integrative *voice* in a human sense. They are the sonically expressive core of the work. Nine male mimes become an adaptive idiosyncratic *score*, as they travel independently about a continuous, mazelike path, always moving but never arriving. The men influence the vocalists and instrumentalists with signals of various sorts but cannot command responses: their cues, that is, are invitations rather than commands. The men move in archetypally expressive ways, functioning as individual yet purposefully linked conductors through the direct expression of their continuing judgments. The instrumentalists provide a harmonic-timbric fabric that supports the vocalists and is based upon the same nineteen pitches that the women sing wordlessly.

The women have three vocal *modes*—solos (SLURS), duos (TONES), and trios (CHORDS)—and three means of alteration that can be appropriately superimposed—dynamics, timbre, and pitch inflection. The instrumentalists share the three forms of alteration but have only two performance modes, cyclical and reiterative. Changes in performance mode are signaled by the men through mirror-reflected images projected on the women's faces and through the display of physical quirks in their manner of movement that can be seen by the instrumentalists. The full understanding of any one role within the total is difficult to achieve initially, but its actual performance is quite natural. The web of interrelated roles results in a ritualized social microcosm or, seen from another perspective, a humanized computer. As in life, one may find the comprehension of his own mode of existence difficult but normally manageable, so too with the individual performer in *I/O*. The interactive processes and restraints are devised so that the whole—properly executed in each part—cannot break down or produce unacceptable results, even though the actual content of any given instant is impossible to predict. Each moment has been foreseen, *in theory*, and approved as consistent with the scheme of the work.

I/O consists of four main sections, joined and delineated by three episodes of preverbal expression: Anxiety, Anger, and Mirth. In these episodes, the women are supported by appropriate instrumental textures and asked to generate vocally fundamental states of emotion. They do so independently, on the basis of internal images of their choice, some remembered or imagined experience. The emotional substance of the episodes is felt almost palpably by listeners and functions as a form of nonverbal commentary upon the sung materials of the four main sections and the changing movement modes of the men. The latter are asked to reflect bodily one inner state during each section. Specifically, these correspond to *self-absorbed*, *regimented*, and *indecisive* in the first three sections, and a return to self-absorbed in the last. The attempt is to strike beneath the surface of linguistic formulas that evoke emotion and hence demand explanation. (In the Western world, the attendant limitations of language-based rationale also restrict by wrenching a private state from its natural surroundings into a public, generalized arena.) Nonverbal vocalization and the attitudes of the body speak directly and in a way that transcends many cultural boundaries.

A general reference is provided for all by two additional factors during performance. One is a complex drone structure of electronically generated sounds to which the performers' pitch, timbric, and dynamic expansions are gauged. The other consists of two series of iconic, radiantly intense projections, based upon circle-to-oval and rectangle-to-square processes and displayed in complementary colors. The performers are also provided with other images, carried internally, from which they draw personal motivation for the use of their materials. For the first section, these are growth/ocean; for the second, awareness/rhythms of the body; in the third, abundance/ cities; and lastly, tranquillity/age.

> The program notes for *I/O* include the following message:
> NB: If the individual audience member wishes, he may participate in the performance. Consider two states of attentiveness:
>
> (1) Totally receptive and relaxed, absorbing all that is happening without taking special note of any one element.
> (2) Single-minded concentration on one element (a sound, a face, a moving figure, a projected image, a mirror-reflected signal "), his to the exclusion of all else.
>   Begin with (1). At the moment any particular element catches your attention, enter state (2), concentrating all your attention upon one item until it stops or you are distracted. Then immediately return to (1) and continue alternating between these extremes.

The effort here is to draw all into the fabric of performance while not asking anything of the individual spectator that requires the public—and therefore possibly unsettling—exhibition of skills he might not possess.

The complement to this group-based performance matrix might be found in the total control of individual environment. That is to say, patterns of complex social interaction might be replaced by a thoroughgoing prescription of every element in the lone person's surroundings. If the essentially social matrix may contrive new morphological wholes out of a larger, freshly designed complex of individually responsible participants—in a sense, a mass mind—then the individual might be enlarged and freed for unprecedented invention by a total release from standard patterns of physical restriction—familiar objects, paths, surfaces, faces, and the like.

Figure 32. Will Insley, *Ceremonial Space,* exterior view.

Will Insley: Ceremonial Space (1970)

"Architecture as an instrument of metaphysical speculation," writes Arthur Drexler of Insley's work. The disruption that arises from entirely depriving an organism of input has been mentioned in previous sections, as has been the direct intervention with messages at the cortical level itself. There is in Insley's work another as yet undomesticated notion: the control of all incident stimulation with a knowledgeable precision that might beget as yet unimagined experience. Technology now allows us the theoretical possibility of determining exactly and exhaustively the entire array of externally available experience within which an individual moves. The structure shown in the accompanying photos is, in Drexler's words:

> ... related to an imagined larger complex, much as the village church might be related to Chartres Cathedral. Its straight and narrow paths lead between, through and along the tops of high walls, past sunken rooms to which there is no access, taking the philosophical visitor into expanding or diminishing volumes of space open to the sky. No experience is possible

21. Insley's work is discussed in "Ceremonial Space" by A. Drexler, issued by the Museum of Modern Art, 1971.

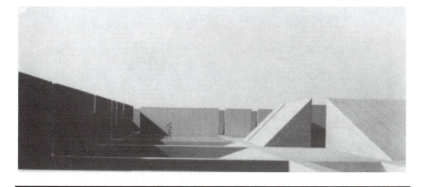

Figure 33. Will Insley, *Ceremonial Space*, interior view.

other than that determined by the architect [and, one would have to add, the previous experience and perceptive capacities of the visitor].[21]

The architect has made notes for far more elaborate ceremonial spaces "where walls of information border corridors and one may set forth upon journeys into one's own informational future." To control the range of eventfulness, of course, is to modify temporal experience, and time is a central preoccupation of Insley. In such a space, perhaps more properly called meditative than ceremonial, one could have intensely subjective experiences, private and yet physically unconstrained aesthetic involvements. Still, it would be possible there to encounter another human being whose acts are *not* a product of either one's own inner invention or that of the directing architect/artist. This might represent a further step beyond both public and private experience as we presently understand them—in a sense, the experience of dream within reality.

Form can derive only from our powers of observation and hence from the depth and range of our personal experience. What we do not recognize does not effectively exist. Morphological innovation depends on a wider willingness to absorb and contemplate experience, no matter what the sensory vehicle. Sounds articulate and populate, but the medium of display is time. Any experience that so presents itself is proper training for new musical experience, just as is any expansion of our ability to discriminate between sounds, however slight the improvement may be. The responsibility and opportunity lie with each listener as much as with the composer.

Index

A

Acceleration: pace and, 4–6; permanence and, 5; *versus* speed, 4–6; value of, 16

Acoustical: probing, 160–62; spaces, 78

Acoustics, x, 77

Aesthetic: intent, 42; response, 11, 22, 165

Aesthetic events, 39; function and meaning of, 41, 45–46

Aesthetic experience: altering of, 59, 62; communications and, 34; forms of, 40–41; memory of, 46–47; modes of perception and, 43–44; morphology and, 145, 185; private consumption and, 3–4, 16, 20, 44; technology use and, 34, 41–42; value and, 7–8

Aesthetic frames of reference, 4, 19; art and, 22; cultural, 29, 37

Altered perception, 57–59

Altered states of consciousness, 48–54; biofeedback, 54–55; brain waves and, 50–54; characteristics of, 49–50; drug use and, 58–59; hypnosis, 56–57; meditation, 55–57; sensory input and, 48–49; short-term, 48

Alternate forms of art, 37–47; aesthetic experience of, 46–47; experience of, 45–46; as process, 42–45

Alternative approaches to art, 47–58; altered states of consciousness and, 48–54; dream interpretation and, 48; drug use and, 47–48; sensory input and, 48–49

Amplification: use of in music, 77–78

Amplitude: changes in, 69–70; envelope and, 72; time and, 72

Analog: signals, 88; synthesis equipment, 86–89

Animation, 11

Antiformalism, 21

Art, 6, 12, 45, 76; alternate forms of (*see* alternate forms of art); alternative

approaches to (*see* alternative approaches to art); audience and, 25–26 (*see also* audience); categories of, 3, 10, 45; commerce and, 19–22; definition of, 21–22, 37; diversity and, 7–8, 29; drug use and, 26–28; as event, 38–42; mixed-media and, 20–21; permanence and, 25–26; private, 44, 126; as process, 42–45; public (*see* public art); public standards and, 22, 24–26

Artisanship, 19–20; art and, 25

Artists, 9, 25; audience and, 40 (*see also* audience); capability and, 8–12; commerce and, 19–22; materials and, 21, 24, 44; skill and, 9, 19, 21–22; technology and, 9, 22, 38

Ashely, Robert, 137–38, 154n.3, 154–55; *in memoriam ... ESTEBAN GÔMEZ*, xii–xiii, 156–58; performance group and, 157–58; reference sonority and, 156–57; "The Place Where the Earth Stood Still," 155

Asian culture: materials and, 73

asynchronous processes: diversity and, 6–7

Attention: nature of, 117–19, 124–25, 129

Audience, xi–x; art and, 25–26; the artist and, 40; broad-spectrum, 25; experience of, 43–44, 46; individual, 40–41; isolation of, 1112; participation, 38, 41–42, 167, 180; passive, 31–32, 180; receptiveness of, 27–28; responsibilities of, 129, 178, 185

Audio-frequency spectrum, 63; resonance and, 71

Audio signals: analog signals and, 88 (*see also* analog)

Auditory system (*see also* ear; hearing): auditory complex, 66–67, 121–22; limits of, 63, 77–78

Austin, Larry, 179

DATE DUE